Manifesting

Saint Germain's

Golden Age

Spiritualizing the World, vol 6

Manifesting Saint Germain's Golden Age

KIM MICHAELS

Copyright © 2017 Kim Michaels. All rights reserved. No part of this book may be used, reproduced, translated, electronically stored or transmitted by any means except by written permission from the publisher. A reviewer may quote brief passages in a review.

MORE TO LIFE PUBLISHING

www.morepublish.com

For foreign and translation rights,

contact info@ morepublish.com

ISBN: 978-87-93297-38-8

The information and insights in this book should not be considered as a form of therapy, advice, direction, diagnosis, and/or treatment of any kind. This information is not a substitute for medical, psychological, or other professional advice, counseling and care. All matters pertaining to your individual health should be supervised by a physician or appropriate health-care practitioner. No guarantee is made by the author or the publisher that the practices described in this book will yield successful results for anyone at any time. They are presented for informational purposes only, as the practice and proof rests with the individual.

For more information: *www.ascendedmasterlight.com* and *www.transcendencetoolbox.com*

CONTENTS

Introduction 7
1 | Transcend the pettiness of inconsequential issues! 11
2 | Invoking the transcendence of petty problems 33
3 | The Next Stage for Modern Democracies 59
4 | Invoking the Next Stage for Democracies 81
5 | Education in the Golden Age 107
6 | Invoking awareness of psychic energy 125
7 | Raising People above Fanaticism 155
8 | Calling forth true cooperation 169
9 | The rise of individuality and individual nations 193
10 | Calling forth true community 211
11 | Making the impossible possible 235
12 | Invoking a new vision of what is possible 259
13 | The power of collective decisions 285
14 | Invoking awareness of collective decisions 303
15 | A new awareness of mental freedom 327
16 | Invoking mental freedom 349
17 | Spiritual communities in the Golden Age 375
18 | Envisioning the money system of the Golden Age 399
19 | Invoking the money system of the Golden Age 427
20 | An economy for the people or for the elite? 471
21 | Invoking an economy for the people 491

INTRODUCTION

This book belongs to the series *Spiritualizing the World*. The books in this series are given by the ascended masters as workbooks that provide the knowledge and practical tools we need in order to make a contribution to solving concrete world problems. This book contains the knowledge and the tools we need in order start manifesting the Golden Age planned by Saint Germain. These books do not contain foundational knowledge about ascended masters and their teachings. In order to make the most efficient use of this book, you need to have a general knowledge of the following topics:

- You need to know who the ascended masters are, how they give their teachings and how you can make the best use of them on a personal and planetary level. You can find extensive teachings on this in the books: *How You Can Help Change the World* and *The Power of Self*.

- You need to know how the earth functions as a cosmic schoolroom. You need to know your own role and the authority you have as a spiritual being in embodiment. You need to know the role of the ascended masters and how only we who are in embodiment can give them the authority to use their unlimited power to affect change on earth. You can find more on these topics in the first book in this series: *How You Can Help Change the World*.

- You need to know how to use the practical tools given by the ascended masters. You can find more on this topic in: *How You Can Help Change the World* and on the website: *www.transcendencetoolbox.com*.

- You need to know about the existence and methods of the dark forces who are ultimately responsible for creating war on earth. You can find foundational teachings on this in: *Cosmology of Evil*.

How to use this book

There is no one way of using the teachings and tools in this book. However, if you want to make a significant contribution to bringing society forward, it is suggested that you start by following this program:

- You read one of the chapters in the book completely in order to increase your understanding of the topic.

- You give the invocation associated with that chapter once a day for nine days while studying the same chapter again.

The reasoning behind this program is that the chapters in the book form a progression. As you give an invocation for one chapter, you are also clearing your own consciousness from certain energies and illusions. This makes it easier for you to absorb and apply the teachings from the next chapter.

You can, of course, also read the book all the way through and then select one or more invocation(s) that you give several times. It is always more powerful to give an invocation once a day for nine or 33 days.

Please note that even though the dictations in this book were given at a conference in Europe (and therefore talk about Europe), the teachings apply to many parts of the world. You can therefore use this book to help people anywhere move towards the Golden Age.

If you feel burdened

The purpose of this book is not to merely give you intellectual knowledge. The real purpose is that you give the invocations, whereby you give the ascended masters the authority to remove the dark forces and energies that cause people to be stuck in repeating old patterns. These forces will not be happy that you contribute to the process of removing them from the earth. They may therefore seek to direct psychic energy at you that can make you feel burdened in various ways. Their purpose is to make you stop (or prevent you from starting) your efforts.

If you feel burdened, you can use some of the decrees and invocations for spiritual protection found on *www.transcendencetoolbox.com*. Most people can quickly come to a point where they are no longer vulnerable to the attacks from dark forces.

The dark forces will always seek to inflate any condition in our personal lives that makes us vulnerable. If you have particular issues, it may be helpful to use other tools that address those issues in a more direct manner. The ascended masters have given many invocations and decrees that can help you deal with specific topics, and you can find most of them on *www.transcendencetoolbox.com*. Some tools are found in the other books by Kim Michaels, and you can find them on *www.morepublish.com*.

NOTE: The first dictations in this book were given during a conference in Holland in the summer of 2016. The last two dictations were given after the financial crisis in 2008.

1 | TRANSCEND THE PETTINESS OF INCONSEQUENTIAL ISSUES!

I AM the Ascended Master Mother Mary, and I am eternally grateful for the service you have given today and the service you gave last year in allowing me a platform to bring forth the dictation I gave that has now been turned into this timeless and universal invocation for helping all people on earth overcome one of the major problems for the manifestation of a Golden Age, namely, the ability to love themselves as God created them and even love themselves as they are, as they have created themselves through the outplaying of free will.

The treadmill of analyzing indefinitely

Truly, my beloved, the outplaying of free will may get you into all kinds of trouble, but what is it that will get you out of the trouble again? Only that you continue to outplay free will. It is when you think that it was free will that got you into trouble (and therefore, free will is dangerous) that you become subject to the illusions and lies of the fallen beings who tell you that there is something fundamentally wrong with you. You need to compensate for it by following one of the schemes that they have defined in order to keep you going around in a circle eternally.

There are people who would object to the teachings I gave last year, the teachings that are in this invocation. They will say that it is not true that we should love the outer self, for surely it is something we need to transcend or bind or consume or destroy. But my beloved, I am not saying you should *not* transcend the outer self. I am saying that there comes a point where the outer self you have left is just enough to keep you in embodiment, and therefore you need to love it.

Do you understand, my beloved, that the fallen beings want to keep you thinking that you are making progress on the spiritual path, and they want to keep you thinking this indefinitely? We have earlier talked about the concept that you can divide the space between zero and one into infinitely smaller increments. It was also spoken about by one of the ancient Greek philosophers who said that, in order to go from here to there, you first have to go halfway. From the halfway point, you need to go to the next halfway point, and you can keep doing this indefinitely. This is what the fallen beings want you to do so that you are on a treadmill that does not bring you to your ascension because you are continually analyzing the outer self.

Do you not see that the outer self is of this world, and you can continue to analyze and divide it into smaller and smaller increments, smaller and smaller segments, and you can continue to do this indefinitely? There is a point on the path where you need to focus on the outer self. That is why we have given teachings on this, on the ego and overcoming the ego. We have given you tools for this, as well. But there also comes that point where you have to ask yourself: "Do I need to continue to analyze and divide into smaller and smaller segments? Or do I need to just take that last step?"

Cover the remaining distance in one quantum leap

Do you not understand that the solution to the riddle presented by the Greek philosopher is very simple? It is true that in order to get from here to there, you need to first walk to the halfway point. Then, you walk to the halfway point of the remaining distance. Then, you walk to the halfway point of the remaining distance. If you started out wanting to go to a place that was a 100 kilometers away, it can take you quite a number of steps to go to the halfway point. Theoretically, you will never make it, unless you realize that it is not necessary to continue to divide the remaining distance, for the simple reason that there comes a point where you are so close to your destination that you can cover the remaining distance in one step. Why, then, is there a need to divide that distance into smaller increments?

This is the way it is on the spiritual path. There are many, many times, many, many stages, where you need to take smaller and smaller steps in order to get close to a certain level. In order to make that final leap, that quantum leap to the next level, you simply need to take that one last step, and that one last step is not some technique, not some understanding. It is the conscious recognition of the issue you are dealing with at your present step and then the conscious decision: "This no longer defines me. This is not who I am." Then, you have taken that step. You, unfortunately, see many people on the spiritual path who find a valid teaching, who apply a valid approach (of course, there are many, many valid teachings and many valid approaches that can help you grow on the spiritual path), but they get stuck in thinking they have to keep applying that teaching indefinitely. They have to keep looking at themselves, looking at the ego, over-analyzing everything instead of simply stepping back, looking at themselves and saying: "This is no longer who I am. This is not the experience I want. I am accepting that I am beyond this."

This is what you need to keep doing until you are at that point where you are so close to the ascended state that you can cover the remaining distance in one quantum leap, which, again, requires one conscious recognition and decision. There are people who think about the ascension and think that there is some kind of conveyor belt. If they find the true teaching of the ascended masters and apply it, it is like being on a conveyor belt and they will go all the way until they are suddenly dumped into the ascended state. That is not the way it happens. You can actually be so close to ascending that you could ascend if you made that last decision, but until you make it you will not ascend, my beloved.

Decide to be in the golden age consciousness

This applies equally to the manifestation of a Golden Age. There are, of course, stages that lead to the manifestation of a Golden Age, and there are stages that the planet needs to go through. There are physical stages, there are certain physical developments. You can see in the world today that there are many nations that are at such a low level of development (where so many people live in poverty or have no possibility of getting an education) that you cannot expect them to jump into a golden age state in a very short period of time. They need to go through a gradual evolution, like what you have seen in the more developed countries. You also have to realize that, even in the more developed countries, you can say that there are many, many things that need to be developed further and need to be refined. You cannot allow yourself to think that this needs to go on forever.

There does come a point where a nation has to consciously step up to a higher level, and how is a nation going to come to this point? It can only do so when the top ten percent of the people in that nation come the point in their own consciousness where they can look at themselves and say: "Regardless of the conditions I see in the physical world, regardless of the problems I see, I am now deciding and accepting that I am in the Golden Age and I am in the golden age consciousness."

My beloved, if you cannot make that decision, how can your nation? We need those among the top ten percent to come to that recognition. They don't all need to find this teaching in order to do so, but it is a matter of leaving certain things behind, of looking at certain things and saying: "I no longer want to experience this. How am I going to avoid experiencing this? Only by changing my own consciousness and my own perception so that I do not any longer perceive the world, perceive life, through that perception filter."

The Golden Age requires a shift in perception

Am I thereby saying that manifesting the Golden Age is a matter of shifting perception? Yes, I am! Certainly, there are physical changes that need to happen, but what have we been telling you in the teachings through this messenger and other messengers for now over a century? We have been telling you that there are higher levels than the physical, material world, and therefore, changes in the physical must start at the higher levels. They must start in consciousness. There has never been a physical change that was not preceded by a change in the emotional, mental, and identity levels, and that change was made by some people.

Jesus, 2,000 years ago, made such a powerful shift of perception that he was able to shift the entire collective consciousness to some degree, and the many people who followed his teachings also helped. Of course, as we have said before, the official Christian churches, started by the Catholic Church, tried to reverse that trend and have to some degree been successful in doing so. Nevertheless, we are now in an age where this reversal created by the fallen beings is being reversed again, and people are becoming free to accept higher, New Age ideas, Golden Age ideas.

The shift in perception comes first and then the physical changes will follow. You, of course, are the forerunners for a shift in perception when you are willing to shift your own perception, which I know that you all are to some degree. I am simply asking you to consider where you have not shifted your perception so that you have shifted into the golden age consciousness.

The delicate balance of giving a dictation

There are, of course, many things that need to be transcended, many shifts that need to happen, but I want to bring one particular issue to your attention in this release. You see, my beloved, when we give our dictations, we are walking a delicate balance. First of all, if we gave a dictation from a level that was much higher than the people we are hoping to reach, then those people would not be able to grasp it. There is not much point in giving a dictation that no one on earth is capable of grasping. When we give a dictation, we are always stepping our vision and our energies down to a level that some people can grasp.

We are always aiming to reach a certain percentage of the collective consciousness. I am not necessarily talking about people who are physically present for a dictation or who are likely to read it or hear it shortly afterwards. As I am giving this dictation, I am looking at a cross-section of the people on earth. I am evaluating carefully the collective consciousness, and I am stepping it down to a level where I know that, even though they have never heard of ascended masters, there are still enough people out there who are capable of accepting this release at inner levels. Therefore, it has the potential to filter through to their conscious awareness, even if they never hear or read this dictation.

How the Divine Mother looks at earth

This is the one consideration we have, and that means you can say that, when we give a dictation, we are stepping our own consciousness down, and we are not giving you the fullness of how we actually look at life on earth or how we look at certain issues. What I will do here is that I will raise the curtain, so to speak, a little bit and give you a more direct worded expression of how I, as the representative of the Divine Mother, look at earth.

First of all, you need to recognize (and I know this is difficult to recognize but you need to at least consider it) that there is a huge gap between the collective consciousness, the consciousness of the average person on earth, and the ascended consciousness. I know it is very difficult to grasp, but those of you who are ascended master students have grasped elements of this. You know that we are not in fear. You know we are not angry beings. You know we are not lying to you or manipulating you. You know we have a different state of consciousness because we are not threatened by anything you do or don't do. We don't need or want anything from you. We don't want to control or manipulate you, and therefore, we have no reason to scare you.

The pettiness of human issues

Still, I want you to think even further. When I look at earth as the representative of the Divine Mother, I see very clearly the state of consciousness that people are in. Last year I told you that, no matter how I look at you, I love you. I love the totality of your being. I do not want you to misconstrue what I am saying as being any kind of critical or condemning statement, but when I look at the collective consciousness and look at the average person on earth, what I see is that they are still so trapped in issues and problems that, from my ascended perspective, are completely and utterly insignificant.

There are many, many people who can look at other people and see that these other people have concerns, issues and problems that you think are petty. It is simply pettiness to worry about this or that or the next thing. You all have seen that there are many other things that the average person is involved with that you no longer want to be involved with. You know it can only be a hindrance on your spiritual path and you have let it go. What I aim to show you here is that in order for this planet, and specifically, this continent of Europe, to shift into the golden age consciousness, people need to overcome this tendency to focus on all of these petty problems and issues. I am not trying to put people down, but I am trying to awaken people to see that most of the concerns they have are petty problems.

They are petty in the sense that they have no more hold over them than the power they themselves are giving to the problem. It is by people focusing their attention, their consciousness, on these problems that the problems are kept alive. They have no significance in terms of manifesting a Golden Age or in terms of taking this planet down into an undesirable state. They are really inconsequential. They are not really taking the planet up or down. They are simply like mud where people keep walking around in the same mud and it is so deep that they cannot pull themselves out of it onto higher ground. They keep spending all of their energy struggling in this mud hole, expending a lot of energy but really getting nowhere. This goes for the vast majority of the people on this planet and the people on this continent.

Look, as just one example, to the debate going on in the UK right now about whether the UK should stay in the EU or not. The arguments raised from both sides of the issue are, from my perspective as an ascended master, as the representative of the Divine Mother, inconsequential. They are petty. Should the future of the UK or of the European Union be decided by the number of hospital beds or the size of a pension or other issues that really are not consequential in the long run?

What I am trying to help you see here is that there are so many of the issues that people are occupied with that are not consequential for bringing a Golden Age. The same goes for the rest of this continent where so many people are still stuck in the past. We talked about this last year. We gave these invocations that created a powerful impetus for creating change in the collective consciousness. By putting them out as a book and as people give them more, we will make that momentum roll on, but we need to add on to it [published as *Help People Overcome the Past*].

We need to build more of an awareness that, for Europe to really move into a Golden Age, the people in all nations need to look at certain issues that they are today very occupied with and realize that they are not consequential. They are only serving to keep them stuck in the mud of the past. What does it really matter what happened 50 years, 100 years, 200 years or 700 years ago? What does it matter who lost or won a battle several hundred years ago? What does it matter today? It is inconsequential for the future.

The fallen beings will try to pull you into petty issues

What you need to do is raise your own vision and see that there are many of the issues that people are concerned with that really are not consequential. They are not a concern of Saint Germain for bringing the Golden Age. You also need to make the calls, of course, that people are awakened. You also need to recognize that there are many dark forces on this continent and, of course, throughout the world, who have fallen beings in embodiment, those who are completely sucked into the fallen consciousness. They have demons and discarnates in the astral plane and fallen beings in the mental and identity realms. They are all working to create these artificial petty problems and to project out there that they are so important that people should focus their energies and attention on them. Maybe they even need to take physical action because this problem absolutely must be solved, or some greater calamity will happen or some greater good will not happen. This is what they always project: "You need to do something to prevent a disaster, or you need to do something to stop the destruction of something good."

This is just a treadmill. It is a treadmill created to engage people indefinitely in this inconsequential struggle. Of course, the fallen beings are never happier than when they can pull someone from the top ten percent into this kind of struggle. I can tell you that many ascended master students over the last 100 years have been pulled into using energy, time and even taking physical action to promote certain causes or to fight certain other causes or threats that were not consequential. Where does this lead you, as the spiritual people?

Step back from the inconsequential struggles

What I am asking you to do is to first of all look at yourself, look at your own state of consciousness, look at your own daily life and see if you are involved with issues, such as conflicts with other people. It may be conditions at your workplace that are inconsequential for your Divine plan, that are just these ongoing squabbles or struggles that really get you nowhere. Then, of course, pull yourself out of them.

You may need to look a little bit at your psychology and why you think this is so important, why you were pulled into it. If you do some work with our invocations and some conscious work by looking at yourself, you can quickly come to that point where you are ready to step back, take a look at yourself, and say: "I no longer want this experience. This no longer defines me." Then, you can take that quantum leap into a state where you are simply free of this consciousness.

My beloved, when you are free of this consciousness, you will find to your surprise that you will meet very few of the people who are still trapped in it. If you do meet them, they have no power to pull you into their games. It is simply as if you are throwing water on a goose; it just runs off. Now there may be instances where you will, after making this shift, be tested. Someone will come to you and be very clever or very aggressive in trying to pull you back in, but if you resist this once, maybe two times, maybe three times, then you will be free.

You will be surprised at how, all of a sudden, these issues go away. These people disappear from your life, or you move on to an entirely different situation where you are no longer engaged in this struggle. For you to be free of the outer situation, you must start by being free in consciousness. You must be willing to look at this and look at why you think this is so important, why you feel that this problem must be addressed or this problem must be solved.

Free yourself from problems that have no solution

Do you see, my beloved, that I am trying to get you to the point where you can see that there is a certain number of problems on this planet and on this continent that are not real problems? They are created by the fallen beings to divert your attention and to suck your energy into a downward spiral. At the same time, they are projecting into your mind that these are real problems and that you need to do something about them, but these problems have no solution. *They have no solution!*

The fallen beings are very clever at projecting that they have a solution, and that solution usually involves forcing or even killing other people, but they have no solution. Whenever you see a problem where the solution called for requires the use of force against other people or another group of people, you know this is an artificial problem created by the fallen beings. We of the ascended masters would never, ever suggest a solution that requires forcing or killing other human beings.

How could we, when we know that this planet and the beings upon it will only make progress through the outplaying of free will?

You need to recognize that whatever argument they have used to pull you into this struggle is a false argument. You need to look at it. There is, my beloved, only one thing you can really do to free yourself from the downward spiral of one of these problems, and it is to simply walk away from it. There is no solution. There is nothing you can do to solve it. There is nothing you *need* to do. There is nothing you *have* to do, other than seeing: "I no longer want to experience life through this perception filter, and I will no longer let this state of consciousness define me." Then you can make the quantum leap.

Nothing can undo the past

These problems are just like what I have talked about: You can keep dividing the distance between where you are and where the solution is into smaller and smaller increments indefinitely without ever arriving at the solution. There are many problems of this sort that are timeless. They are continually reinforced, but there is also a certain amount of these problems that are problems relating to the past. This, of course, is true very much so in Europe where you have the many wars and the many conflicts between people.

Look at the situation that we had you make the calls on last year about the second world war and the Holocaust. You cannot undo what happened. There is no amount of actions you could take that could undo what happened. Now listen carefully. It would, of course, be a great advantage if a sufficient number of people would use decrees and invocations to invoke light and direct it into the energetic records of these events, consuming these energetic records. This is a necessary step, and it is a beneficial step, but what I am saying is that, in your consciousness (in people's perception, in the way they look at the problem), there is nothing that could change what happened in the past. Nothing can change, nothing can undo, what was done.

How can you be free of it? By realizing that you do not need to change what happened. You do not need to undo what was done. You need to simply identify the consciousness that caused it to be done, then you need to say: "I see you. I see this consciousness, and I no longer want to experience life through your perception filter. I no longer want to let you define me, and therefore, I am taking the quantum leap above this consciousness." Surely, open debate, open talk about these issues, would help people make that shift, but again, it is a very, very delicate issue.

Meting out karma is not your job

I understand that there are many people who still look back at the Holocaust and they say: "The German people did this. The German people need to know what they did. They need to acknowledge what they did. They need to recognize and admit what they did." Many people will say: "They also need to be punished for it."

First of all, the idea that someone needs to be punished for what they did does not come from the ascended realm. The people have made karma for what they did—true. That karma they will have to deal with one way or another, but that is not your concern as a human being in embodiment. You are not on the Karmic Board, and you are not on the Karmic Board precisely because you are still in embodiment. Therefore, you do not have the perspective that you need to have in order to be on the Karmic Board. You are not meting out people's karma or withholding people's karma.

Therefore, as the Bible even says: "Vengeance is mine, I will repay, sayes the Lord," which means that you do not have to worry about vengeance, repayment and punishment. It is not *your* job. Thank God that it is not your job because, as you meter out to others, it shall be metered out to you. If you want others to be punished for their transgressions, you are saying to the universe that you want to be punished for yours. Do you know what your transgressions were in a distant past life?

The aggressive consciousness of punishment

I can assure you that those people who are in the state of consciousness where they want to punish others, they have some very severe transgressions from a past life, for they have not overcome the consciousness of aggression against others. The desire to punish others is an act of aggression. I know some will say: "But so was the Holocaust! The Germans committed an act of aggression against innocent people, and they need to be punished for it." I say that if those "innocent people" are still in the consciousness where they want to punish others, they are not so innocent, my beloved.

They are, in fact, trapped in what I just talked about, the consciousness that just keeps you stuck in the mud because when will it ever be enough punishment? Could you imagine that the world decided: "We have now the military power to inflict any kind of punishment that we want on those who are responsible for the Holocaust." What kind of punishment should the world then inflict upon the German people? Should you create concentration camps for the German people and have them work themselves to death and go into the gas chambers?

Would you think this would make the world a better place, my beloved? I think not, from the perspective of an ascended master. I know that you who are here do not think so either, but I am putting this into the collective consciousness. I assure you that there are people who think this way. They just have not thought through to the logical consequence of what they believe. They have not consciously thought: "Well, if our feeling that the Germans should be punished should really be carried out, how would this then look? What kind of a scenario would we create, and is this really what we want to do?"

You see, my beloved, it should be so that those who have suffered much at the hands of others would say to themselves: "We never want to do to others what others have done to us." That is a state of innocence, but when you either want to punish the others or when you are doing the same to others that others did to you (as quite frankly some of the people in Israel are doing to the Palestinians), then you are not as innocent as you want to make it out that you are. This means that whatever happened was not some aggressor that attacked some completely innocent people.

It was on a very large scale the outplaying of these artificial problems and conflicts created by the fallen beings. They had created such a powerful, downward energetic spiral that most of the German people were sucked into it. Mind you, those who were the victims of the Holocaust and the war were sucked into it as well, even those who fought the Germans in England, the United States and other countries. They too were sucked into the downward spiral of war created by the fallen beings.

Look forward with Christ Discernment

You cannot come out and look at a problem like this as a black-and-white issue where there are the "good guys" on one side and they are completely good, and the "bad guys" on the other side and they are completely bad. This is what the fallen beings want you to think because then you never attain Christ discernment, and without Christ discernment, how shall we build a Golden Age? How shall we rise above the past without the Christ discernment that says: "I see what happened in the past. I see that what happened in the past was the outplaying of a certain state of consciousness. I no longer want to be in this state of consciousness. I no longer want to be affected by the perception filter of that state of consciousness. So what do I have to do? What do I have to do to be free? I have to change myself! As long as I think it is those other people, those 'bad people' who have to change, then I am just as trapped in the downward spiral as they are. Do I want to be trapped in this downward spiral anymore?"

If you do not have Christ discernment, you will actually want to continue in the spiral because you will think that there is something that has to be done, some punishment that has to be inflicted on those others before you can free yourself from the spiral. It is only Christ discernment that allows you to have the vision that says: "There is something more. I see there is something more, and I see that it is more important to me than what I think needs to be done down here with these old problems. I see there is the potential of a Golden Age. I want to be part of manifesting that Golden Age, and in order to be part of manifesting the Golden Age, I have to let go of the old state of consciousness. I have to let go of the pettiness of looking at the past of these inconsequential problems or this desire to punish. I just have to let it go!" When you come to that point of realization, which is the essential realization of the Christ consciousness, then all of the fallen beings tremble because now they are afraid that they will lose their hold on you.

Let me recall to you the situation of how Jesus chose his disciples. It is hinted at in the Bible. There is the situation where the fishermen are standing at the Sea of Galilee. They are mending their nets. They are completely occupied by their daily tasks of catching fish and cleaning their nets so they are ready for the next day or the next night of fishing. They are completely focused on their daily lives. Suddenly, a stranger (whom they have never seen before) walks up to them, looks at them with a strong gaze, and says: "Leave your nets and follow me, and I will make you fishers of men!" Those who left their nets immediately and followed Jesus became his disciples. Those who stood there and thought about it could never catch up with him.

You have also the story of Lot's wife who was told not to look back or she would be turned into a pillar of salt. This is, of course, not a true, physical, linear story, but it is a symbol of the fact that she had an attachment. She could not let go of the old. She had to look back. When you have Christ discernment, you do not look back. You look forward and you say: "All of these other things no longer define me, and therefore, I say to you: 'Get thee behind me, Satan, for thou art an offence to me! Thou savors not the things that be of God but the things that be of men.'" This, my beloved, is what the people of Europe, at least a critical mass of them, need to do if we are to manifest a Golden Age on this continent in the foreseeable future.

Leave the unsolvable problems behind

You, of course, are the ones we look at to help them do so by creating a trail in the collective consciousness that they can follow, for without it, they will remain stuck in the mud. They need to be in mud and see: "Oh, there is a path there that leads to higher ground. I want to follow that path. How do I do it?" They yell at you: "How did you get out of the mud?" You look back and say: "I just left it all behind!" If they get it, they can do the same.

When you give an invocation that speaks this into the collective consciousness (as I have now been speaking into it and as you will reinforce it by speaking into it), then you will make it possible for more and more people to simply leave the quagmire behind. They can leave the unsolvable problems behind and say: "We don't need to solve these problems. We need to manifest something higher."

There is a story that was told many years ago about the city of New York in the late 1800s that was facing a major logistical problem. Most of the transportation in the city was with horse carts, and you know what horses leave behind all over the streets. There were some very clever engineers who calculated that, if the horses kept doing their thing for the indefinite future at the current rate, then it was only a matter of so and so many years and then New York city would drown in horse manure, for there was no way to clear it out of the streets. As those who have been to New York City will see, although there may be other kinds of manure in the streets, there is not much horse manure. The reason for this was, of course, that a new technology was invented that made horses obsolete as a means of transportation.

This is the central idea of Saint Germain's Golden Age. Saint Germain knows very well that there are problems here that cannot be solved. Even *he* cannot solve them. Even infinite amounts of violet flame could not solve these problems because people would just recreate them as long as they haven't shifted their perception. The only way to bring a Golden Age is to bring new ideas that simply transcend the old problems so that people can see: "Oh, of course, I don't want a horse cart when I can ride a car. Of course, I don't want this petty old problem when there is something better."

Envision a positive future for the European Union

This is the vision that is missing right now in the European Union. There is hardly anybody who has a positive vision of what the European Union can become. Very, very few people have grasped it, and most of the average people look upon it as something that was somehow forced upon them.

My beloved, if you had a public referendum and a majority of the people in your country voted to join the European Union, how was that forced upon you? My beloved people in Britain, how was it forced upon you that you voted to join the EU? Why do you, then, need to withdraw for a lack of vision and a lack of remembrance of the choices you made? Work to make the EU better from a positive platform, and I say the same to all other nations.

Of course, Saint Germain does not sponsor or support the EU in its' current form, but, of course, Saint Germain wants the European nations to cooperate and eventually unite in a United States of Europe, which he has envisioned since the 1600's. It is not that you need to envision that the EU needs to be preserved or the Euro needs to be preserved by all costs.

1 | *Transcend the pettiness of inconsequential issues!* 31

You need to envision that the people step up to a positive vision of what can be achieved through peaceful cooperation, rather than the petty squabbles that have taken place on this continent now for hundreds and hundreds of years.

I know that some will be highly objective to this, but when I say petty squabbles, I include the Cold war, World War II, World War I, the massacres of the Cathars, the Inquisition, the Crusades, and all of these other wars and squabbles. They were petty from the perspective of the Divine Mother who sees how much more her children are capable of manifesting. Therefore, this is nothing but pettiness, and the consciousness is petty. It is a petty consciousness, and it can only be transcended by being seen for what it is so you see that there is nothing to solve here. We need to look in a new direction and follow a higher vision.

There is nothing petty about making the calls and raising your vision. That is why you are here. That is why I am here. I want to tell you that your calls to me on that last Sunday of every month do make a difference and have made a tremendous difference in this last year where you have done it. It is one of the most powerful forces that are shaping the earth right now.

Conferences such as this make a tremendous difference. The people who give their invocations and decrees in their homes, they make a tremendous difference. I know you do not always see it. I know you do not always feel it. That is why I am telling you so that you can at least hear it because, from my perspective, there is nothing petty about giving rosaries, invocations, decrees, coming together at conferences, creating groups that support each other, raising your vision and supporting each other in raising your vision.

My beloved, be positive about the future, for I am positive about the future. You will only grasp my vision and Saint

Germain's vision if you too are positive. It is not a matter of infinitely analyzing problems; it is a matter of grasping the vision of a whole new reality where the problems have become inconsequential and obsolete.

Thus, I thank you for your attention and your love and your willingness to make the calls that go into the collective consciousness and sometimes create like a tsunami of positive energy that sweeps away much of the darkness and the dross that keeps people stuck in the mud. I am grateful!

2 | INVOKING THE TRANSCENDENCE OF PETTY PROBLEMS

In the name I AM THAT I AM, Jesus Christ, I call to all ascended masters working on manifesting the Golden Age, especially Mother Mary, to radiate into the collective consciousness a new awareness of how to leave behind all inconsequential and petty problems. Help people see that we can build a new future by working with the ascended masters and letting go of the old way of looking at life, including…

[Make personal calls.]

Part 1

1. Mother Mary, radiate into the collective consciousness the awareness that the outplaying of free will may get us *into* trouble, but it can also get us out of trouble again.

> O blessed Mary, Mother mine,
> there is no greater love than thine,
> as we are one in heart and mind,
> my place in hierarchy I find.
>
> **O Mother Mary, generate,**
> **the song that does accelerate,**
> **the earth into a higher state,**
> **all matter does now scintillate.**

2. Mother Mary, radiate into the collective consciousness the awareness that when we think free will is dangerous, we become subject to the lies of the fallen beings. They tell us that there is something fundamentally wrong with us and that we need to follow the schemes they have defined in order to keep us going around in a circle eternally.

> I came to earth from heaven sent,
> as I am in embodiment,
> I use Divine authority,
> commanding you to set earth free.
>
> **O Mother Mary, generate,**
> **the song that does accelerate,**
> **the earth into a higher state,**
> **all matter does now scintillate.**

2 | *Invoking the transcendence of petty problems*

3. Mother Mary, radiate into the collective consciousness the awareness that although it is necessary to analyze problems, there comes a point where we need to go beyond analysis and leave certain issues behind.

> I call now in God's sacred name,
> for you to use your Mother Flame,
> to burn all fear-based energy,
> restoring sacred harmony.

> **O Mother Mary, generate,**
> **the song that does accelerate,**
> **the earth into a higher state,**
> **all matter does now scintillate.**

4. Mother Mary, radiate into the collective consciousness the awareness that many nations are at such a low level of development that they cannot jump into a golden age state in a very short period of time.

> Your sacred name I hereby praise,
> collective consciousness you raise,
> no more of fear and doubt and shame,
> consume it with your Mother Flame.

> **O Mother Mary, generate,**
> **the song that does accelerate,**
> **the earth into a higher state,**
> **all matter does now scintillate.**

5. Mother Mary, radiate into the collective consciousness the awareness that there does come a point where a nation has to consciously step up to a higher level and take a leap into the Golden Age.

> All darkness from the earth you purge,
> your light moves as a mighty surge,
> no force of darkness can now stop,
> the spiral that goes only up.
>
> **O Mother Mary, generate,**
> **the song that does accelerate,**
> **the earth into a higher state,**
> **all matter does now scintillate.**

6. Mother Mary, radiate into the collective consciousness the awareness that a nation can make this leap only when enough people say: "Regardless of the conditions I see in the physical world, regardless of the problems I see, I am now deciding and accepting that I am in the Golden Age and I am in the golden age consciousness."

> All elemental life you bless,
> removing from them man-made stress,
> the nature spirits are now free,
> outpicturing Divine decree.
>
> **O Mother Mary, generate,**
> **the song that does accelerate,**
> **the earth into a higher state,**
> **all matter does now scintillate.**

2 | *Invoking the transcendence of petty problems*

7. Mother Mary, radiate into the collective consciousness the awareness that the spiritual people need to say: "I no longer want to experience this. How am I going to avoid experiencing this? Only by changing my own consciousness and my own perception so that I do not any longer perceive the world through that perception filter."

> I raise my voice and take my stand,
> a stop to war I do command,
> no more shall warring scar the earth,
> a golden age is given birth.
>
> **O Mother Mary, generate,**
> **the song that does accelerate,**
> **the earth into a higher state,**
> **all matter does now scintillate.**

8. Mother Mary, radiate into the collective consciousness the awareness that manifesting the Golden Age is a matter of shifting perception.

> As Mother Earth is free at last,
> disasters belong to the past,
> your Mother Light is so intense,
> that matter is now far less dense.
>
> **O Mother Mary, generate,**
> **the song that does accelerate,**
> **the earth into a higher state,**
> **all matter does now scintillate.**

9. Mother Mary, radiate into the collective consciousness the awareness that because there are higher levels than the material world, changes in the physical must start at the higher levels. They must start in consciousness. There has never been a physical change that was not preceded by a change in the emotional, mental, and identity levels.

> In Mother Light the earth is pure,
> the upward spiral will endure,
> prosperity is now the norm,
> God's vision manifest as form.
>
> **O Mother Mary, generate,**
> **the song that does accelerate,**
> **the earth into a higher state,**
> **all matter does now scintillate.**

Part 2

1. Mother Mary, radiate into the collective consciousness the awareness that a shift in perception comes first and then the physical changes will follow.

> O blessed Mary, Mother mine,
> there is no greater love than thine,
> as we are one in heart and mind,
> my place in hierarchy I find.

2 | Invoking the transcendence of petty problems

**O Mother Mary, generate,
the song that does accelerate,
the earth into a higher state,
all matter does now scintillate.**

2. Mother Mary, radiate into the collective consciousness the awareness that many people have concerns, issues and problems that from a larger perspective are petty. It is pettiness to worry about some of these issues.

I came to earth from heaven sent,
as I am in embodiment,
I use Divine authority,
commanding you to set earth free.

**O Mother Mary, generate,
the song that does accelerate,
the earth into a higher state,
all matter does now scintillate.**

3. Mother Mary, radiate into the collective consciousness the awareness that in order for people to shift into the golden age consciousness, we need to overcome the tendency to focus on petty problems and issues. We need to awaken and see that most of the concerns we have are petty problems.

I call now in God's sacred name,
for you to use your Mother Flame,
to burn all fear-based energy,
restoring sacred harmony.

> **O Mother Mary, generate,**
> **the song that does accelerate,**
> **the earth into a higher state,**
> **all matter does now scintillate.**

4. Mother Mary, radiate into the collective consciousness the awareness that petty problems have no more hold over us than the power we ourselves are giving to the problem. It is by focusing our attention on these problems that the problems are kept alive.

> Your sacred name I hereby praise,
> collective consciousness you raise,
> no more of fear and doubt and shame,
> consume it with your Mother Flame.

> **O Mother Mary, generate,**
> **the song that does accelerate,**
> **the earth into a higher state,**
> **all matter does now scintillate.**

5. Mother Mary, radiate into the collective consciousness the awareness that such problems have no significance in terms of manifesting a Golden Age or in terms of taking this planet down into an undesirable state. They are really inconsequential.

> All darkness from the earth you purge,
> your light moves as a mighty surge,
> no force of darkness can now stop,
> the spiral that goes only up.

2 | Invoking the transcendence of petty problems

**O Mother Mary, generate,
the song that does accelerate,
the earth into a higher state,
all matter does now scintillate.**

6. Mother Mary, radiate into the collective consciousness the awareness that many of the issues people are occupied with are not consequential for bringing a Golden Age, but they keep people stuck in the past.

> All elemental life you bless,
> removing from them man-made stress,
> the nature spirits are now free,
> outpicturing Divine decree.

**O Mother Mary, generate,
the song that does accelerate,
the earth into a higher state,
all matter does now scintillate.**

7. Mother Mary, radiate into the collective consciousness the awareness that for the world to move into a Golden Age, the people in all nations need to look at certain issues and realize that they are not consequential. They are only serving to keep them stuck in the mud of the past.

> I raise my voice and take my stand,
> a stop to war I do command,
> no more shall warring scar the earth,
> a golden age is given birth.

**O Mother Mary, generate,
the song that does accelerate,
the earth into a higher state,
all matter does now scintillate.**

8. Mother Mary, radiate into the collective consciousness the awareness that it doesn't really matter what happened 50, 100 or 700 years ago. It is inconsequential for the future.

As Mother Earth is free at last,
disasters belong to the past,
your Mother Light is so intense,
that matter is now far less dense.

**O Mother Mary, generate,
the song that does accelerate,
the earth into a higher state,
all matter does now scintillate.**

9. Mother Mary, radiate into the collective consciousness the awareness that many of the issues that people are concerned with are not consequential. They are not a concern of Saint Germain for bringing the Golden Age.

In Mother Light the earth is pure,
the upward spiral will endure,
prosperity is now the norm,
God's vision manifest as form.

**O Mother Mary, generate,
the song that does accelerate,
the earth into a higher state,
all matter does now scintillate.**

Part 3

1. Mother Mary, radiate into the collective consciousness the awareness that the fallen beings in embodiment and the dark forces in the higher realms are all working to create these artificial petty problems and to project that they are so important that people should focus their energies and attention on them.

> O blessed Mary, Mother mine,
> there is no greater love than thine,
> as we are one in heart and mind,
> my place in hierarchy I find.
>
> **O Mother Mary, generate,**
> **the song that does accelerate,**
> **the earth into a higher state,**
> **all matter does now scintillate.**

2. Mother Mary, radiate into the collective consciousness the awareness that the dark forces project that people need to take physical action because this problem absolutely must be solved, or some greater calamity will happen or some greater good will not happen.

> I came to earth from heaven sent,
> as I am in embodiment,
> I use Divine authority,
> commanding you to set earth free.

> **O Mother Mary, generate,**
> **the song that does accelerate,**
> **the earth into a higher state,**
> **all matter does now scintillate.**

3. Mother Mary, radiate into the collective consciousness the awareness that this is a treadmill created to engage people indefinitely in this inconsequential struggle. The fallen beings are never happier than when they can pull someone from the top ten percent into this struggle.

> I call now in God's sacred name,
> for you to use your Mother Flame,
> to burn all fear-based energy,
> restoring sacred harmony.

> **O Mother Mary, generate,**
> **the song that does accelerate,**
> **the earth into a higher state,**
> **all matter does now scintillate.**

4. Mother Mary, radiate into the collective consciousness the awareness that the spiritual people need to pull ourselves away from our involvement with such petty problems, including conflicts with other people that are inconsequential for our Divine plans.

> Your sacred name I hereby praise,
> collective consciousness you raise,
> no more of fear and doubt and shame,
> consume it with your Mother Flame.

2 | Invoking the transcendence of petty problems

> **O Mother Mary, generate,**
> **the song that does accelerate,**
> **the earth into a higher state,**
> **all matter does now scintillate.**

5. Mother Mary, radiate into the collective consciousness the awareness that we need to look at our psychology and why we think this is so important, why we were pulled into it. We need to say: "I no longer want this experience. This no longer defines me."

> All darkness from the earth you purge,
> your light moves as a mighty surge,
> no force of darkness can now stop,
> the spiral that goes only up.

> **O Mother Mary, generate,**
> **the song that does accelerate,**
> **the earth into a higher state,**
> **all matter does now scintillate.**

6. Mother Mary, radiate into the collective consciousness the awareness that for us to be free of an outer situation, we must start by being free in consciousness. We must be willing to look at why we think this is so important, why we feel that this problem must be solved.

> All elemental life you bless,
> removing from them man-made stress,
> the nature spirits are now free,
> outpicturing Divine decree.

**O Mother Mary, generate,
the song that does accelerate,
the earth into a higher state,
all matter does now scintillate.**

7. Mother Mary, radiate into the collective consciousness the awareness that a certain number of problems are not real problems. They are created by the fallen beings to divert our attention and to suck our energy into a downward spiral.

I raise my voice and take my stand,
a stop to war I do command,
no more shall warring scar the earth,
a golden age is given birth.

**O Mother Mary, generate,
the song that does accelerate,
the earth into a higher state,
all matter does now scintillate.**

8. Mother Mary, radiate into the collective consciousness the awareness that the fallen beings are projecting into our minds that these are real problems and that we need to do something about them. In reality, these problems have no solution.

As Mother Earth is free at last,
disasters belong to the past,
your Mother Light is so intense,
that matter is now far less dense.

**O Mother Mary, generate,
the song that does accelerate,
the earth into a higher state,
all matter does now scintillate.**

9. Mother Mary, radiate into the collective consciousness the awareness that the fallen beings are very clever at projecting that they have a solution, and that solution usually involves forcing or killing other people. In reality, these problems have no solution.

In Mother Light the earth is pure,
the upward spiral will endure,
prosperity is now the norm,
God's vision manifest as form.

**O Mother Mary, generate,
the song that does accelerate,
the earth into a higher state,
all matter does now scintillate.**

Part 4

1. Mother Mary, radiate into the collective consciousness the awareness that when solving a problem requires the use of force against other people, this is an artificial problem created by the fallen beings.

> O blessed Mary, Mother mine,
> there is no greater love than thine,
> as we are one in heart and mind,
> my place in hierarchy I find.
>
> **O Mother Mary, generate,**
> **the song that does accelerate,**
> **the earth into a higher state,**
> **all matter does now scintillate.**

2. Mother Mary, radiate into the collective consciousness the awareness that whatever argument they have used to pull us into this struggle, it is a false argument. The only way to free ourselves from the downward spiral is to simply walk away from it.

> I came to earth from heaven sent,
> as I am in embodiment,
> I use Divine authority,
> commanding you to set earth free.
>
> **O Mother Mary, generate,**
> **the song that does accelerate,**
> **the earth into a higher state,**
> **all matter does now scintillate.**

3. Mother Mary, radiate into the collective consciousness the awareness that there is no solution to unreal problems. There is nothing we can do to solve them. We only need to see: "I no longer want to experience life through this perception filter, and I will no longer let this state of consciousness define me."

2 | Invoking the transcendence of petty problems

I call now in God's sacred name,
for you to use your Mother Flame,
to burn all fear-based energy,
restoring sacred harmony.

**O Mother Mary, generate,
the song that does accelerate,
the earth into a higher state,
all matter does now scintillate.**

4. Mother Mary, radiate into the collective consciousness the awareness that many artificial problems relate to the past and the many conflicts on every continent.

Your sacred name I hereby praise,
collective consciousness you raise,
no more of fear and doubt and shame,
consume it with your Mother Flame.

**O Mother Mary, generate,
the song that does accelerate,
the earth into a higher state,
all matter does now scintillate.**

5. Mother Mary, radiate into the collective consciousness the awareness that no amount of actions could undo what happened in the past. In our consciousness, in our perception, in the way we look at the problem, there is nothing that could change what happened in the past. Nothing can undo what was done.

All darkness from the earth you purge,
your light moves as a mighty surge,
no force of darkness can now stop,
the spiral that goes only up.

**O Mother Mary, generate,
the song that does accelerate,
the earth into a higher state,
all matter does now scintillate.**

6. Mother Mary, radiate into the collective consciousness the awareness that we can be free of the past only by realizing that we do not need to change what happened. We need to identify the consciousness that caused it and say: "I see you. I see this consciousness, and I no longer want to experience life through your perception filter. I no longer want to let you define me, and therefore, I am taking the quantum leap above this consciousness."

All elemental life you bless,
removing from them man-made stress,
the nature spirits are now free,
outpicturing Divine decree.

**O Mother Mary, generate,
the song that does accelerate,
the earth into a higher state,
all matter does now scintillate.**

7. Mother Mary, radiate into the collective consciousness the awareness that the idea that someone needs to be punished for what they did comes from the fallen beings. We do not have to worry about vengeance, repayment and punishment because the Law of Karma takes care of it.

> I raise my voice and take my stand,
> a stop to war I do command,
> no more shall warring scar the earth,
> a golden age is given birth.

> **O Mother Mary, generate,**
> **the song that does accelerate,**
> **the earth into a higher state,**
> **all matter does now scintillate.**

8. Mother Mary, radiate into the collective consciousness the awareness that those who have suffered much at the hands of others need to say to themselves: "We never want to do to others what others have done to us." That is a state of innocence.

> As Mother Earth is free at last,
> disasters belong to the past,
> your Mother Light is so intense,
> that matter is now far less dense.

> **O Mother Mary, generate,**
> **the song that does accelerate,**
> **the earth into a higher state,**
> **all matter does now scintillate.**

9. Mother Mary, radiate into the collective consciousness the awareness that most of the conflicts of the past were, on a very large scale, the outplaying of the artificial problems and conflicts created by the fallen beings. People on both sides of a conflict were sucked into the downward spiral created by the fallen beings.

> In Mother Light the earth is pure,
> the upward spiral will endure,
> prosperity is now the norm,
> God's vision manifest as form.
>
> **O Mother Mary, generate,**
> **the song that does accelerate,**
> **the earth into a higher state,**
> **all matter does now scintillate.**

Part 5

1. Mother Mary, radiate into the collective consciousness the awareness that the fallen beings want us to think that other people are wholly bad and we are wholly good. Instead, we need to use Christ discernment and say: "I see what happened in the past. I see that what happened in the past was the outplaying of a certain state of consciousness. I no longer want to be in this state of consciousness. I no longer want to be affected by the perception filter of that state of consciousness."

2 | *Invoking the transcendence of petty problems*

O blessed Mary, Mother mine,
there is no greater love than thine,
as we are one in heart and mind,
my place in hierarchy I find.

**O Mother Mary, generate,
the song that does accelerate,
the earth into a higher state,
all matter does now scintillate.**

2. Mother Mary, radiate into the collective consciousness the awareness that if we want to be free, we have to say: "I have to change myself! As long as I think it is those other people, those 'bad people' who have to change, then I am just as trapped in the downward spiral as they are. Do I want to be trapped in this downward spiral anymore?"

I came to earth from heaven sent,
as I am in embodiment,
I use Divine authority,
commanding you to set earth free.

**O Mother Mary, generate,
the song that does accelerate,
the earth into a higher state,
all matter does now scintillate.**

3. Mother Mary, radiate into the collective consciousness the awareness that only Christ discernment allows us to say: "There is something more. I see there is something more, and I see that it is more important to me than what I think needs to be done down here with these old problems. I see there is a potential of a Golden Age. In order to be part of manifesting the Golden Age, I have to let go of the old state of consciousness. I have to let go of the pettiness of looking at the past of these inconsequential problems or this desire to punish. I just have to let it go!"

> I call now in God's sacred name,
> for you to use your Mother Flame,
> to burn all fear-based energy,
> restoring sacred harmony.
>
> **O Mother Mary, generate,**
> **the song that does accelerate,**
> **the earth into a higher state,**
> **all matter does now scintillate.**

4. Mother Mary, radiate into the collective consciousness the awareness that if we are to manifest a Golden Age, a critical mass of people need to say: "All of these other things no longer define me, and therefore, I say to you: 'Get thee behind me, Satan, for thou art an offence to me! Thou savors not the things that be of God but the things that be of men.'"

> Your sacred name I hereby praise,
> collective consciousness you raise,
> no more of fear and doubt and shame,
> consume it with your Mother Flame.

**O Mother Mary, generate,
the song that does accelerate,
the earth into a higher state,
all matter does now scintillate.**

5. Mother Mary, radiate into the collective consciousness the awareness that the central idea of Saint Germain's Golden Age is that there are problems that cannot be solved. The only way to bring a Golden Age is to bring new ideas that simply transcend the old problems.

All darkness from the earth you purge,
your light moves as a mighty surge,
no force of darkness can now stop,
the spiral that goes only up.

**O Mother Mary, generate,
the song that does accelerate,
the earth into a higher state,
all matter does now scintillate.**

6. Mother Mary, radiate into the collective consciousness the awareness that what is missing in the European Union is that not enough people are holding a positive vision of what the European Union can become.

All elemental life you bless,
removing from them man-made stress,
the nature spirits are now free,
outpicturing Divine decree.

**O Mother Mary, generate,
the song that does accelerate,
the earth into a higher state,
all matter does now scintillate.**

7. Mother Mary, radiate into the collective consciousness the awareness that we need to work to make the EU better from a positive platform. Saint Germain wants the European nations to cooperate and eventually unite in a United States of Europe, which he has envisioned since the 1600's.

I raise my voice and take my stand,
a stop to war I do command,
no more shall warring scar the earth,
a golden age is given birth.

**O Mother Mary, generate,
the song that does accelerate,
the earth into a higher state,
all matter does now scintillate.**

8. Mother Mary, radiate into the collective consciousness the awareness that we need to step up to a positive vision of what can be achieved through peaceful cooperation, rather than the petty squabbles that have taken place for hundreds of years.

As Mother Earth is free at last,
disasters belong to the past,
your Mother Light is so intense,
that matter is now far less dense.

**O Mother Mary, generate,
the song that does accelerate,
the earth into a higher state,
all matter does now scintillate.**

9. Mother Mary, radiate into the collective consciousness the awareness that even the Cold war, World War I, World War II and other conflicts were petty from the perspective of the Divine Mother who sees how much more her children are capable of manifesting. The petty consciousness can only be transcended by being seen for what it is so we see that there is nothing to solve. We need to look in a new direction and follow a higher vision.

In Mother Light the earth is pure,
the upward spiral will endure,
prosperity is now the norm,
God's vision manifest as form.

**O Mother Mary, generate,
the song that does accelerate,
the earth into a higher state,
all matter does now scintillate.**

Sealing

In the name of the Divine Mother, I call to all ascended masters for the sealing of myself and all people in my circle of influence in the creative flow of the Divine Mother, the River of Life. I call for the multiplication of my calls by all ascended masters so that we form the perfect figure-eight flow of "As Above, so below." Thus, I accept that this is fully manifest, because the mouth of the Lord, the Divine Mother that I AM, has spoken it. Amen.

3 | THE NEXT STAGE FOR MODERN DEMOCRACIES

I am the Ascended Master MORE, and why am I more? Because long ago I had a vision and I saw the beauty of the Will of God. I decided to surrender myself, my will, my being, into the flow of the Will of God.

When you surrender yourself unconditionally into a particular God quality, you become one with that quality, we might say, but it would be more accurate to say that you *become* the God quality. I became the Will of God, and as I ascended on that ray of the Will of God, I found myself as an ascended being, one with the Will of God, which truly is not static but is an ever-flowing stream of consciousness. It was natural for me to then accept the position as the Chohan of the First Ray whereby I came to represent the Will of God to planet earth.

The challenge of adaptability

The Will of God is, of course, a many-faceted Being, a many-faceted state of consciousness. It cannot be limited to words. It can be represented by words but as you know, a representation is not the real thing. So it is, with the kind of democracy that you know in Europe, and in other parts of the world, that you often call representative democracy. You elect representatives who are supposed to carry out the will of the people. Of course, they are not the people, are they? Therein lies the problem, as we might say.

However, before I go into that, I wish to pick up on what this beloved Being, Mother Mary, said last night. You see, my beloved, before there can be any change, before anything can become more, there must be an act of will. Now you do, I hope, understand that I have changed my name to Master MORE in order to signal that the Will of God always wants more. You might from a human perspective think that if you always want more, you are never satisfied with what is.

This is not the case and this is the perspective I wish to give you. When you look at the world, you see so often that people have an incredible ability to adapt. This is both good and not so good. It is good in the sense that it allows them to survive very difficult conditions that may only be temporary. They can still survive, they can stay in embodiment, they can keep some kind of composure. When the outer conditions change, they can go on with life, they can have some continuity.

The downside of this ability is that they can also become so used to current conditions that they no longer want more because they have adapted so well that they think either that this is the only way that things can be, that this is the way it is supposed to be or that they really do not want to run the risk of upsetting the apple cart because you never know where the apples might fall. Some of them might fall far from the tree. There are fears in people's beings against upsetting status quo, and they cling to status quo because for many people a known misery is better than an uncertainty.

How then can there be positive change when people cling to status quo? Now, you understand that, I am one with the Will of God, I *am* the Will of God for earth and the Will of God is that everything transcends itself. When I talk about change, I am not talking about a change that goes into a negative and creates less, I am talking about the change that creates more. All change that I desire to see is the change towards more and this, my beloved, cannot be a loss. It cannot be a loss to anyone except, perhaps, those who form a power elite and have taken on special privileges and powers by limiting the people and stealing the people's light. They are the ones who can lose when status quo is changed, but the majority of the people on earth do not lose when there is a change that brings forth more.

How change happens

There are two ways that change can come about. One is, as we have talked about many times, the second law of thermodynamics and the fact that a closed system will self-destruct. When there is resistance to change, the clinging to status quo, then you do enter a downward spiral. It is only a matter of how difficult, how dysfunctional, conditions become before people wake up and decide that things are now so bad that they cannot live with it and therefore they have a will to change. This is, of course, not the way that we of the ascended masters desire to see change come about. When people close their minds, it is not that we do anything to accelerate a negative cycle. We are forced by the Law of Free Will to step back and say that if people do not want to open their minds to new ideas, we must let the spiral unfold until they get to that point where they again have the will for something different.

This is, we might say, the negative way that change can come about. You first have no will to change status quo because you have a clinging to status quo and then, when things get so bad, finally something breaks and now there is a will to change. The problem with this process is that when people change this way, it is not really that they have a vision of wanting something better than what they have. It is more that things have gotten so bad that they want to get away from the misery they are experiencing.

Why did things get so bad, why did the downward spiral go so far down? It was because people did not have a vision of something more and thus they could not even long for it, they could not manifest it. When they get to a low point and things finally break, they still have no vision of what they want instead of their misery. They just want to get away from the misery.

That is precisely what the fallen beings want because then they can step in and promise the people something better, if they only will give up something, such as freedom, such as control over their own lives. This is what you have seen in several totalitarian states where the people have been promised some mythical, magical state if only they would give up their freedom to that totalitarian government. Of course then, can the totalitarian government deliver? Well, as you have seen within the last century, where several totalitarian governments collapsed, you know that they can never deliver the promised land.

3 | *The Next Stage for Modern Democracies*

Things could be much better

What I desire to see for earth is an awakening where you find a positive way to long for change. Of course, you who are listening to this have already started this process. I desire you to hold the vision that many more people catch on to the possibility of a positive change. It is not a matter of letting things go so far that they get broken, it is not even a matter of saying that current conditions are bad, it is just a matter of catching the vision that there is something more, there is something higher.

Mother Mary talked about the people who are stuck in a mud hole and they are walking around in mud, all covered in mud and getting nowhere. Many of the nations of Europe have already climbed out of the mud hole of previous ages. You have a condition where many people have not only a tolerable life but have a very affluent life. They have great economic freedom to do many things that their parents and grandparents could not even dream about. It is not a matter of these people coming to see that current conditions are bad.

It is a matter of them coming to see that current conditions could be a springboard, a stepping stone, to something even better—in fact, far better. So much better that their parents could not even dream about it and that they themselves have so far not really dared to dream about it. It is time for them to dream about it, to dare to dream about what a society really could be when we do not have many of these problems we saw a generation or two ago, such as a world-wide war or two or wide-spread poverty, diseases or many other conditions.

Why external problems do not define you

You see, my beloved, many people in Europe today have a commodity that was actually the greatest luxury just a century or two ago, and it is free time. That free time could be used, instead of empty entertainment, for grasping a higher vision and working on implementing it. What would it then require that people can make this transition and adopt a positive view of the future and of the potential for changing current conditions into a Golden Age? It will require what mother Mary talked about, this willingness to see that so many of the problems that eat up people's attention are inconsequential. They are just petty problems that need to be let go.

How can you then do this? Well, we have talked about it many times before for you who are the spiritual students. It can start with a recognition that there are, currently, certain physical, material conditions manifest on earth, manifest in your society. You, as an individual (whether you are spiritual or not) have limited powers to change these conditions because they are created by the collective. What you can realize is that you are not living in these conditions in the sense that the conditions are defining you. Your relationship to the conditions is that you are *experiencing* the conditions.

What you are experiencing is not the outer conditions; you are experiencing something that is created in your own mind. We have talked about it before, how everything is energy and everything is an energy field. There is a certain physical condition but contrary to the sensory experience and the common understanding, that physical condition is still vibrating energy. It is an energy field and when you are experiencing the condition, your personal energy field is interacting with that other energy field. What you experience inside your mind is that interaction, that interference pattern, between the energy field that is external to you and your own energy field. This means that even if you cannot change the energy field that is external, you can change your own field and by doing this you change your experience of the conditions.

That is how you can come to see that a certain problem, that you may have been brought up (by your parents, your peers or your society) to see as being very important, is not really that important because it does not define you anymore than you allow it to define you by focusing your attention upon it. It is indeed possible that you can come to perceive the problem in a different way and therefore, you will see that your experience of it changes. It no longer has any hold over you, and that is when you can come to see it as truly insignificant. It cannot prevent you from going where you want to go. It is not a matter of you coming to the realization (as it has been projected at you from the traditional religions) that you are a sinner and that something is so terrible or so bad. This is not what I am asking you to do.

I am asking you, instead, to realize that you are currently at a good space but the question is: "Is there more you would like to experience on this earth while you are still in embodiment?" Then, how can you have that experience? Do you not see that the entire illusion created by the fallen beings is that the only way for you to change your life experience is to change the external conditions? The reality (that we have been telling you now for years) is that the only way to change your life experience is to change your internal condition.

Adopting a positive outlook on life

This is the way to adopt a positive outlook on life and on the future. You realize that when you begin with yourself, you are not only changing your own life experience, you are at the same time changing the totality of the collective consciousness. If there is a problem in your particular country that most people are very concerned about, then if you change your own perception of that problem, you will shift the collective consciousness.

You may say: "But is it so much that it is significant?" My beloved, it is significant because you are not an isolated individual. Each one of you (who is open to spiritual teachings and especially ascended master teachings) have many other people who are tied to you in a structure similar to a pyramid. When you raise your consciousness, you will pull up on those below you and make it easier for them to shift their perception.

They, on the other hand, have their own pyramid under them, and that means that when they move up, they pull on all those below them. This is how even one person can start a chain reaction that gradually spreads to an entire society. This is how consciousness changes. This is how consciousness has always changed. It starts with one, then two, then three, then more. All of a sudden, there is that shift where it becomes obvious to the majority of the people in a society that something has changed, or something needs to change and they want change.

We are not looking for a Golden Age to be born on the ashes of the current society collapsing. We are looking for those who can grasp the vision of bringing about positive change by building on what has been achieved. Certainly, my beloved, you can look at a society such as Europe (or the United States) and you can see that even though they have a higher level of development, there is *this* problem, there is *that* problem, there is the next problem. You could focus on the problems and think that society is on the brink of an imminent collapse. You could also shift your perception and realize that regardless of the problems that are there (and I am not asking you to go into denial), compared to how society was fifty or a hundred years ago, tremendous progress has been made. You cannot really deny this. If you are not appreciative, then I suggest you go and talk to your grandparents if they are still alive, and ask them to tell you how it was when they were children, and you will see that there has been progress. I am just asking you to focus on that, to adopt the attitude that we have made much progress.

We have a good foundation for making even more progress, and for shifting into the positive where we are no longer enacting change in order to get away from something that is bad and intolerable. We are enacting change because we see that there is so much more that could be done, that could be experienced, that could be manifested. This is truly what I look for. I desire you, who are the spiritual people and you who are my beloved students, to make that switch, to be positive, to transcend the fear that there could be some collapse tomorrow. I am not saying that there will not be bumps in the road, for there will be, but it is a matter of realizing that the bumps in the road are just that. They are just bumps in the road, but it does not stop your progress. It does not stop the progress of society.

You might even switch your perception even more and realize that the bumps in the road are not even bumps in the road. They are simply manifestations that give people an opportunity to shift their perception. You know very well that there are those who, as I said, cling to status quo, do not want to shift their perception. Sometimes they need to be shaken in order to shift their perception.

If you have already decided to shift your perception into a positive, why should it bother you? Why should you look at these with fear and trepidation? Why should you be discouraged because you think things are so bad, when in reality they are not any worse than you make them out to be. I am therefore saying: "Make them out to be positive, to be stepping stones to a new experience, individually and collectively." How does the collective experience shift unless some dare to shift their individual experience.

How a Golden Age can come about

Do you not see that there has been much talk in spiritual circles about the Golden Age, a better time, a shift into another dimension or whatever you have? Most people have a completely unrealistic expectation of how this can come about. They think that currently things are very bad and that is why there needs to be a change. Somehow, magically, some force will come in and bring about the change. Have we not told you, over and over again, that the force that can bring about change is not the ascended masters, it is *you* who are in embodiment because your free will is what determines the course of planet earth.

How can you bring about change into a Golden Age if you do not shift into the golden age consciousness. Do you think that in the Golden Age people are fearing about the future? Do you think they are afraid of this or that problem, this or that major calamity or collapse? No, of course not. A Golden Age is, among other things, an age where people do not fear the future. They look to the future with great expectation, anticipation and a joy of waiting to see what is the next wonderful thing that will unfold in the world, not the next calamity, but the next great thing that will open up and give them an even richer experience, an experience of more. What is the Golden Age? Is it something that will come about in one grandiose event where you can say: "Two minutes ago, the Golden Age was not there but now it is there?" Of course not; it is an ongoing process. There will be people who do not even realize that there is a Golden Age. In the past, there have been golden ages, but there was still a certain percentage of the population who never realized that it was a Golden Age. In a sense, you could say that every age is in its own way a Golden Age for those who are focusing on the positive.

Have you not seen a growth in society for centuries and thousands of years? Is it not possible to say that in every age some people became part of the change and other people remained part of the problem? This is always the case, and I would like you to be part of the change and to know that things are positive, that we are moving up, that things are becoming more. How can you do this? You certainly cannot do it by looking at current conditions, but you can do it by attuning to the Presence of one of the ascended masters. *That* will give you a frame of reference.

My beloved, if I was a pessimist about the future of the earth, I would not be speaking. I would be holding my peace and allowing the negative spiral to unfold. If I did not think that speaking could make a difference, what would be the point in expending the energy? So you see, I am positive and you can know this by tuning in to me, or to Saint Germain, or to Mother Mary, or whomever is closest to your hearts. Then, lock on to that and realize: "This is reality."

How do you tune in to us? What did I say in the beginning? I surrendered myself into the flow of the Will of God. What is the Divine quality that is close to your heart? Surrender into the flow of that quality. That is how you attune to the Presence of an ascended master. You cannot resist, there cannot be fear, you cannot tune in through fear or through an act of outer will. It is an act of inner will, which is to surrender into the flow.

Having then had my say about the inner conditions, the psychological conditions, I desire to give you a few things about the other aspects of the First Ray.

The exposure of a power elite

First of all, we have power, and power has, of course, been misused greatly on planet earth. This messenger recently found a book where scientists had studied Danish society and had determined that there are five million people in Denmark, but there are only a little over four hundred people that actually run the country and form a power elite.

They even used the word power elite and the title of the book was *Power Elite*. This, of course, is the same in every country, even though in some countries the power elite that runs the population is even smaller compared to the population. You need to hold the vision, to make the calls, that the people wake up and realize that, regardless of the fact that you have a democracy, there is still a small elite of people who have too much power for their own good and for the good of society.

Why do I say this? Because what does history show you? There is an old saying: "All power corrupts and absolute power corrupts absolutely." The simple equation is that nobody who is in an unascended state of consciousness can handle having too much power. This is very simple, my beloved. I can even speak from personal experience of having had certain leadership positions in my embodiments. I can assure you that when I am honest with myself, I can see that I could not handle having unlimited power, and there is nobody who can handle having power over others. Why do you think Jesus and the Buddha did not take a position of power in society? Because they had realized this and had realized that their mission was to show a different state of consciousness. I am not thereby judging or condemning those who have accepted positions of power and have wrestled with it. For many others it was necessary to experience that. In some cases, our exercise of power was better than the alternative of having a fallen being ascend to the throne of power.

Nevertheless, it is a fact that power that is concentrated in the hands of a few people *will* be misused. Now mind you, this does not mean that power is misused malevolently or with negative intentions. The fact of the matter is that in many modern societies, such as Denmark, there is nobody who has a direct, conscious, malevolent intent. The people who form the power elite are not all fallen beings. They are not necessarily all completely blinded by the fallen consciousness. It is not that they have a lust for personal power, but they can only exercise power through their vision, and why have they made the effort to attain those positions of power? That was because they had a certain vision.

It may not be a malevolent vision but it is still an individual, subjective, limited vision. This is the only thing you can have while you are in embodiment. The people are not necessarily exercising power in a way so you would consider them evil or manipulative. They are, in many cases, doing what they think is good and they are doing it to the best of their ability, but they can only do it to the limitations of their vision. It is almost impossible to want to have a position of power without thinking that you know better than the people how the country should be run.

You may look at almost any leader in history, even those who have been fallen beings and who have later come to be seen as evil. You may look at Adolf Hitler, and everybody today clearly sees him as evil (or I should not say *everybody* but the *majority*, for some still idolize him). Nevertheless, he still thought he was acting for the betterness of society and even mankind.

The problem with representative democracy

Everybody who strives for a position of power thinks they know better than the people how the country should be run. What is the foundational, the essential, idea behind democracy? It is that nobody knows better than the people how the country should be run. That is the essence of democracy.

Back to my starting remark about representative democracy. Why was it necessary to have a phase where there was representative democracy? Well, it was for practical matters mainly. There was no communication. Most people were not educated. Many people could not even read and write when the first democracies came into being. This makes it very difficult for the people to know enough about society to make informed decisions. At the same time, there was no way to communicate and get all of the people who lived isolated out in the country to actually vote for certain issues. Therefore, it was the practical solution that (every four years or so) you have an election where the people elected representatives that then took up their positions in parliament and enacted the laws that the country had to follow.

The weakness of the system is, of course, that it almost inevitably creates a power elite. Surely, some people may not be elected at the next election and there may be a change-over. There will be an elite of elected representatives who have made it their life goal to be in office. They will therefore do anything they can to *stay* in office, and therefore they form an elite. There will also be an elite of people in business, even in the forms of government who are not elected representatives but have positions in government and also form a power elite. In many cases, it is because they think they know better. Of course, this is all subjective. If you are a business leader, you may think you know what is best for the country but how easy is it for your vision to be skewed so that what you think is best for the country is also what is best for your company and not so good for the competition?

This is almost impossible to avoid in a representative democracy. There will be that influence, and of course, the more you see that money plays a part in getting people elected, the more there will be an influence for those who have money. This is no more clearly seen than in the United States where the sums of money necessary to run a campaign have become outright ridiculous. It is a wonder, for me at least, that the American people are not revolting against it.

This is, again, because they cling to status quo, and things have not yet gone so bad that people say: "This cannot go on!" Rest assured, my beloved, that unless people are awakened, they will get to that point where they have to say: "Our political system is no longer working and we need change. We need to throw the lobbyists out of Washington, and out of the electoral process and out of the media and other areas of society." The same, of course, applies to some degree in Europe, although to a lesser degree because money is not as big of an issue in the campaigns of many European nations.

The need for direct democracy

What I propose, what *we* propose, Saint Germain and I, the Darjeeling council, we propose a shift towards something that has generally been called "direct democracy." You see in most democratic nations that there are some issues that cannot be decided by parliament but must be decided by a popular referendum where all of the people vote.

You also see some countries, such as Switzerland, that have already implemented a more direct form of democracy. People have to vote on many more issues and can even overturn laws if they are not happy with what was enacted by parliament. This is what we propose for all of Europe: An awakening of the people to a need for a direct democracy where there are many more issues that are decided by a direct vote by the people.

This, of course, for practical purposes, needs to be done so that people can vote by computer. I know that there are some nations where they are fixated on keeping the vote secret. There are nations where they have the capability to implement a digital voting system, but they say we cannot do it because we cannot guarantee that somebody cannot hack the results and thereby see who voted for what.

My beloved, in a direct democracy, you do not need secrecy in voting. What is wrong with standing up and taking responsibility for the way you cast your vote? Anyway, in the current digital age, you all know that everybody on Facebook can know your personal secrets if you put them on the net. Is it not so that the need to hide has become less important? It is, in fact, so that, to a large degree, privacy has become much less of an issue in today's society. There is a need to shift and say: "I have no problem with standing out in the public and standing behind my views and how I cast my vote." Therefore, this fixation on keeping the vote secret cannot be allowed to stop the implementation of direct democracy and the practical solutions that make it possible.

Now, there is not just one way to implement direct democracy; it can be done in many different ways. Of course, we are not sitting up here with a fixed model, saying that this is how every country should do it. We see that the European countries will do it in different ways. We see that it is an issue that needs to be debated, and how will it be debated unless you, who are the spiritual people, shift your consciousness and make the calls that go into the collective consciousness? Thereby, you pull up on all of the people you are tied to so that there is a greater awakening to the need to talk about this.

Are political parties outdated?

As part of this process, you also need to debate whether the current system of political parties has outlived its usefulness. You need to realize that having political parties so easily becomes taken over by the dualistic consciousness where everything has to be polarized, and you have a right wing and a left wing of parliament.

Can we not look realistically and say that these old systems have outlived their usefulness? What sense does it make that we still today have political parties that go back to a clearly socialist, Marxist approach to the economy? We have other political parties that go back to the opposite view of the economy, call it a capitalist or conservative view.

Can we not transcend these labels, these ideologies? Can we not realize that when the Soviet Union collapsed, the world saw the death, the end, of the age of ideology? What we are moving into now is an age where it is not a matter of ideology, it is a matter of what Mother Mary has called the Wisdom of the Mother. You look at what works and what does not work. It does not matter that we may have a fanciful ideology that says that ideally the economy should work like this. If we can actually observe that the economy does not work according to theory, when do we then say that the theory has to go? If it does not conform to observation, can we not then adopt this scientific approach sponsored by Saint Germain and say: "Let us look of what works and get rid of all of the ideologies."

Truly, it should not be a matter of the economy working one way if you are on the left side of the parliament and another way if you are on the right side. The economy is the economy. There are certain principles. They work this way, and it is just a matter of acknowledging it instead of wanting to force the world into a perception filter based on ideology. It is better to actually adjust your perception filter based on how the world works instead of how some fallen being thought the world *should* work.

You could, of course, also seek the help of the ascended masters. We will also give you a vision, not only of how the world works now but how it *could* work. I am not asking for the majority of the people to come to this point in the near future because I know that is not realistic. It should be realistic that people will start looking at what actually works and realizing that it is completely petty and ridiculous to attempt to make the universe conform to a man-made ideology when it obviously does not work that way.

Overcoming opposition

Thus, I have given you the ideas I wanted to give you for now, but I want to comment on the fact that, when a release like this is given, there is always opposition to it. Some of you may have felt a certain burden before this conference and it is because you are feeling the opposition to the release of light. It is natural that you feel this but it is possible to shift out of it by going through the change that I talked about earlier. You can come to the point where you might still realize that there is an opposition but you do not let it color you. You do not let it drag you down. You realize that the opposition is actually a sign that the dark forces are threatened. If they were not threatened by you, they would not bother you and this is something that you see in society in general. Many people who are just following status quo are not burdened by any particular opposition. Those who stand out against status quo, who dare to speak out against the party line, they are often burdened by opposition. Some, many in fact, have been weighted down by it so that they could not fulfill their missions.

You can learn to switch to a point where you realize there is opposition, but you do not let it get to you. You actually see it as a certain sense of encouragement because you realize that the dark forces feel threatened by what you are engaged in. My beloved, why do they feel threatened? They feel threatened for one reason only: They know that if you keep going, they will lose. Otherwise, they would not feel threatened and they would not even bother to send you any energy. When you realize this, you can say: "Well, it doesn't matter. I am going to keep going. And I am going to be an open door for the light and the light will be victorious."

You see, my beloved, we were winning from the beginning. There is no question at all that the earth (and all other planets in the universe that are still at a lower level) will be raised. There is no question about it. It is inevitable because the earth is not an isolated planet. It is connected to all of the billions of planets that have already entered the upward spiral to a point of no return where it could not be turned back. The earth is being pulled up by all of these planets. It is being pulled up partly because there are people in embodiment on earth who have, in the past, embodied on these planets that are now firmly in the upward spiral. Through your presence here, there is that pull from the planet you came from, and it is pulling up the earth. The dark forces cannot win. *They cannot win.* It is only a matter of how long they will be allowed to influence people's perception. Because people are still clinging to status quo, they do not want to be awakened, they do not want to come up higher, they do not want to be aware, they do not want to be conscious.

You, of course, all know this, perhaps from your own experience when you first found the path of how it could be overwhelming to suddenly know more than you knew before. You also know it when you talk to other people and you see that they cannot handle getting so much information that is beyond their current image of the world.

Nevertheless, you need to realize that the dark forces can only influence people on a temporary basis and there is no question that their influence on this planet is being reduced at a rapid pace. The reason for this is that there is now a critical mass of people in embodiment who have locked in to a new spiral, a new era, the Aquarian age and the leadership of Saint Germain. Many of these people have not heard of Saint Germain, but they have still locked in at inner levels to the winds of change.

We have said many times that we respect free will, but you also realize, do you not, that we actually *respect* free will. That means we want people to be in a position where they can make a free choice, and you cannot make a free choice if you do not know that there is something better than what you are experiencing right now. Therefore, it is not a violation of free will to give them that vision.

The fallen beings are violating people's free will by making them think that they have limited options, that they could not choose anything different. That is not what *we* do. We give them the vision that there is something and then we let them choose freely—and you do the same thing.

We are not asking you, in your minds, to go out and want to force other people to come into the golden age consciousness. We are asking you not to limit yourself in how, first of all, *you* enter the golden age consciousness, but also how you express yourself and be yourself. You are in embodiment, you have individual free will, you have a right to enter the golden age consciousness. You have a right to express that and to demonstrate it to others. This is not violating their free will. It is exercising your own free will. I cannot force people, for I am an ascended master. I am not asking you to force people either but I am asking you not to force yourself to shut yourself down in order to avoid disturbing others, for they have a right to be disturbed.

You have a right, under the Law of Free Will, to be disturbed and to be made aware that there is a higher choice than the one you are making right now. You do not have a right, under the Law of Free Will, to remain ignorant. Ignorance is not a right; it is not a natural state. It is an artificially manufactured state, created by the fallen beings. That is why you do not need to respect people's desire to remain ignorant.

You have a right to express who you are and what you have come to see. Without vision, the people perish and without vision they cannot accept what is actually better for themselves. You understand, I have said many times: "If people knew better, they would do better." But if they do not know better, how can they have the choice?

I have given you the choice of whether you will be more with me, and I hope you will. And so, I thank you.

4 | INVOKING THE NEXT STAGE FOR DEMOCRACIES

In the name I AM THAT I AM, Jesus Christ, I call to all ascended masters working on manifesting the Golden Age, especially Archangel Michael, Elohim Hercules, Master MORE, Divine Director and Saint Germain to radiate into the collective consciousness a new awareness of the next step for democracy. Help people see that we can build a new future by working with the ascended masters and letting go of the old way of looking at life, including…

[Make personal calls.]

Part 1

1. Master MORE, radiate into the collective consciousness the awareness that even though the people elect representatives to carry out the will of the people, they are not the people and herein lies the problem with democracy.

> Michael Archangel, in your flame so blue,
> there is no more night, there is only you.
> In oneness with you, we're filled with your light,
> what glorious wonder, revealed to our sight.
>
> **Michael Archangel, your Knowing so strong,**
> **Michael Archangel, oh sweep us along.**
> **Michael Archangel, we're singing your song,**
> **Michael Archangel, with you we belong.**

2. Master MORE, radiate into the collective consciousness the awareness that before there can be any change, before anything can become more, there must be an act of will.

> Michael Archangel, protection you give,
> within your blue shield, we ever shall live.
> Sealed from all creatures, roaming the night,
> we remain in your sphere, of electric blue light.
>
> **Michael Archangel, your Knowing so strong,**
> **Michael Archangel, oh sweep us along.**
> **Michael Archangel, we're singing your song,**
> **Michael Archangel, with you we belong.**

3. Master MORE, radiate into the collective consciousness the awareness that because of our adaptability, we can become so used to current conditions that we cling to status quo because a known misery is better than an uncertainty.

> Michael Archangel, what power you bring,
> as millions of angels, praises will sing.
> Consuming the demons, of doubt and of fear,
> we know that your Presence, will always be near.
>
> **Michael Archangel, your Knowing so strong,**
> **Michael Archangel, oh sweep us along.**
> **Michael Archangel, we're singing your song,**
> **Michael Archangel, with you we belong.**

4. Master MORE, radiate into the collective consciousness the awareness that all true change will give more to the people and can only be a loss for the power elite, which is why they resist change.

> Michael Archangel, God's will is your love,
> you bring to us all, God's light from Above.
> God's will is to see, all life taking flight,
> transcendence of self, our most sacred right.
>
> **Michael Archangel, your Knowing so strong,**
> **Michael Archangel, oh sweep us along.**
> **Michael Archangel, we're singing your song,**
> **Michael Archangel, with you we belong.**

5. Master MORE, radiate into the collective consciousness the awareness that the negative way for change to happen is that we cling to status quo and only when something breaks, do we manifest the will to change.

> Michael Archangel, you are the best friend,
> from all worldly dangers you do us defend,
> the devil no match for your power of light,
> and therefore our souls can freely take flight.
>
> **Michael Archangel, your Knowing so strong,**
> **Michael Archangel, oh sweep us along.**
> **Michael Archangel, we're singing your song,**
> **Michael Archangel, with you we belong.**

6. Master MORE, radiate into the collective consciousness the awareness that a downward spiral forms because we do not have a vision of something more. The fallen beings then step in and promise something better, if we give up freedom and control.

> Michael Archangel, as children we play,
> we're bringing the earth into a new day,
> we raise it from all of the patterns so old,
> our planet's life story is by us retold.
>
> **Michael Archangel, your Knowing so strong,**
> **Michael Archangel, oh sweep us along.**
> **Michael Archangel, we're singing your song,**
> **Michael Archangel, with you we belong.**

4 | Invoking the Next Stage for Democracies

7. Master MORE, radiate into the collective consciousness the awareness that we need a positive way to bring about change. Help people catch on to the possibility of a positive change and catch the vision that there is something more.

> Michael Archangel, God's power you show,
> that you are invincible, this we do know,
> you are undivided and thus can withstand,
> anything coming from serpentine band.

> **Michael Archangel, your Knowing so strong,**
> **Michael Archangel, oh sweep us along.**
> **Michael Archangel, we're singing your song,**
> **Michael Archangel, with you we belong.**

8. Master MORE, radiate into the collective consciousness the awareness that current conditions are a springboard, a stepping stone, to something even better, so much better that our parents could not dream about it and we have not dared to dream about it.

> Michael Archangel, come raise now the earth,
> giving her thus a complete rebirth,
> collective the mind that we do now raise,
> for this we do give our infinite praise.

> **Michael Archangel, your Knowing so strong,**
> **Michael Archangel, oh sweep us along.**
> **Michael Archangel, we're singing your song,**
> **Michael Archangel, with you we belong.**

9. Master MORE, radiate into the collective consciousness the awareness that it is time to dare to dream about what a society really could be when we do not have many of the problems we saw a generation or two ago, such as war, poverty or diseases.

> Michael Archangel, the earth is now new,
> covered in Blue-flame as the morning dew,
> our planet now sparkles throughout all of space,
> as we are receiving your infinite Grace.
>
> **Michael Archangel, your Knowing so strong,**
> **Michael Archangel, oh sweep us along.**
> **Michael Archangel, we're singing your song,**
> **Michael Archangel, with you we belong.**

Part 2

1. Master MORE, radiate into the collective consciousness the awareness that our greatest luxury is free time, and instead of empty entertainment, it could be used for grasping a higher vision and working on implementing it.

> O Hercules Blue, we're one with your will,
> all space in our beings with Blue Flame you fill,
> a beacon that radiates light to the earth,
> bringing about our planet's rebirth.
>
> **O Hercules Blue, all life you defend,**
> **giving us power to always transcend,**
> **in you the expansion of self has no end,**
> **as we in God's infinite spirals ascend.**

2. Master MORE, radiate into the collective consciousness the awareness that before we can adopt a positive view of the future, we need to see that so many of the problems that eat up our attention are inconsequential. They are petty problems that need to be let go.

> O Hercules Blue, your wisdom so great,
> within us a sense of knowing create,
> a new frame of reference we suddenly gain,
> for going beyond duality's pain.

> **O Hercules Blue, all life you defend,**
> **giving us power to always transcend,**
> **in you the expansion of self has no end,**
> **as we in God's infinite spirals ascend.**

3. Master MORE, radiate into the collective consciousness the awareness that we do not have to let external conditions define us because we have the power to change how we experience those conditions.

> O Hercules Blue, we lovingly raise,
> our voices in giving God infinite praise,
> in feeling your flame, so clearly we see,
> transcending the self is the true alchemy.

> **O Hercules Blue, all life you defend,**
> **giving us power to always transcend,**
> **in you the expansion of self has no end,**
> **as we in God's infinite spirals ascend.**

4. Master MORE, radiate into the collective consciousness the awareness that by changing our perspective on life, we can free our minds from the limitations put upon us by our parents and society and therefore we can go where we want to go.

> O Hercules Blue, all life now you heal,
> enveloping all in your Blue-flame Seal,
> we're grateful for playing a personal part,
> In God's infinitely intricate work of art.
>
> **O Hercules Blue, all life you defend,**
> **giving us power to always transcend,**
> **in you the expansion of self has no end,**
> **as we in God's infinite spirals ascend.**

5. Master MORE, radiate into the collective consciousness the awareness that the fallen beings have created the illusion that the only way for us to change our life experience is to change external conditions. The reality is that the only way to change our life experience is to change our internal condition.

> O Hercules Blue, your Temple of Light,
> revealed to us all through our inner sight,
> your power allows us to forge on until,
> we pierce every veil and climb every hill.
>
> **O Hercules Blue, all life you defend,**
> **giving us power to always transcend,**
> **in you the expansion of self has no end,**
> **as we in God's infinite spirals ascend.**

6. Master MORE, radiate into the collective consciousness the awareness that when we begin with ourselves, we are not only changing our own life experience, we are at the same time changing the totality of the collective consciousness.

> O Hercules Blue, I pledge now my life,
> in helping this planet transcend human strife,
> duality's lies are pierced by your light,
> restoring the fullness of our inner sight.
>
> **O Hercules Blue, all life you defend,**
> **giving us power to always transcend,**
> **in you the expansion of self has no end,**
> **as we in God's infinite spirals ascend.**

7. Master MORE, radiate into the collective consciousness the awareness that if there is a problem in our particular country that most people are very concerned about, then if we change our own perception of that problem, we will shift the collective consciousness.

> O Hercules Blue, we set all life free,
> from the subtlest lies of duality,
> the prince of this world no more has a bond,
> for with you we go completely beyond.
>
> **O Hercules Blue, all life you defend,**
> **giving us power to always transcend,**
> **in you the expansion of self has no end,**
> **as we in God's infinite spirals ascend.**

8. Master MORE, radiate into the collective consciousness the awareness that even one person can start a chain reaction that gradually spreads to an entire society, and this is how consciousness changes.

> O Hercules Blue, in oneness with thee,
> we open our hearts to your reality,
> your electric-blue fire within us reveal,
> our innermost longing for all that is real.
>
> **O Hercules Blue, all life you defend,**
> **giving us power to always transcend,**
> **in you the expansion of self has no end,**
> **as we in God's infinite spirals ascend.**

9. Master MORE, radiate into the collective consciousness the awareness that a Golden Age will not be born on the ashes of the current society collapsing, but because some grasp the vision of bringing about positive change by building on what has been achieved.

> O Hercules Blue, you fill every space,
> with infinite Power and infinite Grace,
> you embody the key to creativity,
> the will to transcend into Infinity.
>
> **O Hercules Blue, all life you defend,**
> **giving us power to always transcend,**
> **in you the expansion of self has no end,**
> **as we in God's infinite spirals ascend.**

Part 3

1. Master MORE, radiate into the collective consciousness the awareness that most people have a completely unrealistic expectation of how a better age can come about. They think some force will come in and bring about the change, yet the force that can bring about change is we who are in embodiment.

> Master MORE, come to the fore,
> we will absorb your flame of MORE.
> Master MORE, our will so strong,
> our power centers cleared by song.
>
> **Master MORE, your Sacred Heart,**
> **from this we will no more depart,**
> **we are forever in your flow,**
> **of Diamond Will that you bestow.**

2. Master MORE, radiate into the collective consciousness the awareness that a Golden Age is an age where people do not fear the future. They look to the future with great expectation, anticipation and a joy of waiting to see what is the next wonderful thing that will unfold in the world.

> Master MORE, your wisdom flows,
> as our attunement ever grows.
> Master MORE, we have a tie,
> that helps us see through Serpent's lie.

> **Master MORE, your Sacred Heart,**
> **from this we will no more depart,**
> **we are forever in your flow,**
> **of Diamond Will that you bestow.**

3. Master MORE, radiate into the collective consciousness the awareness that there has been growth in society for centuries and millennia. In every age, some people become part of the change and other people remain part of the problem.

> Master MORE, your love so pink,
> there is no purer love, we think.
> Master MORE, you set us free,
> from all conditionality.

> **Master MORE, your Sacred Heart,**
> **from this we will no more depart,**
> **we are forever in your flow,**

4. Master MORE, radiate into the collective consciousness the awareness that in every country, there is a small power elite that runs the country. Even in a democracy, there is a small elite of people who have too much power for their own good, and for the good of society.

> Master MORE, we will endure,
> your discipline that makes us pure.
> Master MORE, intentions true,
> as we are always one with you.

4 | Invoking the Next Stage for Democracies

**Master MORE, your Sacred Heart,
from this we will no more depart,
we are forever in your flow,
of Diamond Will that you bestow.**

5. Master MORE, radiate into the collective consciousness the awareness that history show us that: "All power corrupts and absolute power corrupts absolutely." Nobody can handle having too much power.

Master MORE, our vision raised,
the will of God is always praised.
Master MORE, creative will,
raising all life higher still.

**Master MORE, your Sacred Heart,
from this we will no more depart,
we are forever in your flow,
of Diamond Will that you bestow.**

6. Master MORE, radiate into the collective consciousness the awareness that power that is concentrated in the hands of a few people *will* be misused, not necessarily malevolently or with negative intentions, but because of a limited vision.

Master MORE, your peace is power,
the demons of war it will devour.
Master MORE, we serve all life,
our flames consuming war and strife.

> **Master MORE, your Sacred Heart,**
> **from this we will no more depart,**
> **we are forever in your flow,**
> **of Diamond Will that you bestow.**

7. Master MORE, radiate into the collective consciousness the awareness that leaders can only exercise power through their vision, and they made the effort to attain positions of power because they had a certain vision.

> Master MORE, we are so free,
> eternal bond from you we see.
> Master MORE, we find rebirth,
> in flow of your eternal mirth.

> **Master MORE, your Sacred Heart,**
> **from this we will no more depart,**
> **we are forever in your flow,**
> **of Diamond Will that you bestow.**

8. Master MORE, radiate into the collective consciousness the awareness that even if leaders do not have a malevolent vision, it is still a subjective vision. It is almost impossible to want to have a position of power without thinking that you know better than the people how the country should be run.

> Master MORE, you balance all,
> the seven rays upon our call.
> Master MORE, forever MORE,
> we are the Spirit's open door.

4 | Invoking the Next Stage for Democracies

> **Master MORE, your Sacred Heart,**
> **from this we will no more depart,**
> **we are forever in your flow,**
> **of Diamond Will that you bestow.**

9. Master MORE, radiate into the collective consciousness the awareness that the foundational idea behind democracy is that nobody knows better than the people how the country should be run. That is the essence of democracy.

> Master MORE, your Presence here,
> filling up the inner sphere.
> Life is now a sacred flow,
> God Power we on all bestow.

> **Master MORE, your Sacred Heart,**
> **from this we will no more depart,**
> **we are forever in your flow,**
> **of Diamond Will that you bestow.**

Part 4

1. Master MORE, radiate into the collective consciousness the awareness that representative democracy was a practical necessity because of poor communication and the people's lack of education.

> Divine Director, I now see,
> the world is unreality,
> in my heart I now truly feel,
> the Spirit is all that is real.

**Divine Director, send the light,
from blindness clear my inner sight,
my vision free, my vision clear,
your guidance is forever here.**

2. Master MORE, radiate into the collective consciousness the awareness that the weakness of representative democracy is that it almost inevitably creates a power elite.

Divine Director, vision give,
in clarity I want to live,
I now behold my plan Divine,
the plan that is uniquely mine.

**Divine Director, send the light,
from blindness clear my inner sight,
my vision free, my vision clear,
your guidance is forever here.**

3. Master MORE, radiate into the collective consciousness the awareness that there will be an elite of elected representatives who have made it their life goal to be in office. They will do anything they can to stay in office, and therefore they form an elite.

Divine Director, show in me,
the ego games, and set me free,
help me escape the ego's cage,
to help bring in the Golden Age.

> **Divine Director, send the light,**
> **from blindness clear my inner sight,**
> **my vision free, my vision clear,**
> **your guidance is forever here.**

4. Master MORE, radiate into the collective consciousness the awareness that the more money plays a part in getting people elected, the more there will be an influence for those who have money.

> Divine Director, I'm with you,
> my vision one, no longer two,
> as karma's veil you do disperse,
> I see a whole new universe.

> **Divine Director, send the light,**
> **from blindness clear my inner sight,**
> **my vision free, my vision clear,**
> **your guidance is forever here.**

5. Master MORE, radiate into the collective consciousness the awareness that the next step for democracy is a shift towards direct democracy where more issues are not decided by parliament but must be decided by a popular referendum.

> Divine Director, I go up,
> electric light now fills my cup,
> consume in me all shadows old,
> bestow on me a vision bold.

> **Divine Director, send the light,**
> **from blindness clear my inner sight,**
> **my vision free, my vision clear,**
> **your guidance is forever here.**

6. Master MORE, radiate into the collective consciousness the awareness that in a direct democracy, we do not need secrecy in voting and the fixation on keeping the vote secret cannot be allowed to stop the implementation of direct democracy and the practical solutions that make it possible.

> Divine Director, heart of gold,
> my sacred labor I unfold,
> o blessed Guru, I now see,
> where my own plan is taking me.

> **Divine Director, send the light,**
> **from blindness clear my inner sight,**
> **my vision free, my vision clear,**
> **your guidance is forever here.**

7. Master MORE, radiate into the collective consciousness the awareness that there is a need to debate whether the current system of political parties has outlived its usefulness.

> Divine Director, by your grace,
> in grander scheme I find my place,
> my individual flame I see,
> uniqueness God has given me.

4 | Invoking the Next Stage for Democracies

**Divine Director, send the light,
from blindness clear my inner sight,
my vision free, my vision clear,
your guidance is forever here.**

8. Master MORE, radiate into the collective consciousness the awareness that having political parties so easily becomes taken over by the dualistic consciousness where everything has to be polarized, and we have a right wing and a left wing of parliament.

Divine Director, vision one,
I see that I AM God's own Sun,
with your direction so Divine,
I am now letting my light shine.

**Divine Director, send the light,
from blindness clear my inner sight,
my vision free, my vision clear,
your guidance is forever here.**

9. Master MORE, radiate into the collective consciousness the awareness that it makes no sense to have political parties that go back to a socialist, Marxist approach to the economy and other parties that go back to a capitalist or conservative view.

Divine Director, what a gift,
to be a part of Spirit's lift,
to raise mankind out of the night,
to bask in Spirit's loving sight.

> Divine Director, send the light,
> from blindness clear my inner sight,
> my vision free, my vision clear,
> your guidance is forever here.

Part 5

1. Master MORE, radiate into the collective consciousness the awareness that we need to transcend these labels, these ideologies. When the Soviet Union collapsed, the world saw the end of the age of ideology.

> O Saint Germain, you do inspire,
> my vision raised forever higher,
> with you I form a figure-eight,
> your Golden Age I co-create.
>
> **O Saint Germain, what love you bring,
> it truly makes all matter sing,
> your violet flame does all restore,
> with you we are becoming more.**

2. Master MORE, radiate into the collective consciousness the awareness that it is not a matter of ideology, it is a matter of what works and what does not work. It makes no sense to try to force the economy to fit an ideology. We need to look at how the economy actually works.

> O Saint Germain, what Freedom Flame,
> released when we recite your name,
> acceleration is your gift,
> our planet it will surely lift.
>
> **O Saint Germain, what love you bring,**
> **it truly makes all matter sing,**
> **your violet flame does all restore,**
> **with you we are becoming more.**

3. Master MORE, radiate into the collective consciousness the awareness that the economy is not working one way if you are on the left side of parliament and another way if you are on the right side. There are certain principles, and it is a matter of acknowledging it instead of wanting to force the world into a perception filter based on ideology.

> O Saint Germain, in love we claim,
> our right to bring your violet flame,
> from you Above, to us below,
> it is an all-transforming flow.
>
> **O Saint Germain, what love you bring,**
> **it truly makes all matter sing,**
> **your violet flame does all restore,**
> **with you we are becoming more.**

4. Master MORE, radiate into the collective consciousness the awareness that we need to adjust our perception filter based on how the world works instead of how some fallen being thought the world *should* work.

> O Saint Germain, I love you so,
> my aura filled with violet glow,
> my chakras filled with violet fire,
> I am your cosmic amplifier.
>
> **O Saint Germain, what love you bring,
> it truly makes all matter sing,
> your violet flame does all restore,
> with you we are becoming more.**

5. Master MORE, radiate into the collective consciousness the awareness that we need to start looking at what actually works and realizing that it is completely petty and ridiculous to attempt to make the universe conform to a man-made ideology when it obviously does not work that way.

> O Saint Germain, I am now free,
> your violet flame is therapy,
> transform all hang-ups in my mind,
> as inner peace I surely find.
>
> **O Saint Germain, what love you bring,
> it truly makes all matter sing,
> your violet flame does all restore,
> with you we are becoming more.**

6. Master MORE, radiate into the collective consciousness the awareness that the earth is being raised and the power of the fallen beings and the power elite is being reduced.

> O Saint Germain, my body pure,
> your violet flame for all is cure,
> consume the cause of all disease,
> and therefore I am all at ease.
>
> **O Saint Germain, what love you bring,**
> **it truly makes all matter sing,**
> **your violet flame does all restore,**
> **with you we are becoming more.**

7. Master MORE, radiate into the collective consciousness the awareness that people have a right, under the Law of Free Will, to be disturbed and to be made aware that there is a higher choice than the one they are making right now.

> O Saint Germain, I'm karma-free,
> the past no longer burdens me,
> a brand new opportunity,
> I am in Christic unity.
>
> **O Saint Germain, what love you bring,**
> **it truly makes all matter sing,**
> **your violet flame does all restore,**
> **with you we are becoming more.**

8. Master MORE, radiate into the collective consciousness the awareness that we do not have a right, under the Law of Free Will, to remain ignorant. Ignorance is not a right, it is not a natural state, it is an artificially manufactured state created by the fallen beings. That is why we do not need to respect people's desire to remain ignorant.

O Saint Germain, we are now one,
I am for you a violet sun,
as we transform this planet earth,
your Golden Age is given birth.

**O Saint Germain, what love you bring,
it truly makes all matter sing,
your violet flame does all restore,
with you we are becoming more.**

9. Master MORE, radiate into the collective consciousness the awareness that without vision, the people perish and without vision they cannot accept what is actually better for themselves. If people knew better, they would do better, but if they do not know better, how can they have the choice?

O Saint Germain, the earth is free,
from burden of duality,
in oneness we bring what is best,
your Golden Age is manifest.

**O Saint Germain, what love you bring,
it truly makes all matter sing,
your violet flame does all restore,
with you we are becoming more.**

Sealing

In the name of the Divine Mother, I call to all ascended masters for the sealing of myself and all people in my circle of influence in the creative flow of the Divine Mother, the River of Life. I call for the multiplication of my calls by all ascended masters, so that we form the perfect figure-eight flow of "As Above, so below." Thus, I accept that this is fully manifest, because the mouth of the Lord, the Divine Mother that I AM, has spoken it. Amen.

5 | EDUCATION IN THE GOLDEN AGE

I am the Ascended Master Lanto, the Chohan of the Second Ray. We have each chosen to focus on a particular issue, or a couple of issues, that from our particular ray seems the most important contribution that can be made at this time for bringing Europe into the Golden Age. I will, from the perspective of the Second Ray, which is the Ray of Wisdom, focus on which particular application of wisdom could assist people the most in awakening to the golden age consciousness.

A new awareness about money

In order to explain this, I want to start out by talking about what most people in the more developed part of the world have learned about money. You know, of course, that there are many people who live at such severe levels of poverty that they do not have much money to spend and therefore do not have some of the concerns that you have when you have surplus money,

money that is not needed for the bare physical survival of yourself and your family. You have, in the last generation especially, seen that in many countries the majority of the population has been in this state of affluence. They had more money than was absolutely needed for their physical, material survival and sustenance. This has raised an entirely different way of looking at money where you suddenly have the choices of what to do with your money.

What have many people learned from this experience? They have learned that there are people out there who are out to get your money and who will seek to manipulate the money away from you through various schemes. Some may be relatively innocent, in a sense that they would make you buy something or buy some experience that you don't really need, that isn't very important for you but that gives you maybe some cheap, brief sense of entertainment. Many people have also learned that there are more severe scams and schemes that are aimed at taking money away from you, even to the point of taking more than your surplus but taking everything that you have. This might be anything from various con artist tricks to the greater con artist tricks of the manipulation of the economy, the manipulation of markets, and the manipulation of various pension funds and schemes that were supposed to be there for your retirement but suddenly may not be there due to some manipulation.

What have people learned from all of this? They have learned that they need to be aware of what they do with their money. Before they give their money to someone, they need to consider what those people are going to do with it. Is it still going to be there for you? Is it really going to multiply ten thousand times as they promised you? Or is it just too good to be true? Most people have developed this growing awareness that before you give out money, you need to make a careful, conscious evaluation of what the consequences will be because once the money is out of your hand or bank account, you have no guarantee that you can get it back.

This is, of course, a step up in people's awareness. From the Second Ray of Wisdom we are always looking at how we can increase people's awareness, their level of wisdom. Mother Mary has talked about the Wisdom of the Mother, of what can happen in the physical octave, how things work in the physical octave. What I am talking about, concerning people's awareness of money, is very much an aspect of the Wisdom of the Mother, for you realize that you have to be careful in the material world what you do with your money.

Awareness of how your energy is stolen

If I, as the Chohan of the Second Ray, was to point to one particular thing that could give the most important contribution to the bringing in of the Golden Age in terms of wisdom, it would be that people gained an awareness that is similar to what they have learned about giving away money, but it was applied to the field of giving away their energy. Money is a physical substance, but as you all know, the real currency of the world is energy—your emotional, mental, and identity energy.

Most of the people in the world, of course, are not aware of this. That is why the greatest revolution of thought that we can envision from the Second Ray (and I know that the other chohans can envision their own greatest revolution of thought) would be that people became aware that there are forces in this world that seek to steal their energy. These forces have invented all kinds of schemes in order to take energy away from them. This, of course, begins with a recognition that when you are living in extreme poverty, just physical survival can be such a struggle that it takes up all of your energy. You have no surplus energy to give. It is all tied into just surviving. I am not thereby saying that your energy isn't being stolen by demons because, of course, the people who are in extreme poverty are very much trapped there by demons. What I am pointing out to you is that when you become more physically affluent and have what Master MORE talked about: spare time, you also increase your energy level. You are not spending so much energy on material, physical survival, and therefore you have energy left over. This, of course, now means that you become the target of all of these schemes where forces and people seek to steal your emotional, mental, and identity energy away from you.

Forces that must steal energy

You also need the recognition that there are beings, forces, that are existing in this world that *need* to steal your energy in order to survive. There are people in physical embodiment who need to steal energy from others in order to stay in physical embodiment. There are also those who need to steal energy in order to exercise the power they have. All of the dictators you have seen in history have stolen energy from their followers in order to exercise whatever power they exercised. People also need to become aware that there are beings in the emotional, mental, and identity realms that likewise need to steal their energy in order to continue to survive or in order to continue to exercise power. Why do these beings need to steal energy? Because they have lowered their consciousness to the point where they can no longer receive energy from the spiritual realm.

I realize full well that to give the average person this awareness will require quite a process. It is not something that can happen overnight because people need to know many things.

You need to understand also that you are actually a spiritual being, that there is a level of reality beyond the material and that the entire material realm is created and sustained by a flow of energy from the spiritual realm into the four levels of the material universe. You need to understand that this energy flows into the material world through those beings that are not cut off from the flow because they haven't lowered their consciousness beyond the critical level.

You know well that on the physical level, the more money you have, the more you become a target for those who want to steal it. People need to recognize that the same holds true with energy. Some people have more energy, more light, than others and they are the ones who become a target. Therefore, they are the ones that need to be more aware. Yet all people need to be aware because all people in the more affluent countries are definitely the target of the lower forces that want to steal their energy.

This is such a widespread phenomenon that I almost hesitate to tell you more about it because I know that the vast majority of the people on this planet would be so overwhelmed if they knew how many schemes are created for the sole purpose of stealing people's energy. These schemes may be presented at the physical level as having some necessity or even doing a good deed, serving a good cause, but in reality they are aimed at only one thing: stealing people's energy.

Energy vampires

While it may sound as if it would be a big leap for the average person to come to accept this, I can also tell you that, seen from my perspective, the acceptance of these ideas is not as far off as you might think. Otherwise why would I bother presenting them if only a few could grasp them? Many people know about the idea, the concept, of vampires that will suck your blood. It is not such a big leap to realize that although physical vampires do not exist, there are energy vampires that will steal your energy. There are, of course, also people in the physical who will use physical violence to steal people's energy.

There is also a growing awareness of energy, meaning what we might call mental or psychic energy. More and more people are becoming aware of this, more and more people are becoming sensitive to negative energies or positive energies. You have many people who have even entered a race to get more and more positive energy, to feel good vibrations, to feel a good mood, a good environment. There is already a growing awareness of energy and the importance of energy, and that is why it is time that those of you who are more aware make the calls into the collective consciousness to pull up on those who can be pulled up and to realize that they need to be as careful with how they spend their energy as with how they spend their money.

Physical activities that drain energy

How do you spend energy? Well, you spend energy, of course, through your physical activities. Many physical activities are aimed at stealing your energy. There are many examples, from the very severe to the seemingly benign. One of the most severe is, of course, torture. You realize that while there was a time when torture was being reduced in the world, in recent decades torture has actually increased. The violations of people, their human rights, the application of torture, has increased, and this is even done at a governmental level in many nations. Torture is a physical activity that has the primary purpose of stripping people of their emotional, mental, and identity energy so that the dark forces, the demons, can use it for their survival or to increase their power.

This is why virtually every dictator in the history of the world has had to execute or torture (or both) a certain amount of people in order to get enough energy to feed the demons that give power to the human being in embodiment. You may think, as some do, that Hitler had great power or that Stalin or Mao had great power, but they had very little personal power. They had surrendered themselves to some very powerful demons because they had an ambition of exercising power in the physical world. They were literally willing to sell their souls to the devil in order to have that power here on earth.

Between the extreme ranges of war and torture and the more benign activities, there is a great range of these physical activities. Let me mention just one: many sporting games. When people get completely worked up into a state of frenzy, yelling and screaming, rooting for their home team, rooting against the other team, it has the effect of draining people's energy. Any kind of substance that alters your consciousness, drugs or alcohol, tobacco included, also allows demons and entities to steal your energy.

There are many seemingly benign activities that do the same. Many movies (in fact, I am tempted to say *all* movies, but that is not entirely accurate, as there is a very small percentage of movies that do not steal your energy) are direct energy drains. This applies especially to very violent movies or what you call horror movies that are aimed at scaring you. There are also many ways of stealing your energy through getting your sympathy, through getting you to engage in an activity where you feel empathy or pity with other people.

I am not trying to overwhelm you and get you to feel that you cannot engage in any activity. I am trying to make you more aware and more sensitive, and I am especially speaking to the collective consciousness that there is a need to increase your sensitivity. It is not so black-and-white that an activity can only drain your energy and that, therefore, your only option is to not engage in the activity. There are many of the more benign activities where, if you are in a certain state of consciousness and you are not aware, then your energy can be stolen. At the same time, you can engage in that activity without having your energy stolen so this goes with the increased awareness.

Emotional activities that drain energy

There are many activities that are not directly physical, although they have a physical counterpart. They are truly aimed at creating such an emotional reaction in you that it sets up a pattern in your emotional body. I understand that there are certain activities that create an emotional reaction, such as a sporting game, but there are also certain activities or matrices that are created at the emotional level in order to program your emotional body to respond a certain way when you are exposed to specific situations.

A person who regularly goes to football games and always gets very hyperactive about it, has already created (or had created) certain matrices in his emotional body that cause him to be drawn to the football games and to react a certain way. It causes people to not feel that they are getting enough of it, and they want more and more.

Mental activities that drain energy

There are activities in the mental realm that are aimed at just keeping you engaged, as Mother Mary said, in these petty problems that really have no solution and will not make a contribution to bringing forth a Golden Age. These are so numerous that I will not mention them, but there are many, many such activities that have that singular purpose of engaging your mind in thinking you are working for a good cause, thinking you are actually helping to solve a particular problem, but there is no solution to the problem.

There is, however, also another category of this kind of mental activities that I wish to make you aware of because it is not something we have spoken much about so far. You know that we have talked about the fallen beings seeking to trap you into the epic mindset where there is seemingly some cause that is so important that it is a matter of life and death or the collapse of the planet that this problem is solved. Beyond this, you need to recognize that the function of your mental body is to explain things, to give you an explanation for why something is happening. There is nothing particularly good, bad or evil about this. It is simply the function of the mental body. It is meant to analyze, to understand, to compare, to look at what happens, look at what the consequences of a certain choice are so you can evaluate before you make a choice.

The fallen beings have learned to take advantage of this. They know that whatever you experience, whatever you see on earth, your mental body will want to come up with an explanation. It will want to understand this. The fallen beings have learned that there are many things they can do, many schemes they can create, where they do something that violates people. There is no reason for it other than they want to make people confused because they know that people will seek out an explanation, but there is no explanation.

The fallen beings are doing this deliberately to confuse your mental bodies and to induce a state of doubt (or even in the emotional body a state of fear) because you cannot understand why this is happening. You cannot understand why people are doing this. Why are people behaving like this? You seek a rational explanation, you seek a cause and effect, but you cannot see any cause. You cannot see any rational explanation so your mental body gets engaged in seeking this explanation where there is none. The only way out of it is to realize what the fallen beings are trying to do and then refuse to engage your mental body in always wanting an explanation.

As an obvious example, people have often sought to understand why a serial killer will go on a killing spree and seemingly randomly kill people. The fallen beings know that your rational, intellectual mind wants to understand why this happened so that you can protect yourself or society from this happening again. You think that if something happened, there must be a rational explanation, there must be some sequence of causes that led up to this effect, and if you can understand what the sequence was in that particular instance, you might be able to prevent it in other instances.

Psychologists have engaged in this game of trying to analyze how serial killers think, what their upbringing was, how the subconscious mind works, in order to find a rational explanation, but in many cases there is no rational explanation. The explanation is that some fallen beings were trying to create this confusion, and they were able to have demons take over the mind of a particular person and cause him to go on this killing spree.

This is the only explanation there is. You cannot go in and analyze the mind of the serial killer and find a rational explanation for this because it was not his mind that was doing the killing. It was the mind of the demons who had taken him over, and they have no reason. You cannot go in and say: "Well, why did the demon choose to kill that person and not that person?" There is no rational explanation for this.

Wanting to understand everything

You need to, as the spiritual people, recognize that your mind always wants an explanation. As you become aware of the spiritual path, you want to understand everything. You think that if you have a spiritual teaching, it should be possible to explain everything. You need to be more aware here.

There *is* an explanation for everything. You might look at a serial killer and say: "There is an explanation." I have just given that explanation to you, but, as I said, there is no spiritual teaching that can go into the mind of that person and say why exactly this happened. You can go into the mind of the person, and you can see when that person (most likely in a past life) did start the downward path that caused the person to gradually surrender more and more of its mind to dark forces. You can do this, but you cannot give a direct, analytical, cause-and-effect sequence that is understandable to the intellectual mind. At least you cannot do so by looking at that particular person, that particular lifetime, and any conditions in that person's lifetime that led to this. Therefore, you will see that the scientists, the psychologists, will never get to the bottom of these issues because they are approaching it from a limited perspective.

The same applies to some of the world events you have seen. You can go into the mind of Adolf Hitler and you can try to analyze, based on his upbringing and this and that. Psychologists have been doing this since the 1940s and '50s. But have they gotten anywhere closer to understanding why Hitler did what he did? Not really, in terms of fully understanding it. They all realize (if they have investigated this) that there were other people who had a very similar childhood but who did not become mass murderers. How do you explain this?

Again, as I said earlier, you cannot understand a person like Adolf Hitler without understanding that he had such an ambition about having power on earth that he was willing to sell his soul to the dark forces beyond the physical octave. They could give him that power by literally giving him the power to manipulate people's emotional, mental and identity bodies by making them feel that they were the super humans, belonging to the super race. Therefore, it was perfectly rational, and they had the absolute right to do what they did in terms of suppressing and eradicating other people.

This all started in the identity, mental, and emotional bodies of the German people. You cannot find a physical explanation, and you cannot even find a completely rational explanation. Again, the demons who had taken over Hitler's mind wanted to do certain things that were so outrageous, so nonsensical, so irrational, just to create confusion, just to confuse people's mental bodies. This very much goes along with increasing the awareness of how your energy is stolen because you will see that there are many activities in the world where people are frantically seeking an explanation of many of the events that are, as I have now told you, inexplicable.

How education drains people's energy

Of course, the Second Ray is very much related to the field of education, and if you take these ideas and apply them to education, you will see that there are many activities in the area of education and science that are aimed at trying to explain some of these things that I am now telling you have no explanation. What is the effect of this? It is that all of the people who, with the best of intentions, are focusing their minds on trying to understand the psychology, for example, behind mass murderers or behind certain world events are pouring their energy into a matrix, into a portal that allows the forces in the mental realm to steal their energy.

These forces feed themselves on the energy and therefore gain more power to control and affect the minds of people in embodiment. It becomes a vicious circle where the people in embodiment are feeding the beings in the mental realm, and thereby the beings in the mental realm are getting more power to manipulate people's minds, and they can steal even more energy from them.

It needs to be recognized that there are many areas of education that simply have the effect of draining people's energy. This applies not only to seeking an explanation, but it applies also to the old structure of much of higher education that is based on a more authoritarian model where the university professors and teachers teach from a position of authority and are talking down to the students. They are in essence seeking to program the students to conform to the overall worldview upon which that educational institution is based, or even the overall view upon which most educational institutions are based.

You will recognize, of course, that much of higher education around the world promotes a strictly materialistic view of life. This feeds certain demons or beings in the mental realm. It even feeds many demons in the emotional realm that are stealing people's energy by engaging them in the intellectual pursuit of a rational explanation for how the universe works so that we can put God out of the equation—for now we have this rational theory that explains everything. It also makes many intellectual people have a certain disdain or overbearing feeling towards religious people, and thereby these intellectual people's emotional energies are drained.

Authoritarian education programs people

Much education is not aimed at giving the students wisdom but is aimed at programming their minds to accept a certain worldview that is defined by the dark forces, the very forces of anti-wisdom. This, of course, is an important topic to make calls on because how will we ever bring forth a greater awareness of the Golden Age and the golden age principles unless it involves education? In many cases, it must start with education. It must start by recognizing that the current educational model in many countries is based on not only a Piscean mindset but the perverted Piscean mindset of an authoritarian structure that leads to one person or a few people being at the top and everybody at lower levels having to conform.

You need to open up for an Aquarian Age education where there is no authority as such. It is recognized that both students and teachers are walking a continued path of education and that the teachers are not meant to possess a finite closed box of knowledge. A teacher should actually be a person who is learning throughout his entire life and he or she is learning by teaching and is continually growing and evolving and raising consciousness in order to deserve being called a teacher. You cannot educate yourself for X amount of years and obtain X amount of knowledge and think that it will be enough to teach this for the rest of your life. You are constantly educating yourself, and this means that it needs to be seen in the Aquarian Age that as the students are being taught and educated by the teachers, the teachers are also learning from the students and therefore all are growing together.

This means that the old structure of having a classroom where a teacher is standing at the podium, talking down to the students, is long since obsolete. It needs to be replaced by what you see is beginning to emerge in many fields of education, namely a much more interactive structure. It can become much more interactive when the students and teachers are working together on projects that are not simply aimed at stuffing factual knowledge into the minds of the students. It is aimed at advancing knowledge on an overall level by engaging the students in some kind of project where they are either researching some new field or they are seeking ways to give this knowledge to other people.

Education without materialism

It also needs to be recognized that in the Aquarian Age, education will not be a closed box. It will not be so that you have an educational institution that is set apart from society and only those who choose to fulfill the requirements and become full-time students may enter. In the Aquarian Age, an educational institution is seeking to raise the awareness of all of the people in society by reaching beyond the closed academic circles.

It needs to be recognized that in the Piscean Age an educational institution was a way to bestow a privilege on certain people, but the price they paid for getting that privilege was that they surrendered to the mindset that ran the organization. If you were willing to submit to the materialistic mindset, then you could receive a degree from the university and a well-paid job in some scientific institution. But woe onto you if you questioned the materialistic paradigm. You would become an outcast, as you still do in many fields of science and education. Instead of having these closed institutions that bestow privileges on people, educational institutions need to be much more open and educate people who are not necessarily seeking a degree. They need to seek to raise the general level of education because in the Aquarian Age it needs to be seen that you are educating yourself throughout your entire life. This isn't just a matter of acquiring factual knowledge or skills but of raising your general level of awareness, raising your consciousness, by knowing about your own psychology and how the human psyche works, how the world works, what works and what doesn't work based on the Wisdom of the Mother. This is the aim of the golden age education that I envision.

How a Golden Age is manifest

There is, of course, much more to say about it, many more aspects, but I am not looking to say everything through one messenger. I am looking for those who are spiritually aware and who are willing to tune in and receive the ideas and who can put them into action because they have knowledge of and experience with the educational system. They know firsthand what works and what does not work, and they know that something new is needed. Again, not even all of them need to know about ascended masters and know where the ideas are coming from, but you, as the spiritual students, can make the calls for these people to be cut free and to be open so they can receive these ideas and implement them.

You do understand, I hope, that the Golden Age of Saint Germain will not be brought by thirty or forty people who are following a particular ascended-master teaching. It is not even going to be brought by thousands or ten thousands or millions of people following a particular ascended-master teaching. It is going to be brought by millions of people who are receptive to receiving the ideas that make up the Golden Age. Many of them will not need to know about ascended masters or know where the ideas come from. They will need to have the openness so they can receive that one idea that they can bring forth and put into action because they are in that position in the physical octave where they can bring a particular area of society one step forward.

There are millions of such people around the world, and I know that when you think about this, you realize that you have transcended this ego-based desire that you want to be among the few who bring the Golden Age. I know that you are able to tune in to how we look at this. We are not looking at *who* brings the Golden Age and who gets the credit. We are just looking at bringing in the Golden Age for the benefit of all.

It is when you transcend the desire for personal credit or personal honor, and work for the benefit of all, that you will find that your mind suddenly, magically becomes free of many of the issues that Mother Mary talked about and called petty problems. It was the egoic desire to be someone special that caused you to be drawn into many of these activities. When you let go of it, you will find that it is such a relief to just release this. You are not seeking some outer credit, honor or glory, you are just enjoying being in the flow and finding your place, finding your contribution to manifesting this grand overall scheme envisioned by Saint Germain.

We have in the past seen ascended master groups that thought a few hundred or a few thousand people were the ones who would bring in the Golden Age of Saint Germain. Saint Germain has never seen it that way. He looks to all who have the potential to make some contribution. His mind is grand enough to work with millions and millions of people on this planet and give them exactly what they can receive, each one. If you let go of the desire to be someone special, then you will find that you *will* be special because you will be able to receive the exact idea from Saint Germain that you have the potential to bring forth. That, my beloved, will be your greatest joy, as it is my greatest joy to work with those of you who are sensitive to my Being and to give you the ideas that you can receive from the Second Ray and the Chohan of Wisdom that I AM.

I thank you for putting your attention on me rather than the many things in the world that seek to steal your energy. I do not need your energy. I need you to receive my energy and ideas, for I am a being that does not need to take in. I need to give out, for it is not my need but my greatest joy to give to those who are willing to receive.

6 | INVOKING AWARENESS OF PSYCHIC ENERGY

In the name I AM THAT I AM, Jesus Christ, I call to all ascended masters working on manifesting the Golden Age, especially Archangel Jophiel, Elohim Apollo, Master Lanto, Gautama Buddha, Surya and Saint Germain, to radiate into the collective consciousness a new awareness of the forces that seek to steal our psychic energy. Help people see that we can build a new future by working with the ascended masters and letting go of the old way of looking at life, including…

[Make personal calls.]

Part 1

1. Master Lanto, radiate into the collective consciousness the awareness that as people have learned to be careful about how they give away money, they need to be even more careful about how they give away their psychic energy.

> Jophiel Archangel, in wisdom's great light,
> all serpentine lies exposed to our sight.
> So subtle the lies that creep through the mind,
> yet you are the greatest teacher we find.

> **Jophiel Archangel, exposing all lies,**
> **Jophiel Archangel, cutting all ties.**
> **Jophiel Archangel, clearing the skies,**
> **Jophiel Archangel, the mind truly flies.**

2. Master Lanto, radiate into the collective consciousness the awareness that whereas money is a physical substance, the real currency of the world is energy—our emotional, mental, and identity energy.

> Jophiel Archangel, your wisdom we hail,
> your sword cutting through duality's veil.
> As you show the way, we know what is real,
> from serpentine doubt, we instantly heal.

> **Jophiel Archangel, exposing all lies,**
> **Jophiel Archangel, cutting all ties.**
> **Jophiel Archangel, clearing the skies,**
> **Jophiel Archangel, the mind truly flies.**

3. Master Lanto, radiate into the collective consciousness the awareness that there are forces in this world that seek to steal our energy. These forces have invented all kinds of schemes in order to take energy away from us.

> Jophiel Archangel, your reality,
> the best antidote to duality.
> No lie can remain in your Presence so clear,
> with you on our side, no serpent we fear.
>
> **Jophiel Archangel, exposing all lies,**
> **Jophiel Archangel, cutting all ties.**
> **Jophiel Archangel, clearing the skies,**
> **Jophiel Archangel, the mind truly flies.**

4. Master Lanto, radiate into the collective consciousness the awareness that when we become more physically affluent, we have energy left over, and this makes us targets for schemes where forces and people seek to steal our psychic energy.

> Jophiel Archangel, God's mind in in me,
> and through your clear light, its wisdom we see.
> Divisions all vanish, as we see the One,
> and truly, the wholeness of mind we have won.
>
> **Jophiel Archangel, exposing all lies,**
> **Jophiel Archangel, cutting all ties.**
> **Jophiel Archangel, clearing the skies,**
> **Jophiel Archangel, the mind truly flies.**

5. Master Lanto, radiate into the collective consciousness the awareness that there are beings that need to steal our energy in order to survive. There are people who need to steal energy in order to stay in embodiment or exercise power.

> Jophiel Archangel, now show us the way,
> that leads us beyond duality's fray,
> we long to discern the truth and the lie,
> so we the serpentine knots can untie.

Jophiel Archangel, exposing all lies,
Jophiel Archangel, cutting all ties.
Jophiel Archangel, clearing the skies,
Jophiel Archangel, the mind truly flies.

6. Master Lanto, radiate into the collective consciousness the awareness that all of the dictators seen in history have stolen energy from their followers in order to exercise power.

> Jophiel Archangel, your Presence is here,
> and therefore our minds are perfectly clear,
> in wisdom's great fount we do take a bath,
> and now we withstand the devil's own wrath.

Jophiel Archangel, exposing all lies,
Jophiel Archangel, cutting all ties.
Jophiel Archangel, clearing the skies,
Jophiel Archangel, the mind truly flies.

7. Master Lanto, radiate into the collective consciousness the awareness that there are beings in the emotional, mental and identity realms that need to steal our energy in order to continue to survive or exercise power.

Jophiel Archangel, it is your great task,
to raise all mankind, if only we ask,
so now on behalf of those who are blind,
we ask for your help in wisdom to find.

Jophiel Archangel, exposing all lies,
Jophiel Archangel, cutting all ties.
Jophiel Archangel, clearing the skies,
Jophiel Archangel, the mind truly flies.

8. Master Lanto, radiate into the collective consciousness the awareness that these beings and people need to steal energy because they have lowered their consciousness to the point where they can no longer receive energy from the spiritual realm.

Jophiel Archangel, your Presence we hail,
your Light cutting through the serpentine veil,
the serpents can no longer people deceive,
for all now your Flame of Wisdom receive.

Jophiel Archangel, exposing all lies,
Jophiel Archangel, cutting all ties.
Jophiel Archangel, clearing the skies,
Jophiel Archangel, the mind truly flies.

9. Master Lanto, radiate into the collective consciousness the awareness that we are spiritual beings, that there is a level of reality beyond the material, and that the entire material realm is created and sustained by a flow of energy from the spiritual realm into the four levels of the material universe. This energy flows into the material world through those beings whose minds are open to the flow.

Jophiel Archangel, where else can we go,
when we long the highest wisdom to know?
You share with us gladly all that you are,
and now our vision goes ever so far.

Jophiel Archangel, exposing all lies,
Jophiel Archangel, cutting all ties.
Jophiel Archangel, clearing the skies,
Jophiel Archangel, the mind truly flies.

Part 2

1. Master Lanto, radiate into the collective consciousness the awareness that all people in the more affluent countries are the target of the lower forces that want to steal their energy.

Beloved Apollo, with your second ray,
you open our eyes to see a new day,
We see through duality's lies and deceit,
transcending the mindset producing defeat.

Beloved Apollo, thou Elohim Gold,
your radiant light our eyes now behold,
as pages of wisdom you gently unfold,
our planet is free from all that is old.

2. Master Lanto, radiate into the collective consciousness the awareness that the schemes created for the purpose of stealing people's energy are often presented at the physical level as having some necessity or even doing a good deed, serving a good cause.

Beloved Apollo, in your flame we know,
that your living wisdom is always a flow,
in your light we see our own highest will,
immersed in the stream that never stands still.

**Beloved Apollo, thou Elohim Gold,
your radiant light our eyes now behold,
as pages of wisdom you gently unfold,
our planet is free from all that is old.**

3. Master Lanto, radiate into the collective consciousness the awareness that it is time for all open-minded people to realize that we need to be as careful with how we spend our energy as with how we spend our money.

Beloved Apollo, your light makes it clear,
why we have taken embodiment here,
exposing all lies causing the fall,
you help us reclaim the oneness of all.

**Beloved Apollo, thou Elohim Gold,
your radiant light our eyes now behold,
as pages of wisdom you gently unfold,
our planet is free from all that is old.**

4. Master Lanto, radiate into the collective consciousness the awareness that many physical activities are aimed at stealing our energy. One of the most severe is torture, and its primary purpose is to strip people of their emotional, mental and identity energy so that the dark forces and demons can use it for their survival or to increase their power.

> Beloved Apollo, exposing all lies,
> we hereby surrender all ego-based ties,
> we know our perception is truly the key,
> to transcending the serpentine duality.
>
> **Beloved Apollo, thou Elohim Gold,**
> **your radiant light our eyes now behold,**
> **as pages of wisdom you gently unfold,**
> **our planet is free from all that is old.**

5. Master Lanto, radiate into the collective consciousness the awareness that virtually every dictator has had to execute or torture a certain amount of people in order to get enough energy to feed the demons that give power to the human being in embodiment.

> Beloved Apollo, we heed now your call,
> drawing us into Wisdom's Great Hall,
> working to raise our own cosmic sphere,
> together we form the tip of the spear.
>
> **Beloved Apollo, thou Elohim Gold,**
> **your radiant light our eyes now behold,**
> **as pages of wisdom you gently unfold,**
> **our planet is free from all that is old.**

6. Master Lanto, radiate into the collective consciousness the awareness that Hitler, Stalin or Mao had very little personal power because they had surrendered themselves to demons in order to exercise power in the physical world. They were willing to sell their souls to the devil in order to have power on earth.

Beloved Apollo, your wisdom so clear,
in oneness with you, no serpent we fear,
the beam in our eye we willingly see,
we're free from the serpent's own duality.

**Beloved Apollo, thou Elohim Gold,
your radiant light our eyes now behold,
as pages of wisdom you gently unfold,
our planet is free from all that is old.**

7. Master Lanto, radiate into the collective consciousness the awareness that many sporting games have the effect of draining people's energy. Any kind of substance that alters our consciousness, such as drugs, alcohol or tobacco, also allows demons and entities to steal our energy.

Beloved Apollo, you help us to see
through your knowing eyes we truly are free,
we willingly stand in your piercing gaze,
empowered, we exit duality's maze.

**Beloved Apollo, thou Elohim Gold,
your radiant light our eyes now behold,
as pages of wisdom you gently unfold,
our planet is free from all that is old.**

8. Master Lanto, radiate into the collective consciousness the awareness that the majority of movies are direct energy drains, especially violent movies, horror movies or movies that make us feel sympathy.

> Beloved Apollo, our vision we raise,
> we see that the earth is in a new phase,
> for nothing can stop the knowledge you bring,
> exposing that there's no separate thing.
>
> **Beloved Apollo, thou Elohim Gold,**
> **your radiant light our eyes now behold,**
> **as pages of wisdom you gently unfold,**
> **our planet is free from all that is old.**

9. Master Lanto, radiate into the collective consciousness the awareness that there is a need to increase our sensitivity. Even more benign activities can drain our energy, but if we are sufficiently aware, we can engage in an activity without having our energy stolen.

> Beloved Apollo, in wisdom's great mirth,
> we all are together uplifting the earth,
> as you now the true Flame of Wisdom reveal,
> all of earth's people can see what is real.
>
> **Beloved Apollo, thou Elohim Gold,**
> **your radiant light our eyes now behold,**
> **as pages of wisdom you gently unfold,**
> **our planet is free from all that is old.**

Part 3

1. Master Lanto, radiate into the collective consciousness the awareness that many activities are aimed at setting up a pattern in our emotional bodies, causing us to feel that we are not getting enough and that we need more and more.

> Master Lanto, golden wise,
> expose in us the ego's lies.
> Master Lanto, will to be,
> we will to win our mastery.
>
> **Master Lanto, Wisdom's Fount,**
> **with blessings we can hardly count,**
> **you are for earth a shining light,**
> **your Golden Wisdom oh so bright.**

2. Master Lanto, radiate into the collective consciousness the awareness that there are activities in the mental realm that are aimed at keeping us engaged in petty problems that have no solution and will not make a contribution to bringing forth a Golden Age.

> Master Lanto, balance all,
> for wisdom's balance we do call.
> Master Lanto, help us see,
> that balance is the Golden Key.
>
> **Master Lanto, Wisdom's Fount,**
> **with blessings we can hardly count,**
> **you are for earth a shining light,**
> **your Golden Wisdom oh so bright.**

3. Master Lanto, radiate into the collective consciousness the awareness that there are many activities that have the singular purpose of engaging our minds in thinking we are working for a good cause, thinking we are actually helping to solve a particular problem, but there is no solution to the problem.

> Master Lanto, from Above,
> we call forth discerning love.
> Master Lanto, love's not blind,
> through love, God vision we do find.

> **Master Lanto, Wisdom's Fount,**
> **with blessings we can hardly count,**
> **you are for earth a shining light,**
> **your Golden Wisdom oh so bright.**

4. Master Lanto, radiate into the collective consciousness the awareness that the function of our mental body is to explain things, to analyze, to understand, to compare, to look at the potential consequences.

> Master Lanto, we are sure
> as Christic lamb intentions pure.
> Master Lanto, we'll transcend,
> acceleration is our truest friend.

> **Master Lanto, Wisdom's Fount,**
> **with blessings we can hardly count,**
> **you are for earth a shining light,**
> **your Golden Wisdom oh so bright.**

5. Master Lanto, radiate into the collective consciousness the awareness that the fallen beings have learned to create schemes where they do something that violates people, and there is no reason for it other than they want to make people confused because they know that people will seek an explanation.

> Master Lanto, we are whole,
> no more division in the soul.
> Master Lanto, healing flame,
> all balance in your sacred name.

> **Master Lanto, Wisdom's Fount,**
> **with blessings we can hardly count,**
> **you are for earth a shining light,**
> **your Golden Wisdom oh so bright.**

6. Master Lanto, radiate into the collective consciousness the awareness that the fallen beings are doing this deliberately to confuse our mental bodies and induce a state of doubt because we cannot understand why this is happening.

> Master Lanto, serve all life,
> as we transcend all inner strife.
> Master Lanto, peace you give,
> to all who want to truly live.

> **Master Lanto, Wisdom's Fount,**
> **with blessings we can hardly count,**
> **you are for earth a shining light,**
> **your Golden Wisdom oh so bright.**

7. Master Lanto, radiate into the collective consciousness the awareness that we seek a rational explanation, but there is no rational explanation. The only way out is to realize what the fallen beings are trying to do and then refuse to engage our mental bodies in always wanting an explanation.

> Master Lanto, free to be,
> in balanced creativity.
> Master Lanto, we employ,
> your balance as the key to joy.

> **Master Lanto, Wisdom's Fount,**
> **with blessings we can hardly count,**
> **you are for earth a shining light,**
> **your Golden Wisdom oh so bright.**

8. Master Lanto, radiate into the collective consciousness the awareness that we cannot understand why people do certain things because their actions are directed by demons and fallen beings who are seeking to create chaos and confusion.

> Master Lanto, balance all,
> the seven rays upon our call.
> Master Lanto, we take flight,
> the threefold flame a blazing light.

> **Master Lanto, Wisdom's Fount,**
> **with blessings we can hardly count,**
> **you are for earth a shining light,**
> **your Golden Wisdom oh so bright.**

6 | Invoking awareness of psychic energy

9. Master Lanto, radiate into the collective consciousness the awareness that scientists and psychologists will never get to the bottom of these issues because they are approaching it from a limited perspective.

> Lanto dear, your Presence here,
> filling up the inner sphere.
> Life is now a sacred flow,
> God Wisdom we on all bestow.

> **Master Lanto, Wisdom's Fount,**
> **with blessings we can hardly count,**
> **you are for earth a shining light,**
> **your Golden Wisdom oh so bright.**

Part 4

1. Master Lanto, radiate into the collective consciousness the awareness that we cannot understand a person like Adolf Hitler without seeing that he had such an ambition about having power on earth that he was willing to sell his soul to the dark forces beyond the physical octave.

> Gautama, show my mental state
> that does give rise to love and hate,
> your exposé I do endure,
> so my perception will be pure.

**Gautama, Flame of Cosmic Peace,
unruly thoughts do hereby cease,
we radiate from you and me
the peace to still Samsara's Sea.**

2. Master Lanto, radiate into the collective consciousness the awareness that the dark forces could give Hitler the power to manipulate people's emotional, mental and identity bodies by making them feel that they were the super humans, belonging to the super race. Therefore, it seemed perfectly rational to them that they had the absolute right to suppress and eradicate other people.

Gautama, in your Flame of Peace,
the struggling self I now release,
the Buddha Nature I now see,
it is the core of you and me.

**Gautama, Flame of Cosmic Peace,
unruly thoughts do hereby cease,
we radiate from you and me
the peace to still Samsara's Sea.**

3. Master Lanto, radiate into the collective consciousness the awareness that this started in the identity, mental and emotional bodies. We cannot find a physical explanation, and we cannot find a completely rational explanation.

Gautama, I am one with thee,
Mara's demons do now flee,
your Presence like a soothing balm,
my mind and senses ever calm.

**Gautama, Flame of Cosmic Peace,
unruly thoughts do hereby cease,
we radiate from you and me
the peace to still Samsara's Sea.**

4. Master Lanto, radiate into the collective consciousness the awareness that the demons who had taken over Hitler's mind wanted to do certain things that were outrageous, nonsensical and irrational in order to confuse people's mental bodies.

Gautama, I now take the vow,
to live in the eternal now,
with you I do transcend all time,
to live in present so sublime.

**Gautama, Flame of Cosmic Peace,
unruly thoughts do hereby cease,
we radiate from you and me
the peace to still Samsara's Sea.**

5. Master Lanto, radiate into the collective consciousness the awareness that there are many activities in the area of education and science that are aimed at trying to explain some of the things that have no explanation.

Gautama, I have no desire,
to nothing earthly I aspire,
in non-attachment I now rest,
passing Mara's subtle test.

> **Gautama, Flame of Cosmic Peace,**
> **unruly thoughts do hereby cease,**
> **we radiate from you and me**
> **the peace to still Samsara's Sea.**

6. Master Lanto, radiate into the collective consciousness the awareness that all of the people who, with the best of intentions, are focusing their minds on trying to understand these matters are pouring their energy into a matrix, into a portal, that allows the forces in the mental realm to steal their energy.

> Gautama, I melt into you,
> my mind is one, no longer two,
> immersed in your resplendent glow,
> Nirvana is all that I know.

> **Gautama, Flame of Cosmic Peace,**
> **unruly thoughts do hereby cease,**
> **we radiate from you and me**
> **the peace to still Samsara's Sea.**

7. Master Lanto, radiate into the collective consciousness the awareness that these forces feed themselves on the energy and therefore gain more power to control and affect the minds of people in embodiment.

> Gautama, in your timeless space,
> I am immersed in Cosmic Grace,
> I know the God beyond all form,
> to world I will no more conform.

**Gautama, Flame of Cosmic Peace,
unruly thoughts do hereby cease,
we radiate from you and me
the peace to still Samsara's Sea.**

8. Master Lanto, radiate into the collective consciousness the awareness that this becomes a vicious circle where the people in embodiment are feeding the beings in the mental realm. These beings are getting more power to manipulate people's minds, and they can steal even more energy from them.

Gautama, I am now awake,
I clearly see what is at stake,
and thus I claim my sacred right
to be on earth the Buddhic Light.

**Gautama, Flame of Cosmic Peace,
unruly thoughts do hereby cease,
we radiate from you and me
the peace to still Samsara's Sea.**

9. Master Lanto, radiate into the collective consciousness the awareness that there are many areas of education that have the effect of draining people's energy. This applies to the structure of much of higher education that is based on an authoritarian model where the university professors and teachers teach from a position of authority and are talking down to the students.

Gautama, with your thunderbolt,
we give the earth a mighty jolt,
I know that some will understand,
and join the Buddha's timeless band.

> Gautama, Flame of Cosmic Peace,
> unruly thoughts do hereby cease,
> we radiate from you and me
> the peace to still Samsara's Sea.

Part 5

1. Master Lanto, radiate into the collective consciousness the awareness that the teachers are seeking to program the students to conform to the overall worldview upon which that educational institution is based, or even the view upon which most educational institutions are based.

> Surya, cosmic being bright,
> your balance is my pure delight,
> I am in orbit round God Star,
> in perfect unity we are.
>
> **Surya, banish all extremes,**
> **Surya, shatter Serpent's schemes,**
> **Surya, balance to me bring,**
> **Surya, making my heart sing.**

2. Master Lanto, radiate into the collective consciousness the awareness that much of higher education promotes a strictly materialistic view of life. This feeds certain demons or beings in the mental realm.

Surya, there is more to life,
than human conflict, war and strife,
your balance gives me inner peace,
all outer conflicts do now cease.

Surya, banish all extremes,
Surya, shatter Serpent's schemes,
Surya, balance to me bring,
Surya, making my heart sing.

3. Master Lanto, radiate into the collective consciousness the awareness that this also feeds many demons in the emotional realm. They are stealing people's energy by engaging them in the intellectual pursuit of a rational explanation for how the universe works so that we can put God out of the equation by having a rational theory that explains everything.

Surya, what a wondrous sight,
from Sirius you send the light,
of one mind, I now call to thee,
for your apprentice I would be.

Surya, banish all extremes,
Surya, shatter Serpent's schemes,
Surya, balance to me bring,
Surya, making my heart sing.

4. Master Lanto, radiate into the collective consciousness the awareness that education makes many intellectual people have a certain disdain or overbearing feeling towards religious people, and thereby their emotional energies are drained.

> Surya, radiate your light,
> with balance you set all things right,
> consuming energetic dross,
> my letting go is not a loss.
>
> **Surya, banish all extremes,**
> **Surya, shatter Serpent's schemes,**
> **Surya, balance to me bring,**
> **Surya, making my heart sing.**

5. Master Lanto, radiate into the collective consciousness the awareness that much education is not aimed at giving the students wisdom but is aimed at programming their minds to accept a certain worldview that is defined by the forces of anti-wisdom.

> Surya, your light is alive,
> for inner balance I do strive,
> the alchemy is now begun,
> my heart transformed into a sun.
>
> **Surya, banish all extremes,**
> **Surya, shatter Serpent's schemes,**
> **Surya, balance to me bring,**
> **Surya, making my heart sing.**

6. Master Lanto, radiate into the collective consciousness the awareness that the current educational model is based on the perverted Piscean mindset of an authoritarian structure that leads to one person or a few people being at the top and everybody at lower levels having to conform.

> Surya, come enlighten me,
> duality you help me see,
> extremes they cannot pull me in,
> on Middle Way I always win.
>
> **Surya, banish all extremes,**
> **Surya, shatter Serpent's schemes,**
> **Surya, balance to me bring,**
> **Surya, making my heart sing.**

7. Master Lanto, radiate into the collective consciousness the awareness that in the aquarian-age education, there is no authority as such. Both students and teachers are walking a continued path of education and the teachers are not meant to possess a finite, closed box of knowledge.

> Surya, in your cosmic sphere,
> with Cuzco I your light revere,
> from your perspective o so grand,
> life finally I understand.
>
> **Surya, banish all extremes,**
> **Surya, shatter Serpent's schemes,**
> **Surya, balance to me bring,**
> **Surya, making my heart sing.**

8. Master Lanto, radiate into the collective consciousness the awareness that teachers are learning throughout life and they are learning by teaching. They are continually growing, evolving and raising their consciousness in order to deserve being called teachers.

Surya, show me God's design,
I see that God is all benign,
you calm my feeling body's storm,
I know the God beyond all form.

Surya, banish all extremes,
Surya, shatter Serpent's schemes,
Surya, balance to me bring,
Surya, making my heart sing.

9. Master Lanto, radiate into the collective consciousness the awareness that in the Aquarian Age, the students are being taught and educated by the teachers, but the teachers are also learning from the students and therefore all are growing together.

Surya, I come from afar,
and as you show me my home star,
I see now my internal light,
a star I am in my own right.

Surya, banish all extremes,
Surya, shatter Serpent's schemes,
Surya, balance to me bring,
Surya, making my heart sing.

Part 6

1. Master Lanto, radiate into the collective consciousness the awareness that the old structure of having a classroom where a teacher is standing at the podium, talking down to the students, is obsolete. It needs to be replaced by a much more interactive structure.

> O Saint Germain, you do inspire,
> my vision raised forever higher,
> with you I form a figure-eight,
> your Golden Age I co-create.

> **O Saint Germain, what love you bring,**
> **it truly makes all matter sing,**
> **your violet flame does all restore,**
> **with you we are becoming more.**

2. Master Lanto, radiate into the collective consciousness the awareness that education can become much more interactive when students and teachers are working together on projects that are aimed at advancing knowledge on an overall level by engaging the students in researching some new field or seeking ways to give this knowledge to other people.

> O Saint Germain, what Freedom Flame,
> released when we recite your name,
> acceleration is your gift,
> our planet it will surely lift.

**O Saint Germain, what love you bring,
it truly makes all matter sing,
your violet flame does all restore,
with you we are becoming more.**

3. Master Lanto, radiate into the collective consciousness the awareness that in the Aquarian Age, education will not be a closed box. An educational institution is not set apart from society and is seeking to raise the awareness of all of the people in society by reaching beyond the closed academic circles.

O Saint Germain, in love we claim,
our right to bring your violet flame,
from you Above, to us below,
it is an all-transforming flow.

**O Saint Germain, what love you bring,
it truly makes all matter sing,
your violet flame does all restore,
with you we are becoming more.**

4. Master Lanto, radiate into the collective consciousness the awareness that in the Piscean Age an educational institution was a way to bestow a privilege on certain people, but the price they paid was that they surrendered to the mindset that ran the organization.

O Saint Germain, I love you so,
my aura filled with violet glow,
my chakras filled with violet fire,
I am your cosmic amplifier.

> **O Saint Germain, what love you bring,**
> **it truly makes all matter sing,**
> **your violet flame does all restore,**
> **with you we are becoming more.**

5. Master Lanto, radiate into the collective consciousness the awareness that if you were willing to submit to the materialistic mindset, then you could receive a degree from the university and a well-paid job in some scientific institution. But if you questioned the materialistic paradigm, you would become an outcast.

> O Saint Germain, I am now free,
> your violet flame is therapy,
> transform all hang-ups in my mind,
> as inner peace I surely find.

> **O Saint Germain, what love you bring,**
> **it truly makes all matter sing,**
> **your violet flame does all restore,**
> **with you we are becoming more.**

6. Master Lanto, radiate into the collective consciousness the awareness that instead of having these closed institutions that bestow privileges on people, educational institutions need to raise the general level of education. In the Aquarian Age people will be educating themselves throughout life.

> O Saint Germain, my body pure,
> your violet flame for all is cure,
> consume the cause of all disease,
> and therefore I am all at ease.

**O Saint Germain, what love you bring,
it truly makes all matter sing,
your violet flame does all restore,
with you we are becoming more.**

7. Master Lanto, radiate into the collective consciousness the awareness that true education is not just a matter of acquiring factual knowledge or skills but of raising our general level of awareness, raising our consciousness. We need to know how the human psyche works, how the world works, what works and what doesn't work based on the Wisdom of the Mother.

O Saint Germain, I'm karma-free,
the past no longer burdens me,
a brand new opportunity,
I am in Christic unity.

**O Saint Germain, what love you bring,
it truly makes all matter sing,
your violet flame does all restore,
with you we are becoming more.**

8. Master Lanto, radiate into the collective consciousness the awareness that will awaken all people who are willing to tune in and receive new ideas and who can put them into action because they have knowledge of and experience with the educational system. They know firsthand what works and what does not work, and they know that something new is needed.

O Saint Germain, we are now one,
I am for you a violet sun,
as we transform this planet earth,
your Golden Age is given birth.

**O Saint Germain, what love you bring,
it truly makes all matter sing,
your violet flame does all restore,
with you we are becoming more.**

9. Master Lanto, radiate into the collective consciousness the awareness that will awaken the millions of people who are receptive to receiving the ideas that make up the Golden Age. Help them use their positions in the physical octave to bring a particular area of society one step forward. Help all of us find our contribution to manifesting this grand overall scheme envisioned by Saint Germain.

O Saint Germain, the earth is free,
from burden of duality,
in oneness we bring what is best,
your Golden Age is manifest.

**O Saint Germain, what love you bring,
it truly makes all matter sing,
your violet flame does all restore,
with you we are becoming more.**

Sealing

In the name of the Divine Mother, I call to all ascended masters for the sealing of myself and all people in my circle of influence in the creative flow of the Divine Mother, the River of Life. I call for the multiplication of my calls by all ascended masters, so that we form the perfect figure-eight flow of "As Above, so below." Thus, I accept that this is fully manifest, because the mouth of the Lord, the Divine Mother that I AM, has spoken it. Amen.

7 | RAISING PEOPLE ABOVE FANATICISM

I AM the Ascended Master Paul the Venetian. I am the Chohan of the Third Ray of Love. From our perspective of love, what would be the most important changes that could be made for bringing the Golden Age? Well, the first one I want to address is the absolute need for Europe to overcome fanaticism. When I say the word "fanaticism" in Europe, naturally the first thing that comes to your mind is Nazism. It has been universally recognized that Nazism was a clear and undeniable manifestation of fanaticism. This, of course, I am not going to dispute. I am going to break down the elements that characterized Nazism.

The characteristics of fanaticism

First of all, you have the sense that you are superior to other people, you are the superior group of people. Because of your characteristics, you know better what should happen on this planet. You actually think, when you are in a fanatical mindset, that you are wiser than all others, that you know better, that you know reality. You think your vision, your ideology, your religion – or whatever you have that you are holding on to – is the *superior* way, the *only true* way to look at things.

Are you really wise when you are in this mindset? If you think that you are superior compared to other people who are different from yourselves, then are you not proving that you are in a state of consciousness where you are focused on differences that set people apart? You are demonstrating that you do not see the true reality, namely the underlying oneness of all life. If you do not see reality, how can you be wise? How can you be superior in wisdom? If your ideology is clearly defining some people as superior to others, how can that be the ultimate truth?

Another characteristic of fanaticism is, of course, that you believe that your ideology, your worldview, defines an ideal that should happen and a threat to that ideal. Furthermore, you identify that certain people, yourselves, are working for the manifestation of the ideal condition, and other people, especially a specific group of other people, are working against this. Again, can this be superior wisdom when the underlying reality is that all life, all human beings, came from the same source and are all connected in consciousness?

Another characteristic of fanaticism is that you feel that you have not only a right, but even an obligation, to force those other people to come into compliance with your worldview. You feel that even though this is using force, perhaps even using lethal force, it is justified by the necessity to establish your worldview as the dominant one, or even the *only* one, on earth. Again, can this be superior wisdom when you realize that all human beings are connected in consciousness? When you use force against someone else, you are affecting yourself.

You cannot get away with using violence and force without affecting yourself. Furthermore, you do not see that the purpose of the planet is the outplaying of free will. When you are forcing the free will of others, you have first forced your own free will because you have surrendered your own free will to the system behind your fanatical worldview.

Fanaticism in European history

You now see several elements of fanaticism. The sense of superiority, the sense of an epic right and an epic wrong, the sense that you have a right to use force, that it is necessary to use force, and that you can get away with doing this, perhaps even be rewarded by some force. If you take these elements and look at the history of the European continent, you will see that, although Nazism may be an extreme outpicturing of the fanatical mindset, it is by no means the only one.

Need I point any further than the Catholic Church? It, for the greater part of its existence, has acted out the fanatical mindset by claiming itself to be the only true religion, the only true representative of Christ. It has claimed that it was of epic importance that all people be brought into the Christian faith, and that it was justified to use violence, even killing other people, in order to further the cause of Christ. Can we say today that the Catholic Church has lifted itself out of fanaticism? Well, *I* certainly cannot say that.

Then, look at many other manifestations in European history. Go back to the time before the first World War and see how the three major powers in Europe at the time – England, Germany, and France – had their own version of fanaticism. They thought their nation was superior to all others and they were feeling fully justified in going to war against their neighbors and seeking to use force to establish their own dominance. Was not the British Empire an expression of the fanatical mindset? Was not the entire colonial era (where so many nations of Europe expanded beyond the boundaries of Europe and forcefully suppressed other nations) another expression of the fanatical mindset?

Then, look at other things in Europe. Look how, for example, there was a reaction against the Catholic Church, and as an outcome of this was created materialism. Well, is materialism not also an expression of the fanatical mindset? Some will say: "When did materialism use violence to kill other people?" I would say: "Well, is not Marxism an expression of materialism?" It is certainly a denial of anything spiritual, of anything beyond the material world, saying that everything is determined by the conditions in the material world and by some historical necessity.

Then, look to less violent aspects of materialism, as you find it in many educational institutions. Is there not a clear sense of superiority, a clear sense that we have the only truth, that we know reality, that we know how the universe works, even though we recognize that there is an event horizon that we cannot see beyond? We still feel that we can project that we know what is happening beyond that event horizon and that there is nothing beyond the material world. Is there not a clear sense of superiority towards religious people and those who do not share the materialistic beliefs? Is there not a clear sense of superiority in academic circles where people feel that they are better than all others and that they should be able to impose their view of the world upon all others?

Is it not possible to go even further and see that many nations have a national fanaticism about the superiority of their nation, their way of doing things and how they are better than others? We can even go to the level of seeing how people are fanatical about certain football teams, about certain other sports and about so many other things.

The use of psychic violence

What is the real essence of fanaticism? Well, we have seen in Europe how fanaticism has been allowed to outplay itself. We have seen an extremely violent expression of fanaticism. The result of this is that most European nations have moved beyond the willingness to kill those who have different beliefs than yourself or those who are of another nationality. We have moved to a point where the threat of a war between the European nations has diminished to a level where it is highly unlikely. We have also moved to a point where it is highly unlikely that the European nations would engage in a large-scale war of aggression outside the borders of Europe. Yet, we have not reached a point where the European nations are refusing to use any kind of force outside of their own borders, as you see in the intervention in Syria, Libya and other countries.

We can say that, by and large, Europe has transcended the desire or the sense that the use of violence is justified, at least the use of deadly violence. We do, of course, see that there are other forms of violence, including psychological violence of wanting to force other people to come into a certain view of the world. We see this in religious circles, we see it in materialistic circles, we see it in political circles. It is necessary to make calls that Europe will transcend the use of psychic violence justified by the fanatical mindset.

The next level is where Europe would transcend the sense that there is only one truth, only one way to look at reality, and that this truth (this ideology, religion or political theory) is superior to all others. Some progress has been made in this field. There are many nations that are much more practical and not so caught up in a particular ideology or worldview. Calls are needed, but progress has been made.

The sense of superiority

This leaves us with the most insidious aspect of fanaticism, namely the sense of being superior to other people. This is where, even though Europe has made progress, much is still lacking. There is still a very subtle sense of superiority found not only in nations, but in Europe as a whole. There is a sense of superiority towards the less developed nations. There are even many in Western Europe who have a sense of superiority towards the nations of Eastern Europe. There are still many people in Britain, in Germany and in France who feel that their nations are superior. There is hardly a nation in Europe who does not have some sense of pride or arrogance about their own nation having certain characteristics that makes it unique or superior.

If this sense of superiority could be transcended, it would have an incredible impact on bringing the Golden Age into manifestation in Europe. The reason for this is very subtle but profound. When you have a sense of superiority, what is the underlying psychological mechanism that gives you this outwardly directed sense of superiority? You realize, I am sure, based on our many teachings on psychology, that when you are projecting something *out* upon other people, you are at the same time projecting something *in* upon yourself. When you are projecting upon other people that you are superior to them, what are you projecting inwardly upon yourself? You are projecting, of course, that you are inferior in some way. If you did not feel inferior deep inside, why would you have a need to project superiority outside your own mind? Why would you have a need to compare yourself to others?

The fanatical mindset truly is based on the psychological mechanism of inferiority that finds its outward expression as superiority. What is the effect of this? Well, the effect is that when you go into a state of cooperation with other people, such as you have seen beginning in Europe, you can never fully cooperate because full cooperation can only be done among equals. If one part sees itself as superior, there cannot be full cooperation. If all of the parties have their own sense of superiority, how can there be full cooperation?

There can be a state of what human beings call cooperation, but it is not true cooperation. What human beings look for is: "How can I get an advantage by cooperating with others? What is in it for me? What do I get out of it?" You see this in the European Union. You see it in Britain right now in the debate about whether to stay or exit. You see it in all other nations as well: "What do we get out of EU? What does it do for us?"

This need not be that a nation is only looking for some material advantage, such as money or trade, but it may also be that a nation looks to a sense of superiority where they feel they are the leaders. They do not even mind paying more money out than they get in, in order to give them that sense that they are the leaders. Or it may be that they are looking to get some sense of compensation for what they did in the past, such as is, to some degree, the case with Germany. Even Germany still has a need for superiority, of feeling that they are the good guys. They are the ones who are holding the Union together, who are lifting up the Union and making it all work.

The basis for true cooperation

Of course, there are similar mechanisms in France and in England. Many other nations have their own version of it, even though the smaller nations have overcome this to a larger extent than the big nations. Can you see, my beloved, that this is not what we of the ascended masters call cooperation? Why is it not so? Because when you truly cooperate, you are not coming from a state of: "What is in it for me?" You are coming from a state of: "How can I serve others?" You are not cooperating with others in order to *get*. You are cooperating with others in order to *give*.

What does it take for a nation to move into this state? Well, it has to overcome the major block to true cooperation, which is inferiority. You have to come to a point where you are not seeking to do something with other nations in order to build up your own self-esteem. You have come to the point of recognition inside yourself, inside your national psyche, that you are fully acceptable as you are, as you were created by God. You are not inferior, you were not created inferior. My beloved, you cannot get this sense of self-worth, this true sense of self-worth, through a materialistic worldview.

Where should this sense of self-worth come from? It cannot come from the material world unless you are materially superior to others. It cannot come from a political ideology that sets you apart from other people. It cannot come from a religion that makes you feel superior compared to those who are on the outside. Such a religion is based on the consciousness of separation that separates you from God and separates you from all other people.

It can only come from a true spiritual recognition. This does not have to take the form of an outer spiritual teaching. It comes from an inner recognition that no people are superior to others because all people were created with equal value, equal worth. If you can accept that you have worth from within, that you do not need to get it from this world, then you can look at other people and interact with other people without the need to feel superior.

What is the outcome of realizing that you have worth from within? It is that you realize that you do not need to create an ideal state in this world. You do not need to create the perfect world, the kingdom of God, the Utopian socialist society or whatever model you can come up with. As your value comes from Above, so does the value of everything you do on earth. You are not relating so much to earth as you are relating to the spiritual realm. When you realize how the interaction between Spirit and matter works, you realize that as you give to other people horizontally, you will receive more from Above.

No Golden Age without Spirit

We of the ascended masters will never fail to multiply what you give selflessly to raise the All. Therefore, the best way to get something for yourself is to give to others, because then you will receive more from Above. When you know this, then you can cooperate with others. You are not doing it based on a need to get prestige or even a physical advantage for yourself. You are doing it based on a desire to raise the All. You are not coming from a state of lack that you want to fill or get away from. You are coming from a state of being in the flow, and you know that giving gives you more.

It is true that the ultimate state of egotism is complete altruism because the best thing you can do for yourself is to do something for others. This recognition would be of incredible value in bringing the Golden Age into manifestation.

Basically, we can say that with men it is impossible to bring the Golden Age into manifestation. A Golden Age can be brought only when human beings in embodiment cooperate with the ascended masters so that we can add the increase. We can add the multiplication, and it is this multiplication that manifests a Golden Age.

A Golden Age is not a matter of finding some magical formula that works here on earth. Human beings cannot by themselves create a Golden Age. They can create it only in a symbiotic relationship between those of you in embodiment and those of us Above, where we multiply your selfless efforts. That is the formula for the Golden Age. It cannot be brought about unless you open your minds and hearts to receive what we are longing to give you from Above. You cannot open your minds and hearts when you are in the state of fanaticism, no matter how subtle it might be.

There is a great need to make calls for this. There is even a need for the more spiritually mature people to recognize that you may still have elements of this mindset that sets you apart, that gives you a need for superiority. My beloved, this messenger has been willing to go through this process. It was tempting for him to feel that he was bringing forth a higher teaching that was superior to other teachings on the planet. He has been willing to look at this in himself and raise himself above it, as many of you have also done, which is why you are attracted to this teaching; which is why it resonates with you.

No superior spiritual teaching

It is not that a certain teaching may not have a lot of truth. But it is just that we of the ascended masters are not looking at the teachings – even the teachings we have brought forth through a sponsored messenger – through the dualistic mindset where we evaluate everything based on higher or lower. After all, the teaching that helps a given person take the next step on his or her path is the most valuable teaching at that point of their path. It does you no good to have a so-called superior teaching if you are not ready for that teaching but need something else to step up higher.

We are only looking to help people. We are not looking to help people through some exclusive religion or teaching. It is a complete perversion to think that God or Jesus wants people to see the Catholic Church as the only true religion, or the Muslim religion as the only true religion. It is a complete illusion. We are only looking to raise all life. We hope that you can lock in to that consciousness and realize that your efforts have value, but it is not because of the outer teaching. It is because of your inner multiplication, application and expression of the teaching.

We hope you also realize that it is not a matter of making all other people follow one specific outer teaching. The Christians so often quote the verse where Jesus tells his disciples to go out into all the world and make all people his disciples. He was not speaking as the leader of a particular, exclusivist religion. He was speaking as the embodied representative of the Christ consciousness. What he wanted was for his disciples to lock in to the Christ consciousness, to achieve a degree of Christhood and go out and make all other people disciples of the true Christ, which is to achieve discernment.

Love-based discernment

You do not achieve discernment through an outer teaching, by mechanically following the outer teaching. You achieve discernment by sharpening your ability in your heart to read vibration, to read when something vibrates at the level of love and when something vibrates below that level. There are many teachings on the planet that have some degree of love. There is hardly any teaching that cannot be applied with love by those who have pure hearts. There are Catholics who have such pure hearts that their approach to Catholicism is love-based, and the same goes for most other teachings on the planet.

Again, raise yourself above this need for exclusivity (the need to feel superior to others) and you will, as Lanto said, feel like another weight will drop from you. You will feel so much freer, so much lighter. Instead of being concerned about how other people look at you and whether they see and validate your need to feel superior, you have given up that need. You are free to be who you are and flow with the Spirit, flow with the impulses from your I AM Presence. You flow with that River of Life where you see that the more you do to raise the All, the more you receive from Above. The more you receive from Above, the more this pulls you towards the source of what you are receiving. You realize that what you are receiving from Above is only a small fragment of what is there up Above. In order to receive the fullness of it, you have to go Above and become one with the source as we who are Above have become one with the source.

There comes a point where, even though you are feeling a stream of receiving love from Above, it is not enough for you. You want more. You want oneness with the source. That is where I and all the other representatives of the Third Ray are willing to help you, as is every representative from every ray and any ascended master. We love to see you come into oneness with the source with which we are one. We long to feel that oneness with you that is only possible when we are all ascended and have shed the last remnants of that human consciousness that must, of necessity, keep unascended beings somewhat apart.

While you are still on earth, open yourself up to the flow of love from Above. When you come to the point where you feel that it is time to unite with the source of that love, then let go of those last attachments and join us in the ascended realm.

8 | CALLING FORTH TRUE COOPERATION

In the name I AM THAT I AM, Jesus Christ, I call to all ascended masters working on manifesting the Golden Age, especially Archangel Chamuel, Elohim Heros, Paul the Venetian, Sanat Kumara and Saint Germain to radiate into the collective consciousness a new awareness of how to free people from all remnants of the fanatical mindset and bring true cooperation. Help people see that we can build a new future by working with the ascended masters and letting go of the old way of looking at life, including...

[Make personal calls.]

Part 1

1. Paul the Venetian, radiate into the collective consciousness the awareness that there is an absolute need for people to overcome fanaticism.

Chamuel Archangel, in ruby ray power,
we know we are taking a life-giving shower.
Love burning away all perversions of will,
we suddenly feel our desires falling still.

Chamuel Archangel, descend from Above,
Chamuel Archangel, with ruby-pink love,
Chamuel Archangel, so often thought-of,
Chamuel Archangel, o come Holy Dove.

2. Paul the Venetian, radiate into the collective consciousness the awareness that people need to overcome the mindset that: "We are superior to other people, we are the superior group of people."

Chamuel Archangel, a spiral of light,
as ruby ray fire now pierces the night.
All forces of darkness consumed by your fire,
consuming all those who will not rise higher.

Chamuel Archangel, descend from Above,
Chamuel Archangel, with ruby-pink love,
Chamuel Archangel, so often thought-of,
Chamuel Archangel, o come Holy Dove.

3. Paul the Venetian, radiate into the collective consciousness the awareness that people need to overcome the mindset that: "We know better what should happen on this planet, we are wiser than all others, we know better, we know reality."

Chamuel Archangel, your love so immense,
with clarified vision, our lives now make sense.
The purpose of life you so clearly reveal,
immersed in your love, God's oneness we feel.

Chamuel Archangel, descend from Above,
Chamuel Archangel, with ruby-pink love,
Chamuel Archangel, so often thought-of,
Chamuel Archangel, o come Holy Dove.

4. Paul the Venetian, radiate into the collective consciousness the awareness that people need to overcome the mindset that: "Our vision, our ideology, our religion is the superior way, the *only* true way to look at things."

Chamuel Archangel, what calmness you bring,
we see now that even death has no sting.
For truly, in love there can be no decay,
as love is transcendence into a new day.

Chamuel Archangel, descend from Above,
Chamuel Archangel, with ruby-pink love,
Chamuel Archangel, so often thought-of,
Chamuel Archangel, o come Holy Dove.

5. Paul the Venetian, radiate into the collective consciousness the awareness that when we think we are superior compared to other people who are different from ourselves, we are only proving that we are focused on differences that set people apart and we do not see the underlying oneness of all life.

> Chamuel Archangel, God't Love Flame bestow,
> on all those longing God's true love to know,
> conditions we know can never be real,
> and this is the love you always reveal.
>
> **Chamuel Archangel, descend from Above,**
> **Chamuel Archangel, with ruby-pink love,**
> **Chamuel Archangel, so often thought-of,**
> **Chamuel Archangel, o come Holy Dove.**

6. Paul the Venetian, radiate into the collective consciousness the awareness that people need to overcome the mindset that: "Our ideology or worldview defines an ideal that should happen and a threat to that ideal. We are working for the manifestation of the ideal condition, and a specific group of other people are working against this.

> Chamuel Archangel, love's seed you have sown,
> in hearts of all those who don't seek to own,
> for love that possesses is nothing but fear,
> that pierces the heart with duality's spear.
>
> **Chamuel Archangel, descend from Above,**
> **Chamuel Archangel, with ruby-pink love,**
> **Chamuel Archangel, so often thought-of,**
> **Chamuel Archangel, o come Holy Dove.**

7. Paul the Venetian, radiate into the collective consciousness the awareness that people need to overcome the mindset that: "We have not only a right, but even an obligation, to force other people to come into compliance with our worldview. Using force is justified by the necessity to establish our worldview as the dominant one.

Chamuel Archangel, we don't want control,
for this is the devil's hold on the soul,
your love will now break the serpentine chain,
so we are set free God's love to reclaim.

Chamuel Archangel, descend from Above,
Chamuel Archangel, with ruby-pink love,
Chamuel Archangel, so often thought-of,
Chamuel Archangel, o come Holy Dove.

8. Paul the Venetian, radiate into the collective consciousness the awareness that when we use force against someone else, we are affecting ourselves because we cannot get away with using force without creating consequences.

Chamuel Archangel, you are so adept,
at helping us God's true love to accept,
we know that the love for which we so yearn,
is not something we on earth have to earn.

Chamuel Archangel, descend from Above,
Chamuel Archangel, with ruby-pink love,
Chamuel Archangel, so often thought-of,
Chamuel Archangel, o come Holy Dove.

9. Paul the Venetian, radiate into the collective consciousness the awareness that the purpose of the planet is the outplaying of free will. When we are forcing the free will of others, we have first forced our own free will because we have surrendered our own free will to the system behind our fanatical worldview.

> Chamuel Archangel, for love to accept,
> we do not need to be so perfect,
> for love is not static but always a flow,
> demanding only we're willing to grow.
>
> **Chamuel Archangel, descend from Above,**
> **Chamuel Archangel, with ruby-pink love,**
> **Chamuel Archangel, so often thought-of,**
> **Chamuel Archangel, o come Holy Dove.**

Part 2

1. Paul the Venetian, radiate into the collective consciousness the awareness that although Nazism may be an extreme outpicturing of the fanatical mindset, it is by no means the only one in history.

> O Heros-Amora, in your love so pink,
> we care not what others about us may think,
> in oneness with you, we claim a new day,
> as innocent children, we frolic and play.
>
> **O Heros-Amora, we reap what we sow,**
> **yet this is Plan B for helping us grow,**
> **for truly, Plan A is that we join the flow,**
> **immersed in the Infinite Love you bestow.**

2. Paul the Venetian, radiate into the collective consciousness the awareness that the Catholic Church has also acted out the fanatical mindset by claiming to be the only true religion, the only true representative of Christ.

O Heros-Amora, a new life begun,
we laugh at the devil, the serious one,
the serpent is stuck in his duality,
but we are set free by Love's reality.

**O Heros-Amora, we reap what we sow,
yet this is Plan B for helping us grow,
for truly, Plan A is that we join the flow,
immersed in the Infinite Love you bestow.**

3. Paul the Venetian, radiate into the collective consciousness the awareness that the Catholic Church has claimed that it was of epic importance that all people be brought into the Christian faith, and that it was justified to use violence, even killing other people, in order to further the cause of Christ.

O Heros-Amora, awakened we see,
in true love is no conditionality,
we bathe in your glorious Ruby-Pink Sun,
knowing our God allows life to be fun.

**O Heros-Amora, we reap what we sow,
yet this is Plan B for helping us grow,
for truly, Plan A is that we join the flow,
immersed in the Infinite Love you bestow.**

4. Paul the Venetian, radiate into the collective consciousness the awareness that during the first World War, the three major powers in Europe had their own version of fanaticism. They thought their nation was superior and was justified in going to war, using force to establish their own dominance.

O Heros-Amora, life is such a joy,
we see that the world is like a great toy,
whatever the mind into it projects,
the mirror of life exactly reflects.

O Heros-Amora, we reap what we sow,
yet this is Plan B for helping us grow,
for truly, Plan A is that we join the flow,
immersed in the Infinite Love you bestow.

5. Paul the Venetian, radiate into the collective consciousness the awareness that the British Empire was an expression of the fanatical mindset. The colonial era was another expression of the fanatical mindset.

O Heros-Amora, conditions you burn,
we know we are free to take a new turn,
Immersed in the stream of infinite Love,
we know that the Spirit came from Above.

O Heros-Amora, we reap what we sow,
yet this is Plan B for helping us grow,
for truly, Plan A is that we join the flow,
immersed in the Infinite Love you bestow.

6. Paul the Venetian, radiate into the collective consciousness the awareness that materialism is also an expression of the fanatical mindset through its denial of anything spiritual.

O Heros-Amora, we feel that at last,
we've risen above the trap of the past,
in true love we claim our freedom to grow,
forever we're one with Love's Infinite Flow.

8 | Calling forth true cooperation

**O Heros-Amora, we reap what we sow,
yet this is Plan B for helping us grow,
for truly, Plan A is that we join the flow,
immersed in the Infinite Love you bestow.**

7. Paul the Venetian, radiate into the collective consciousness the awareness that Marxism is an expression of materialism, which is also based on a fanatical claim that everything is determined by the conditions in the material world and by some historical necessity.

O Heros-Amora, conditions are ties,
forming a net of serpentine lies,
but you have the antidote setting us free,
you take us beyond conditionality.

**O Heros-Amora, we reap what we sow,
yet this is Plan B for helping us grow,
for truly, Plan A is that we join the flow,
immersed in the Infinite Love you bestow.**

8. Paul the Venetian, radiate into the collective consciousness the awareness that materialism in many educational institutions is based on a sense of superiority, a sense that we have the only truth, that we know reality, that we know how the universe works.

O Heros-Amora, your love is no bond,
for love only wants to take us beyond,
your love has no bounds, forever it flies,
raising all life into Ruby-Pink skies.

> **O Heros-Amora, we reap what we sow,**
> **yet this is Plan B for helping us grow,**
> **for truly, Plan A is that we join the flow,**
> **immersed in the Infinite Love you bestow.**

9. Paul the Venetian, radiate into the collective consciousness the awareness that in academic circles there is a sense of superiority towards religious people, making people feel they should be able to impose their view of the world upon all others.

> O Heros-Amora, love bathing the earth,
> filling all people with infinite mirth,
> for fear and despair there is no more room,
> as all are awakened by love's sonic boom.

> **O Heros-Amora, we reap what we sow,**
> **yet this is Plan B for helping us grow,**
> **for truly, Plan A is that we join the flow,**
> **immersed in the Infinite Love you bestow.**

Part 3

1. Paul the Venetian, radiate into the collective consciousness the awareness that many nations have a national fanaticism about the superiority of their nation, their way of doing things, and how they are better than others. People are even fanatical about sports and many other things.

8 | Calling forth true cooperation

Master Paul, venetian dream,
your love for beauty's flowing stream.
Master Paul, in love's own womb,
your power shatters ego's tomb.

Master Paul, your love so true,
and therefore we apply to you,
to set all free in the great love,
that you are shining from Above.

2. Paul the Venetian, radiate into the collective consciousness the awareness that even though the world has seen an extremely violent expression of fanaticism, the developed nations have not reached the point where they are refusing to use any kind of force outside of their own borders.

Master Paul, your counsel wise,
our minds are raised to lofty skies.
Master Paul, in wisdom's love,
such beauty flowing from Above.

Master Paul, your love so true,
and therefore we apply to you,
to set all free in the great love,
that you are shining from Above.

3. Paul the Venetian, radiate into the collective consciousness the awareness that even though many nations have transcended the sense that the use of physical violence is justified, there are other forms of violence, including psychological violence of wanting to force other people to come into a certain view of the world.

Master Paul, love is an art,
it opens up the secret heart.
Master Paul, love's rushing flow,
our hearts awash in sacred glow.

Master Paul, your love so true,
and therefore we apply to you,
to set all free in the great love,
that you are shining from Above.

4. Paul the Venetian, radiate into the collective consciousness the awareness that people need to transcend the use of psychic violence justified by the fanatical mindset.

Master Paul, accelerate,
upon pure love we meditate.
Master Paul, intentions pure,
our self-transcendence will ensure.

Master Paul, your love so true,
and therefore we apply to you,
to set all free in the great love,
that you are shining from Above.

5. Paul the Venetian, radiate into the collective consciousness the awareness that people need to transcend the sense that there is only one truth, only one way to look at reality, and that this truth, this ideology, religion or political theory is superior to all others.

> Master Paul, your love will heal,
> our inner light you do reveal.
> Master Paul, all life console,
> with you we're being truly whole.
>
> **Master Paul, your love so true,
> and therefore we apply to you,
> to set all free in the great love,
> that you are shining from Above.**

6. Paul the Venetian, radiate into the collective consciousness the awareness that the most insidious aspect of fanaticism is the sense of being superior to other people. There is still a very subtle sense of superiority found not only in nations, but in Europe and the world as a whole.

> Master Paul, you serve the All,
> by helping us transcend the fall.
> Master Paul, in peace we rise,
> as ego meets its sure demise.
>
> **Master Paul, your love so true,
> and therefore we apply to you,
> to set all free in the great love,
> that you are shining from Above.**

7. Paul the Venetian, radiate into the collective consciousness the awareness that there is a sense of superiority towards the less developed nations. Many in Western Europe have a sense of superiority towards the nations of Eastern Europe. Many people in Britain, Germany and France feel their nations are superior. Many nations have a sense that their own nation has certain characteristics that makes it unique or superior.

> Master Paul, love all life free,
> your love is for eternity.
> Master Paul, you are the One,
> to help us make the journey fun.
>
> **Master Paul, your love so true,**
> **and therefore we apply to you,**
> **to set all free in the great love,**
> **that you are shining from Above.**

8. Paul the Venetian, radiate into the collective consciousness the awareness that if this sense of superiority could be transcended, it would have an incredible impact on bringing the Golden Age into manifestation.

> Master Paul, you balance all,
> the seven rays upon our call.
> Master Paul, you paint the sky,
> with colors that delight the I.
>
> **Master Paul, your love so true,**
> **and therefore we apply to you,**
> **to set all free in the great love,**
> **that you are shining from Above.**

9. Paul the Venetian, radiate into the collective consciousness the awareness that when you are projecting something *out* upon other people, you are at the same time projecting something *in* upon yourself. When you are projecting upon other people that you are superior to them, you are projecting upon yourself that you are inferior in some way.

Master Paul, your Presence here,
filling up the inner sphere.
Life is now a sacred flow,
God Love we do on all bestow.

Master Paul, your love so true,
and therefore we apply to you,
to set all free in the great love,
that you are shining from Above.

Part 4

1. Paul the Venetian, radiate into the collective consciousness the awareness that the fanatical mindset truly is based on the psychological mechanism of inferiority that finds its outward expression as superiority.

Sanat Kumara, Ruby Fire,
I seek my place in love's own choir,
with open hearts we sing your praise,
together we the earth do raise.

Sanat Kumara, Ruby Ray,
bring to earth a higher way,
light this planet with your fire,
clothe her in a new attire.

2. Paul the Venetian, radiate into the collective consciousness the awareness that the effect of the inferiority-superiority dynamic is that you can never fully cooperate because full cooperation can only be done among equals.

Sanat Kumara, Ruby Fire,
initiations I desire,
I am for you an electrode,
Shamballa is my true abode.

**Sanat Kumara, Ruby Ray,
bring to earth a higher way,
light this planet with your fire,
clothe her in a new attire.**

3. Paul the Venetian, radiate into the collective consciousness the awareness that this leads to false cooperation, where people are only cooperating in order to get an advantage for themselves.

Sanat Kumara, Ruby Fire,
I follow path that you require,
initiate me with your love,
the open door for Holy Dove.

**Sanat Kumara, Ruby Ray,
bring to earth a higher way,
light this planet with your fire,
clothe her in a new attire.**

4. Paul the Venetian, radiate into the collective consciousness the awareness that when you truly cooperate, you are not coming from a state of: "What is in it for me?" You are coming from a state of: "How can I serve others?" You are not cooperating with others in order to get but in order to give.

Sanat Kumara, Ruby Fire,
your great example all inspire,
with non-attachment and great mirth,
we give the earth a true rebirth.

**Sanat Kumara, Ruby Ray,
bring to earth a higher way,
light this planet with your fire,
clothe her in a new attire.**

5. Paul the Venetian, radiate into the collective consciousness the awareness that for a nation to move into this state, it has to overcome the major block to true cooperation, which is inferiority.

Sanat Kumara, Ruby Fire,
you are this planet's purifier,
consume on earth all spirits dark,
reveal the inner Spirit Spark.

**Sanat Kumara, Ruby Ray,
bring to earth a higher way,
light this planet with your fire,
clothe her in a new attire.**

6. Paul the Venetian, radiate into the collective consciousness the awareness that in order to overcome inferiority, a nation has to recognize that it is fully acceptable as it is. We cannot get this true sense of self-worth through a materialistic worldview.

Sanat Kumara, Ruby Fire,
you are a cosmic amplifier,
the lower forces can't withstand,
vibrations from Venusian band.

**Sanat Kumara, Ruby Ray,
bring to earth a higher way,
light this planet with your fire,
clothe her in a new attire.**

7. Paul the Venetian, radiate into the collective consciousness the awareness that true self-worth cannot come from the material world, it cannot come from a political ideology that sets you apart from other people, it cannot come from a religion based on the consciousness of separation that separates you from God and from other people.

Sanat Kumara, Ruby Fire,
I am on earth your magnifier,
the flow of love I do restore,
my chakras are your open door.

**Sanat Kumara, Ruby Ray,
bring to earth a higher way,
light this planet with your fire,
clothe her in a new attire.**

8. Paul the Venetian, radiate into the collective consciousness the awareness that self-worth can come only from a true spiritual recognition, an inner recognition that no people are superior to others because all people were created with equal value, equal worth.

Sanat Kumara, Ruby Fire,
Venusian song the multiplier,
as we your love reverberate,
the densest minds we penetrate.

**Sanat Kumara, Ruby Ray,
bring to earth a higher way,
light this planet with your fire,
clothe her in a new attire.**

9. Paul the Venetian, radiate into the collective consciousness the awareness that if we can accept that we have worth from within, that we do not need to get it from this world, then we can look at other people and interact with other people without the need to feel superior.

Sanat Kumara, Ruby Fire,
you are for all the sanctifier,
the earth is now a holy place,
purified by cosmic grace.

**Sanat Kumara, Ruby Ray,
bring to earth a higher way,
light this planet with your fire,
clothe her in a new attire.**

Part 5

1. Paul the Venetian, radiate into the collective consciousness the awareness that when we know we have worth from within, we do not need to create an ideal state in this world. We do not need to create the perfect world, the kingdom of God or the utopian socialist society.

> O Saint Germain, you do inspire,
> my vision raised forever higher,
> with you I form a figure-eight,
> your Golden Age I co-create.
>
> **O Saint Germain, what love you bring,**
> **it truly makes all matter sing,**
> **your violet flame does all restore,**
> **with you we are becoming more.**

2. Paul the Venetian, radiate into the collective consciousness the awareness that when our value comes from Above, so does the value of everything we do on earth. We are not relating so much to earth as we are relating to the spiritual realm.

> O Saint Germain, what Freedom Flame,
> released when we recite your name,
> acceleration is your gift,
> our planet it will surely lift.
>
> **O Saint Germain, what love you bring,**
> **it truly makes all matter sing,**
> **your violet flame does all restore,**
> **with you we are becoming more.**

3. Paul the Venetian, radiate into the collective consciousness the awareness that when we realize how the interaction between Spirit and matter works, we know that as we give to other people horizontally, we will receive more from Above.

> O Saint Germain, in love we claim,
> our right to bring your violet flame,
> from you Above, to us below,
> it is an all-transforming flow.

> **O Saint Germain, what love you bring,**
> **it truly makes all matter sing,**
> **your violet flame does all restore,**
> **with you we are becoming more.**

4. Paul the Venetian, radiate into the collective consciousness the awareness that the best way to get something for ourselves is to give to others because then we will receive more from Above. When we know this, we can cooperate with others.

> O Saint Germain, I love you so,
> my aura filled with violet glow,
> my chakras filled with violet fire,
> I am your cosmic amplifier.

> **O Saint Germain, what love you bring,**
> **it truly makes all matter sing,**
> **your violet flame does all restore,**
> **with you we are becoming more.**

5. Paul the Venetian, radiate into the collective consciousness the awareness that a Golden Age can be brought only when human beings in embodiment cooperate with the ascended masters so that you can add the multiplication that manifests a Golden Age.

> O Saint Germain, I am now free,
> your violet flame is therapy,
> transform all hang-ups in my mind,
> as inner peace I surely find.
>
> **O Saint Germain, what love you bring,**
> **it truly makes all matter sing,**
> **your violet flame does all restore,**
> **with you we are becoming more.**

6. Paul the Venetian, radiate into the collective consciousness the awareness that a Golden Age cannot be brought about unless we open our minds and hearts to receive what the ascended masters are longing to give us from Above. We cannot open your minds and hearts when we are in the state of fanaticism, no matter how subtle it might be.

> O Saint Germain, my body pure,
> your violet flame for all is cure,
> consume the cause of all disease,
> and therefore I am all at ease.
>
> **O Saint Germain, what love you bring,**
> **it truly makes all matter sing,**
> **your violet flame does all restore,**
> **with you we are becoming more.**

7. Paul the Venetian, radiate into the collective consciousness the awareness that there is a need for the more spiritually mature people to recognize that we may still have elements of the mindset that sets us apart, that gives us a need for superiority.

O Saint Germain, I'm karma-free,
the past no longer burdens me,
a brand new opportunity,
I am in Christic unity.

**O Saint Germain, what love you bring,
it truly makes all matter sing,
your violet flame does all restore,
with you we are becoming more.**

8. Paul the Venetian, radiate into the collective consciousness the awareness that if people could rise above the need to feel superior, people would feel as if a huge weight had been lifted from them and they would feel truly free.

O Saint Germain, we are now one,
I am for you a violet sun,
as we transform this planet earth,
your Golden Age is given birth.

**O Saint Germain, what love you bring,
it truly makes all matter sing,
your violet flame does all restore,
with you we are becoming more.**

9. Paul the Venetian, radiate into the collective consciousness the awareness that the more we do to raise the All, the more we receive from Above. The more we receive from Above, the more this pulls us towards the source of what we are receiving and oneness with Source is the ultimate freedom.

> O Saint Germain, the earth is free,
> from burden of duality,
> in oneness we bring what is best,
> your Golden Age is manifest.
>
> **O Saint Germain, what love you bring,**
> **it truly makes all matter sing,**
> **your violet flame does all restore,**
> **with you we are becoming more.**

Sealing

In the name of the Divine Mother, I call to all ascended masters for the sealing of myself and all people in my circle of influence in the creative flow of the Divine Mother, the River of Life. I call for the multiplication of my calls by all ascended masters, so that we form the perfect figure-eight flow of "As Above, so below." Thus, I accept that this is fully manifest, because the mouth of the Lord, the Divine Mother that I AM, has spoken it. Amen.

9 | THE RISE OF INDIVIDUALITY AND INDIVIDUAL NATIONS

I AM the Ascended Master Serapis Bey, and I will give a personal message to each one of you. The message is this: "I love you."

What else of a personal message could you possibly need because all the rest is detail. You see, if there was a change that I envision happening on earth that would bring the Golden Age, it would be precisely that more and more people on earth would come to the acceptance of the fact that we who are in the ascended realm love you unconditionally. If you could come to understand that all of the very subtle ideas spread around the world that present God as an angry, remote, conditional being are fabrications of the fallen beings, deliberately set up to separate you from God, then that would be a tremendous step forward towards the Golden Age.

Satanic ideas

If you know that God loves you, then everything else, everything that is happening on earth, becomes insignificant in comparison. Is it not so that human beings have a great need – desire – for love? Is it not so that most people believe that they have to find this love on earth? Where else would they find it when they have been brought up to believe that either there is no God or there is an angry God up there in the sky who is more eager to judge them and punish them than to love them? If people could be brought to understand a very simple fact, namely that Spirit does not conform to conditions in matter, then that would be a huge leap forward.

You know, of course, that the Fourth Ray has often been presented as the Ray of Purity, and we have often talked about various kinds of impurities on earth. The essence of impurity is actually that you take current conditions in matter (the conditions you observe on earth) and you use these conditions to project what conditions are like in the spiritual realm. You are seeking to force Spirit to conform to some condition in matter. This is the essence of the satanic consciousness.

It is why Jesus said to Peter: "Get thee behind me, Satan!" Peter was wanting Jesus to conform to his idea of what should or should not happen to the Living Christ. This is the essence of what the fallen beings want to do with everyone. They want all people to conform to their ideas, but they especially want those who are the more spiritual people (those who are beginning to attain some measure of Christhood) to conform to their ideas.

They are absolutely desperate to make you accept that there is some condition on earth to which you need to conform, some limitation you cannot go beyond, some chain that you cannot break, some mistake you have made that you cannot get away from. This is, of course, promoted in many ways. One of the primary ways has been the Christian religion, the Catholic Church, but certainly also materialism, which says that you are not even a spiritual being.

All of these impurities, that are around in the world, have the effect of changing, distorting, making dirty, your vision of the spiritual realm, your vision of Spirit—and thereby your vision of yourself as a spiritual being. If people could come to understand that nothing on earth is permanent – nothing on earth has power over them as spiritual beings – then they could avoid being so attached to conditions on earth. Of course, as we have said, it is this attachment that leads to the fanaticism that causes so much violence and conflict.

How to overcome impurity

Any attachment to any condition on earth is an impurity. The trick is to realize that you do not free yourself from an impurity by destroying the impurity, by removing the impurity or by doing something to the impurity. This can be subtle to understand.

We tell you that, as ascended master students, you need to take responsibility for yourselves and your own path. Of course, part of taking responsibility is to realize that you may have made a mistake. You may have done something that you now see was not the highest possible. Therefore, you realize that you did this because you have a certain mechanism in your consciousness, a certain attachment, a certain wound from the past that caused you to act this way. You need to do something about this.

There are even spiritual teachings that talk about the fact that if you make a certain action, you make karma and then you have to overcome the karma. While it is not false to say that you have to transform the energy you created through that action, you are not actually fully overcoming the karma, as we have said before, unless you overcome the consciousness that led you to act this way.

How do you overcome an impurity? Not by focusing on the impurity, but by focusing on what it is in your consciousness that causes the impurity to stick to you. You can take the sentence: "The prince of this world comes and has nothing in me." You could imagine yourself walking through one of these gauntlets from olden times where there are rows of people on both sides who are trying to hit you with any kind of instrument. Instead of trying to hit you, they are throwing various things at you and the question is: "Do they stick to you or do they just fall off like water on a goose?"

It is the wounds, the illusions, the impurities in your consciousness that cause the impurities on earth to stick to you. They pull you into a reactionary pattern where you become trapped, and perhaps you become trapped for the rest of that lifetime (or for many lifetimes) into reacting. This is what you see going on all over the world where groups of people have been in a reactionary pattern with each other for centuries, for thousands of years. You can see this in Europe as well.

It would be a tremendous help, a tremendous progress towards the Golden Age, if people could realize that they will never be free in their own minds as long as they are trapped in these reactionary spirals. Also, they would need to realize that the only way to be free of these spirals is to stop trying to change those other people or even outer conditions, but to focus on changing themselves.

A new era of community

Another aspect that I want to present from the perspective of the Fourth Ray is that we have before said that the Aquarian Age is an age of community. This is a very subtle concept to fully understand. Normally, when you talk about community, you are talking about a group of people working together for some common purpose. They are working in a group. This raises the question of the interplay between the individual and the group.

What you have seen (not only in the Piscean Age but also in previous ages) is that the kind of groups that have formed on earth have been what we might call karmic groups where people had a similar state of consciousness that magnetized them together. That consciousness was dualistic so that you had one group of people that were sticking together, but the main thing that made them stick together was that they were in opposition to another group. In order to avoid being overrun by the other group, they had to stick together to defend themselves. This is how you have seen many groupings form.

To some degree, you see in the European community a formation of this in a certain reaction against something else, against those who are on the outside. This could be the Eastern Bloc (as was the case when the European Union was formed) or it can be a sense that we are a group of nations who are superior, or who are able to work together, but those other nations are not at our level and we do not want to work with them. Or if we work with them, we cannot be equal partners. In so many individual and national groupings, there is this sense that some have to be superior to others. It is, of course, not this kind of groupings that we envision as the basis for the community of the Aquarian Age and the Golden Age of Aquarius.

We foresee a whole new approach to groups. The strange or the subtle thing is that, in order to get to the point where you can form Aquarian groups, humanity (especially in the more developed world) first had to go through a phase where they were focusing on individuality. You will see that you have grown up in a culture in Europe that very much focuses on the individual person. You all have been told you have individual human rights, and you all have been brought up to educate yourself, to look out for your own interests, get the best possible education, job, income and so on.

The reality is that this is just a temporary phase. It was not a phase that was absolutely necessary. You will see that Jesus, when he inaugurated the Age of Pisces, had his disciples and other followers form a community. In the *Book of Acts* you can see the formation of a community where the disciples lived together and shared many things. This was a pattern that could have continued throughout the Piscean Age.

What happened instead was that the Catholic Church was formed and thereby Christianity was dominated by the fallen beings. The fallen beings can only conceive of a community of unequals; they cannot conceive of a community of equals. They want to set themselves up as the unquestioned leaders who have a number of obedient followers. This, of course, is not the community that Jesus started. He started a community of the spirit, of the Holy Spirit, where it was recognized that there was no single leader because it was a matter of who was the open door for the Spirit, and that could change from moment to moment. If this pattern had continued, you could have built a much greater sense of community in the Age of Pisces. Because of the takeover of the fallen beings, you created this new perverted form of community where the many follow the leader, and they follow the leader without questioning what the leader says and does. You saw this in the kings in the Middle Ages. You saw how this was broken only by the advent of democracy, which is based on individual human rights.

A new concept of individuality

This has been used also by the fallen beings. We have talked before about the established power elite, which was the Catholic Church, and the aspiring power elite. When scientific ideas and principles became more accepted, the aspiring power elite immediately started using this to create materialism and create a whole different set of ideas. They perverted the idea of individuality, making it seem like the individual was the superior unit of society, and that the individual had the right to do whatever it wanted. This was partly based on the concept of "survival of the fittest" and that some individuals were simply more fit than others and therefore were fit to rule. This has filtered down so that most people in Europe today have grown up with this idea that they only need to consider themselves and their own interests and do what is best for themselves. This has led to, as we have talked about, in the European community each nation is looking at "What can I get" rather than "What can I give."

However, even though this has been perverted, it was still necessary for Europe and other parts of the world to go through this phase of focusing on individuality. It was the only way that some people could pull themselves away from the domination of the fallen beings in the Catholic Church. Some then became subject to other fallen beings, but some have managed to use their individuality to say: "I will follow neither this nor that extreme, I will look for a middle way." That is why you are here as spiritual students. That is why many other people are looking for new ideas, a new awareness of what is the next step in the evolution of society.

What then *is* the next step? It is the recognition that you are an individual, but you are not meant to live as an individual for an entire lifetime. You are, however, meant to follow a spiritual path that leads you to get to know who you are as an individual, as a *spiritual* individual.

Ideally, if a society was set up the way it will be in the Golden Age, you would start this process as a young child. Everything from kindergarten forward would help you go on a journey of self-discovery. Instead of just educating yourself about facts, you would also educate yourself about yourself, about who you are. You would discover who you are, what is your Divine plan, what you are here to bring forth. Ideally, this process should be completed in the early twenties. You should then have an education that allows you to go out in society and find your place there. That is the time where you also realize that once you have manifested a certain degree of Christhood, it is actually time to no longer be so focused on yourself but to be focused on serving others.

There is a phase where you need to pull away from the mass consciousness because if you just follow the mass consciousness, you cannot manifest Christhood, you cannot raise yourself above the mass consciousness. You go within, you focus on yourself. You focus on discovering and developing your individuality and your individual talents. Once you have done that, once you have come to a certain step of initiation (having passed these initiations), then you realize that the true way to grow from there is to no longer do something for yourself but to do something for others. It is only in serving others that you progress further. You cannot go beyond a certain level on your individual path by only focusing on yourself and your own growth. This is one of the illusions that has trapped many sincere spiritual students in a blind alley where they continue to be so focused on themselves.

They do what Mother Mary said: They are dividing the distance between here and there into smaller and smaller increments, focusing on more and more little issues about their body, about their mind, about their psychology, about their past lives, about this or that. It is all focused on themselves and it just keeps them trapped in a treadmill and prevents them from taking that quantum leap where they are no longer focused on themselves but focused on serving the whole in some way. You are either serving other people, you are serving society, you are serving the vision of the ascended masters, you are serving some purpose that is beyond personal interest.

Mental illness in affluent nations

This, of course, can be taken to the level of nations. As we have said, the European nations (especially the more developed and affluent of them) have decades ago come to a point where they can grow no further unless they begin to look at how they can serve others. If they do not take this step, they will see more and more internal problems come up that pull on their resources and their attention, but it does not help the nation progress. One example of this is what we talked about yesterday, namely mental illness. This is an example of how, when a nation has no goal that reaches beyond itself, more and more people manifest a sense of hopelessness, a sense of despair. They go into depression or other forms of mental illness or substance abuse.

The reason is simple. When a nation reaches the level where it has the resources to help others, there will be a wave of souls that come into embodiment because they know it is their Divine plan to serve in this capacity, and they see that this nation is an opportunity for them to fulfill this. When they come into embodiment, they forget who they are. There is nothing in their nation that stimulates their desire to help the whole. Then, what can they do other than feel an inner tension, feel like life has no meaning? "Why am I here? What is the purpose of it all?" They go into this downward spiral of more and more severe mental illness.

Again, this is not a matter of analyzing it. It is, in many cases, a matter of channeling your energies into a constructive direction so that you do what you came here to do. This is what the nations of Europe have not been willing to recognize. The reason being that they have not been willing to free themselves from the paradigm, the worldview, of both materialism and the Christian churches.

It is clear that in order for there to be a Golden Age in Europe, the nations of Europe need to transcend the mindset that took over Christianity and the mindset that has taken over materialism. It is not a matter of withdrawing, going into the opposite extreme or rejecting all religion. It is a matter of realizing that the only alternative to the Catholic Church is *not* materialism or atheism. There is a middle way, a different approach where you recognize that life does have a purpose that is not contained within the material realm.

The fallen beings (the prince of this world, the consciousness of Satan) want you to believe that the world is a separate unit. Either there is no God, or the world is separated from God. Therefore, the world in a way is enough in itself. It is a purpose in itself. It is a closed circle. There are very, very few people who can be satisfied in this closed circle for an entire embodiment. Most people have a desire for something that reaches beyond, but when they cannot find it, then what can they do but feel depressed?

A nation can be depressed

The same thing happens with nations. If you actually look at the nations of Europe today, you will see that if you considered certain nations as individuals, you would say that this person suffers from depression. There are many nations (the majority of the nations) that suffer from a form of depression. This needs to be recognized. It needs to be recognized that a nation can actually look at its national psyche and can see that a change is needed. The change is that you start looking beyond yourself and what Mother Mary called all of the petty problems that consume people's attention. You start looking at how you can help the whole. How can you do something for someone else? How can you find a higher vision and dedicate yourself to bringing that vision into manifestation in your nation and outside your nation?

Going back to what I said about the phase of individuality, you can see that nations have also had a need to go through this phase where they were individual nations that were focusing on their growth. Saint Germain has taught before (in fact, here in Holland) about nation states and that this was a necessary phase but it also has certain problems. First of all, it gave rise to war between nation states.

It was necessary to create the nation states in order to avoid a situation where all people had become the subject of the fallen beings under one overall leadership. It was therefore better to have individual nations than to have everyone ruled by what the fallen beings were trying to do through the Catholic

Church in the Middle Ages: create a sort of religious-political state that was ruled by the church. This, of course, meant that we had to break this up by creating individual nations so that it was possible that some nations could at least be open to a different approach to Christianity or a different approach to science. Otherwise, how else would there be change if everything had been under the dictatorial rule of the Catholic Church?

You need to recognize, again, that there was a time where the individual nations served a purpose. It wasn't the highest possible purpose but it was an adaptation to conditions. What you realize is that for there to be a true Golden Age in Europe, the nations of Europe need to recognize that they have gone past the point of focusing on themselves (where they need to realize who they are) so that they can enter a new phase of cooperation with each other.

The cooperation we are looking for is, of course, a true form of community. This has several aspects, but one of the most important ones is that a true community can only exist among equals. It can exist among individuals who realize that they are all spiritual beings, that they all come from the same source, that they all have an I AM Presence and spiritual individuality that is of infinite value. Therefore, no one is more important, more valuable, more worthy than anyone else. People may have different functions but it does not mean that they have different value.

It is the same with nations. As we have said, there is still this spirit of superiority in Europe, and for a true community of European nations to emerge, it needs to be overcome. Of course, the inferiority that we see in some of the smaller nations must also be overcome. This will require some changes here and there where there are actually nations that will merge with each other because they realize they have so much in common that there really is little point in having these national boundaries that were drawn artificially on a map decades or centuries ago based on conditions that existed back then but are completely irrelevant today. These are things to make calls for as the spiritual people. These are things to focus your mind on.

A new type of spiritual community

It is important that, as the spiritual people, you also keep in mind how you as individuals can come together and form a true community of the spirit. A community of equals where no one is superior, no one is more valuable, no one is above anyone else. No one is above the Law, and no one is above common sense. No one is above the need to treat others with respect.

I am not here talking about forming a spiritual community, as the many communities you have seen in the past, where you set yourselves apart and define yourselves in opposition to or as being different from others. I am talking about a different form of community, an Aquarian Age community that is not a separatist, elitist, sectarian community but is a universalist, inclusive community. You still find a way to support each other and have certain common goals and visions, but you do not do it by setting yourself apart from society, apart from others and especially not by setting yourself *above* others.

I realize this is a delicate challenge to put before you. I hope you also realize that we do not put any challenge before you that you are not capable of meeting if you are willing to transcend whatever impurity in yourself that blocks the manifestation of the goal. We have often said that any condition in the material world can be changed, and it is true but only if you transcend the consciousness that manifested that condition.

Of course, you are capable of transcending the issues that we bring to your attention.

Spiritual people and a new view of matter

One last comment I want to make is that it would also be extremely beneficial to the bringing forth of the Golden Age if people could come to rethink their attitude towards the matter realm, the Mother realm. This must begin with the spiritual people because you are the ones who have the greatest awareness. You are also the ones who, in many cases, face this very subtle challenge of how do you, on one hand, recognize that you are a spiritual person, you have a spiritual goal, but on the other hand, you have to live an everyday life in a society that is very far from your spiritual vision. How do you bridge that gap?

Traditionally, you saw in the Age of Pisces that many spiritual people would withdraw from society because they could not maintain any sense of spirituality or harmony when they were living in society. This is not what we are asking in the Age of Aquarius. We are asking you to find a way to live in society and still be spiritual. If you can do this, as the spiritual people, you can be the forerunners for creating a shift in the collective consciousness where people realize that the Mother is not their enemy. The Mother is not a limitation of their creative efforts.

It needs to be recognized that the fallen beings have done everything they can to promote what we have called hatred of the Mother. You hate the Mother realm because you think the Mother realm is the one that is punishing you, that is putting limitations in your way, that is making life such a struggle on this planet. You have already made that change, but by making the calls and by working on yourselves even more, you can bring forth a new trend in the collective consciousness where people realize that the Mother is the mirror.

Conditions in the material realm are a mirror of conditions in the collective consciousness. If you experience that life is a struggle, it is because there is a struggle in the collective consciousness that has created certain physical conditions. People need to begin to question whether it is actually possible to change conditions by changing consciousness. This, of course, is what the fallen beings have done everything to prevent, both through religion and materialism, but it is beginning to break up.

You can make the calls for the breakthrough of a new approach to science where scientists officially recognize the need to incorporate consciousness in all scientific theories. They begin to research consciousness (as some of them have already done) and people begin to realize that there is already enough scientific evidence to prove that everything is linked to consciousness.

Nations looking at their national psyche

When people begin to realize this, then they can stop blaming their misfortune on the Mother realm and instead realize that it is a product of consciousness. This begins at the individual level, but there will come a point where nations can begin to look at it collectively and say: "What is it in our collective consciousness that has manifested the current limitations and problems we face, and what can we do to shift this? How can we change?"

You may think that this is way beyond what the nations are willing to do, but is it really? Have not many nations already started this process to some degree? Why is there greater affluence today in many nations than there was a generation or two ago? Is it not because something has changed in the collective psyche of that nation that has set the stage for the emergence of greater physical prosperity? Could we not take this further? Why is there more political freedom? Why is there more tolerance?

Could we not take this further? Could we not become more aware of how we react to certain conditions? Could we not consciously change that reaction and realize that thereby we could manifest a higher degree of freedom, prosperity and tolerance? Could we not recognize that when we are faced with external challenges, such as terrorism or refugees, it is because there is something in our consciousness that we have not resolved. Instead of focusing exclusively on the outer crisis, we can focus on that element of the national and even international psyche and thereby we can transcend the problem rather than solving the problem or destroying the cause of the problem. The fallen beings can see no other solution than to destroy the physical cause of the problem or to somehow find a solution that is in the material world where the problem is. What we are telling you over and over is that there is no solution to material problems in the material world. There is only the solution of the transcendence of consciousness.

This, of course, is a big mouthful, but I hope you are beginning to realize that at this conference we are giving teachings that reach far beyond this conference. They are meant to create a shift in the collective consciousness both when we speak them and when they are spoken by the people who will give the invocations and study and hear these dictations.

You who are here at this conference have chosen to be here because you wanted to hold the spiritual balance for the bringing forth of this release of light and teaching. We are grateful that you are here and that you give us this platform. I can tell you that each one of you is being used, your chakras are being used, as a broadcasting station, as a sort of amplifier that amplifies in the physical the signal that is coming from us. The impulse that is coming from us is being amplified in your chakras and thereby broadcast horizontally in the collective consciousness with a greater force than the law would allow us to do alone.

We, of course, have the power. We could release the energy that would instantly force a change in the collective consciousness, but the Law of Free Will does not allow us to do this, and we have no desire to do this. You who are in physical embodiment, you can allow yourself to be a broadcasting station for this signal. Of course, those of you who will study the dictations and give the invocations will also become amplifiers for the signal. The many people who might just pick up on these ideas when the collective consciousness is raised, they will also become amplifiers, and this is how real change comes about on earth. It begins with a few and then spreads like rings in the water.

I know that it is not necessarily easy for those of you who are here to hold this balance, and it can seem somewhat heavy, somewhat tedious. Nevertheless, I tell you, we are grateful that you have given us this platform. With this I give you, once again, my unconditional love, each one.

10 | CALLING FORTH TRUE COMMUNITY

In the name I AM THAT I AM, Jesus Christ, I call to all ascended masters working on manifesting the Golden Age, especially Archangel Gabriel, Elohim Astrea, Serapis Bey, Shiva and Saint Germain to radiate into the collective consciousness a new awareness of how to create a community of equals in the world. Help people see that we can build a new future by working with the ascended masters and letting go of the old way of looking at life, including…

[Make personal calls.]

Part 1

1. Serapis Bey, radiate into the collective consciousness the awareness that the ascended masters love us unconditionally and that the angry, remote, conditional God is a fabrication of the fallen beings, deliberately set up to separate us from God.

> Gabriel Archangel, your light we revere,
> immersed in your Presence, nothing we fear.
> Disciples of Christ, we do leave behind,
> the ego's desire for responding in kind.
>
> **Gabriel Archangel, of this we are sure,**
> **Gabriel Archangel, Christ light is the cure.**
> **Gabriel Archangel, intentions so pure,**
> **Gabriel Archangel, in you we're secure.**

2. Serapis Bey, radiate into the collective consciousness the awareness that seeking to force Spirit to conform to some condition in matter is the essence of the satanic consciousness.

> Gabriel Archangel, we fear not the light,
> in purifications' fire, we delight.
> With your hand in ours, each challenge we face,
> we follow the spiral to infinite grace.
>
> **Gabriel Archangel, of this we are sure,**
> **Gabriel Archangel, Christ light is the cure.**
> **Gabriel Archangel, intentions so pure,**
> **Gabriel Archangel, in you we're secure.**

3. Serapis Bey, radiate into the collective consciousness the awareness that the fallen beings are desperate to make us accept that there is some condition on earth to which we need to conform, some limitation we cannot go beyond, some chain that we cannot break, some mistake we have made that we cannot get away from.

> Gabriel Archangel, your fire burning white,
> ascending with you, out of the night.
> The ego has nowhere to run and to hide,
> in ascension's bright spiral, with you we abide.

> **Gabriel Archangel, of this we are sure,**
> **Gabriel Archangel, Christ light is the cure.**
> **Gabriel Archangel, intentions so pure,**
> **Gabriel Archangel, in you we're secure.**

4. Serapis Bey, radiate into the collective consciousness the awareness that the impurities in the world have the effect of distorting our vision of ourselves as spiritual beings. Nothing on earth has power over us as spiritual beings so we do not need to be so attached to conditions on earth.

> Gabriel Archangel, your trumpet we hear,
> announcing the birth of Christ drawing near.
> In lightness of being, we now are reborn,
> rising with Christ on bright Easter morn.

> **Gabriel Archangel, of this we are sure,**
> **Gabriel Archangel, Christ light is the cure.**
> **Gabriel Archangel, intentions so pure,**
> **Gabriel Archangel, in you we're secure.**

5. Serapis Bey, radiate into the collective consciousness the awareness that we do not free ourselves from an impurity by destroying the impurity, by removing the impurity, or by doing something to the impurity.

> Gabriel Archangel, the earth is now free,
> embracing a nondual reality,
> the judgment of Christ upon forces so dark,
> who deny that all have a spiritual spark.
>
> **Gabriel Archangel, of this we are sure,**
> **Gabriel Archangel, Christ light is the cure.**
> **Gabriel Archangel, intentions so pure,**
> **Gabriel Archangel, in you we're secure.**

6. Serapis Bey, radiate into the collective consciousness the awareness that we do not overcome an impurity by focusing on the impurity, but by focusing on what it is in our consciousness that causes the impurity to stick to us.

> Gabriel Archangel, with angels so white,
> raising our planet out of the dark night,
> as we now intone the Word of the Lord,
> the beings who fell are bound by your sword.
>
> **Gabriel Archangel, of this we are sure,**
> **Gabriel Archangel, Christ light is the cure.**
> **Gabriel Archangel, intentions so pure,**
> **Gabriel Archangel, in you we're secure.**

7. Serapis Bey, radiate into the collective consciousness the awareness that it is the wounds, the illusions, the impurities in our consciousness that cause the impurities on earth to stick to us.

> Gabriel Archangel, we call now to you,
> the astral plane your light burning through,
> entities, demons, discarnates are bound,
> as you and we intone Sacred Sound.

> **Gabriel Archangel, of this we are sure,**
> **Gabriel Archangel, Christ light is the cure.**
> **Gabriel Archangel, intentions so pure,**
> **Gabriel Archangel, in you we're secure.**

8. Serapis Bey, radiate into the collective consciousness the awareness that our wounds pull us into a reactionary pattern where we become trapped. This is going on all over the world where groups of people have been in a reactionary pattern with each other for thousands of years.

> Gabriel Archangel, what glorious day,
> your radiant angels have come here to stay,
> your purifications fire burning white,
> intentions so pure, our hearts taking flight.

> **Gabriel Archangel, of this we are sure,**
> **Gabriel Archangel, Christ light is the cure.**
> **Gabriel Archangel, intentions so pure,**
> **Gabriel Archangel, in you we're secure.**

9. Serapis Bey, radiate into the collective consciousness the awareness that we will never be free in our own minds as long as we are trapped in these reactionary spirals. The only way to be free of these spirals is to stop trying to change other people but to focus on changing ourselves.

> Gabriel Archangel, our planet so pure,
> in our bright new future we do feel secure,
> with your band of light encircling the earth,
> Saint Germain's Golden Age is now given birth.
>
> **Gabriel Archangel, of this we are sure,**
> **Gabriel Archangel, Christ light is the cure.**
> **Gabriel Archangel, intentions so pure,**
> **Gabriel Archangel, in you we're secure.**

Part 2

1. Serapis Bey, radiate into the collective consciousness the awareness that groups often form, as is the case in the European community, as a reaction against something else, against those who are on the outside.

> Beloved Astrea, your heart is so true,
> your Circle and Sword of white and blue,
> cut all life free from dramas unwise,
> on wings of Purity our planet will rise.

> Beloved Astrea, in oneness with you,
> your circle and sword of electric blue,
> with Purity's Light cutting right through,
> raising the earth into all that is true.

2. Serapis Bey, radiate into the collective consciousness the awareness that in many individual and national groupings, there is this sense that some have to be superior to others. This kind of groupings cannot be the basis for the community of the Golden Age of Aquarius.

> Beloved Astrea, in God Purity,
> accelerate all of our life energy,
> we're rising beyond every impurity,
> as Purity's Light forever we see.

> **Beloved Astrea, in oneness with you,
> your circle and sword of electric blue,
> with Purity's Light cutting right through,
> raising the earth into all that is true.**

3. Serapis Bey, radiate into the collective consciousness the awareness that the fallen beings can only conceive of a community of unequals; they cannot conceive of a community of equals. They want to set themselves up as the unquestioned leaders who have a number of obedient followers.

> Beloved Astrea, from Purity's Ray,
> send forth deliverance to all life today,
> acceleration to Purity, we are now free
> from all that is less than love's Purity.

> **Beloved Astrea, in oneness with you,**
> **your circle and sword of electric blue,**
> **with Purity's Light cutting right through,**
> **raising the earth into all that is true.**

4. Serapis Bey, radiate into the collective consciousness the awareness that Jesus started a community of the spirit, of the Holy Spirit, where it was recognized that there was no single leader because it was a matter of who was the open door for the Spirit.

> Beloved Astrea, accelerate us all,
> as for your deliverance we fervently call,
> set all life free from vision impure
> beyond fear and doubt, we're rising for sure.

> **Beloved Astrea, in oneness with you,**
> **your circle and sword of electric blue,**
> **with Purity's Light cutting right through,**
> **raising the earth into all that is true.**

5. Serapis Bey, radiate into the collective consciousness the awareness that the fallen beings created a perverted form of community where the many follow the leader, and they follow the leader without questioning the leader.

> Beloved Astrea, we're willing to see,
> all of the lies that keep us unfree,
> we surrender all lies causing the fall,
> forever affirming the oneness of All.

**Beloved Astrea, in oneness with you,
your circle and sword of electric blue,
with Purity's Light cutting right through,
raising the earth into all that is true.**

6. Serapis Bey, radiate into the collective consciousness the awareness that this was broken only by the advent of democracy, which is based on individual human rights.

Beloved Astrea, accelerate life
beyond all duality's struggle and strife,
consume all division between God and man,
accelerate fulfillment of God's perfect plan.

**Beloved Astrea, in oneness with you,
your circle and sword of electric blue,
with Purity's Light cutting right through,
raising the earth into all that is true.**

7. Serapis Bey, radiate into the collective consciousness the awareness that the fallen beings perverted the idea of individuality, making it seem like the individual is the superior unit of society, and that the individual has the right to do whatever it wants, partly based on the concept of survival of the fittest.

Beloved Astrea, we lovingly call,
break down separation's invisible wall,
raising our minds into true unity
with the Masters of love in Infinity.

> Beloved Astrea, in oneness with you,
> your circle and sword of electric blue,
> with Purity's Light cutting right through,
> raising the earth into all that is true.

8. Serapis Bey, radiate into the collective consciousness the awareness that this has caused most people in Europe to have grown up with the idea that they only need to consider themselves. This has led to a European community where each nation is looking at what it can get rather than what it can give.

> Beloved Astrea, help all of us find,
> the secret that we create with the mind,
> and thus what in ignorance we decreate,
> in knowledge we easily can recreate.

> Beloved Astrea, in oneness with you,
> your circle and sword of electric blue,
> with Purity's Light cutting right through,
> raising the earth into all that is true.

9. Serapis Bey, radiate into the collective consciousness the awareness that it was necessary for people to go through the phase of focusing on individuality so we could pull ourselves away from the domination of the fallen beings.

> Beloved Astrea, we all do aspire,
> to learning to use your purity's fire,
> to raise every form in infamy sown,
> as Saint Germain makes this planet his own.

> **Beloved Astrea, in oneness with you,**
> **your circle and sword of electric blue,**
> **with Purity's Light cutting right through,**
> **raising the earth into all that is true.**

Part 3

1. Serapis Bey, radiate into the collective consciousness the awareness that the next step in the evolution of society is the recognition that we are not meant to live as individuals for an entire lifetime. We are meant to follow a path that leads us to see ourselves as spiritual individuals.

> Serapis Bey, what power lies,
> behind your purifying eyes.
> Serapis Bey, it is a treat,
> to enter your sublime retreat.
>
> **Serapis Bey, we call to you,**
> **to help us dual lies see through,**
> **come purify our inner sight,**
> **we see the earth in your great light.**

2. Serapis Bey, radiate into the collective consciousness the awareness that in a golden age society, everything is set up to help children complete a journey of self-discovery.

> Serapis Bey, what wisdom found,
> your words are always most profound.
> Serapis Bey, we tell you true,
> our minds have room for naught but you.

> **Serapis Bey, we call to you,**
> **to help us dual lies see through,**
> **come purify our inner sight,**
> **we see the earth in your great light.**

3. Serapis Bey, radiate into the collective consciousness the awareness that children need to discover who they are and what is their Divine plans, what they can bring forth in serving others and society.

> Serapis Bey, what love beyond,
> our hearts do leap, as we respond.
> Serapis Bey, your life a poem,
> that calls us to our starry home.

> **Serapis Bey, we call to you,**
> **to help us dual lies see through,**
> **come purify our inner sight,**
> **we see the earth in your great light.**

4. Serapis Bey, radiate into the collective consciousness the awareness that both individuals and nations need to grow to a point where they start serving others.

> Serapis Bey, your guidance sure,
> our base is clear and white and pure.
> Serapis Bey, no longer trapped,
> by soul in which the self was wrapped.

> **Serapis Bey, we call to you,**
> **to help us dual lies see through,**
> **come purify our inner sight,**
> **we see the earth in your great light.**

5. Serapis Bey, radiate into the collective consciousness the awareness that the more affluent nations are at the point where they can grow no further unless they begin to look at how they can serve others.

> Serapis Bey, what healing balm,
> in mind that is forever calm.
> Serapis Bey, our thoughts are pure,
> your discipline we shall endure.
>
> **Serapis Bey, we call to you,**
> **to help us dual lies see through,**
> **come purify our inner sight,**
> **we see the earth in your great light.**

6. Serapis Bey, radiate into the collective consciousness the awareness that if nations do not take this step, they will see more and more internal problems come up that pull on their resources and their attention, but it does not help the nation progress.

> Serapis Bey, what secret test,
> for egos who want to be best.
> Serapis Bey, expose the "me,"
> that takes away our harmony.
>
> **Serapis Bey, we call to you,**
> **to help us dual lies see through,**
> **come purify our inner sight,**
> **we see the earth in your great light.**

7. Serapis Bey, radiate into the collective consciousness the awareness that when a nation has no goal that reaches beyond itself, more and more people manifest a sense of hopelessness and go into depression or other forms of mental illness or substance abuse.

> Serapis Bey, what moving sight,
> the self ascends to sacred height.
> Serapis Bey, forever free,
> in sacred synchronicity.

> **Serapis Bey, we call to you,**
> **to help us dual lies see through,**
> **come purify our inner sight,**
> **we see the earth in your great light.**

8. Serapis Bey, radiate into the collective consciousness the awareness that when a nation reaches the level where it has the resources to help others, there will be a wave of souls that come into embodiment because they know it is their Divine plan to serve in this capacity, and they see that this nation is an opportunity for them to fulfill this.

> Serapis Bey, you balance all,
> the seven rays upon our call.
> Serapis Bey, in space and time,
> the pyramid of self, we climb.

> **Serapis Bey, we call to you,**
> **to help us dual lies see through,**
> **come purify our inner sight,**
> **we see the earth in your great light.**

9. Serapis Bey, radiate into the collective consciousness the awareness that if there is nothing in their nation that stimulates their desire to help the whole, then people go into a downward spiral of more and more severe mental illness.

> Serapis Bey, your Presence here,
> filling up the inner sphere.
> Life is now a sacred flow,
> God Purity we do bestow.
>
> **Serapis Bey, we call to you,**
> **to help us dual lies see through,**
> **come purify our inner sight,**
> **we see the earth in your great light.**

Part 4

1. Serapis Bey, radiate into the collective consciousness the awareness that many nations have not been willing to recognize this because they have not been willing to free themselves from the paradigms of materialism and Christianity.

> O Shiva, God of Sacred Fire,
> It's time to let the past expire,
> I want to rise above the old,
> a golden future to unfold.
>
> **O Shiva, clear the energy,**
> **O Shiva, bring the synergy,**
> **O Shiva, make all demons flee,**
> **O Shiva, bring back peace to me.**

2. Serapis Bey, radiate into the collective consciousness the awareness that in order for there to be a Golden Age, the nations need to transcend the mindset that took over Christianity and the mindset that has taken over materialism.

> O Shiva, come and set me free,
> from forces that do limit me,
> with fire consume all that is less,
> paving way for my success.

> **O Shiva, clear the energy,**
> **O Shiva, bring the synergy,**
> **O Shiva, make all demons flee,**
> **O Shiva, bring back peace to me.**

3. Serapis Bey, radiate into the collective consciousness the awareness that it is not a matter of going into the opposite extreme or rejecting all religion. It is a matter of realizing that there is a different approach and that life does have a purpose that reaches beyond the material realm.

> O Shiva, Maya's veil disperse,
> clear my private universe,
> dispel the consciousness of death,
> consume it with your Sacred Breath.

> **O Shiva, clear the energy,**
> **O Shiva, bring the synergy,**
> **O Shiva, make all demons flee,**
> **O Shiva, bring back peace to me.**

4. Serapis Bey, radiate into the collective consciousness the awareness that a nation has a national psyche, and some of the more developed nations suffer from a national depression.

> O Shiva, I hereby let go,
> of all attachments here below,
> addictive entities consume,
> the upward path I do resume.
>
> **O Shiva, clear the energy,**
> **O Shiva, bring the synergy,**
> **O Shiva, make all demons flee,**
> **O Shiva, bring back peace to me.**

5. Serapis Bey, radiate into the collective consciousness the awareness that the emergence of nation states was a necessary phase in the evolution of the world. For there to be a Golden Age, the more developed nations need to recognize that they have gone past the point of focusing on themselves so they can enter a new phase of cooperation with each other.

> O Shiva, I recite your name,
> come banish fear and doubt and shame,
> with fire expose within my mind,
> what ego seeks to hide behind.
>
> **O Shiva, clear the energy,**
> **O Shiva, bring the synergy,**
> **O Shiva, make all demons flee,**
> **O Shiva, bring back peace to me.**

6. Serapis Bey, radiate into the collective consciousness the awareness that a true community can only exist among equals. For a true community of nations to emerge, the spirit of superiority and inferiority needs to be overcome.

> O Shiva, I am not afraid,
> my karmic debt hereby is paid,
> the past no longer owns my choice,
> in breath of Shiva I rejoice.
>
> **O Shiva, clear the energy,**
> **O Shiva, bring the synergy,**
> **O Shiva, make all demons flee,**
> **O Shiva, bring back peace to me.**

7. Serapis Bey, radiate into the collective consciousness the awareness that this will lead to some nations that will merge with each other because they realize they have so much in common that there is little point in having these national boundaries that were drawn artificially on a map based on conditions that are irrelevant today.

> O Shiva, show me spirit pairs,
> that keep me trapped in their affairs,
> I choose to see within my mind,
> the spirits that you surely bind.
>
> **O Shiva, clear the energy,**
> **O Shiva, bring the synergy,**
> **O Shiva, make all demons flee,**
> **O Shiva, bring back peace to me.**

8. Serapis Bey, radiate into the collective consciousness the awareness that spiritual people need to rethink our attitude towards the matter realm, the Mother realm.

> O Shiva, naked I now stand,
> my mind in freedom does expand,
> as all my ghosts I do release,
> surrender is the key to peace.
>
> **O Shiva, clear the energy,**
> **O Shiva, bring the synergy,**
> **O Shiva, make all demons flee,**
> **O Shiva, bring back peace to me.**

9. Serapis Bey, radiate into the collective consciousness the awareness that the spiritual people can be the forerunners for creating a shift in the collective consciousness where people realize that the Mother is not their enemy. The Mother is not a limitation of their creative efforts.

> O Shiva, all-consuming fire,
> with Parvati raise me higher,
> when I am raised your light to see,
> all men I will draw onto me.
>
> **O Shiva, clear the energy,**
> **O Shiva, bring the synergy,**
> **O Shiva, make all demons flee,**
> **O Shiva, bring back peace to me.**

Part 5

1. Serapis Bey, radiate into the collective consciousness the awareness that the fallen beings have done everything they can to promote hatred of the Mother. People hate the Mother realm because they think the Mother realm is punishing us and making life a struggle.

> O Saint Germain, you do inspire,
> my vision raised forever higher,
> with you I form a figure-eight,
> your Golden Age I co-create.
>
> **O Saint Germain, what love you bring,**
> **it truly makes all matter sing,**
> **your violet flame does all restore,**
> **with you we are becoming more.**

2. Serapis Bey, radiate into the collective consciousness the awareness that the Mother is the mirror. Conditions in the material realm are a mirror of conditions in the collective consciousness. It is possible to change physical conditions by changing consciousness.

> O Saint Germain, what Freedom Flame,
> released when we recite your name,
> acceleration is your gift,
> our planet it will surely lift.

**O Saint Germain, what love you bring,
it truly makes all matter sing,
your violet flame does all restore,
with you we are becoming more.**

3. Serapis Bey, radiate into the collective consciousness the awareness that there needs to be a breakthrough of a new approach to science where scientists officially recognize the need to incorporate consciousness in all scientific theories. There is already enough scientific evidence to prove that everything is linked to consciousness.

O Saint Germain, in love we claim,
our right to bring your violet flame,
from you Above, to us below,
it is an all-transforming flow.

**O Saint Germain, what love you bring,
it truly makes all matter sing,
your violet flame does all restore,
with you we are becoming more.**

4. Serapis Bey, radiate into the collective consciousness the awareness that nations need to say: "What is it in our collective consciousness that has manifested the current limitations and problems we face, and what can we do to shift this? How can we change?"

O Saint Germain, I love you so,
my aura filled with violet glow,
my chakras filled with violet fire,
I am your cosmic amplifier.

**O Saint Germain, what love you bring,
it truly makes all matter sing,
your violet flame does all restore,
with you we are becoming more.**

5. Serapis Bey, radiate into the collective consciousness the awareness that there is greater affluence today because something has changed in the collective psyche of nations that has set the stage for the emergence of greater physical prosperity.

O Saint Germain, I am now free,
your violet flame is therapy,
transform all hang-ups in my mind,
as inner peace I surely find.

**O Saint Germain, what love you bring,
it truly makes all matter sing,
your violet flame does all restore,
with you we are becoming more.**

6. Serapis Bey, radiate into the collective consciousness the awareness that by becoming more aware of how they react to certain conditions, nations could consciously change that reaction and manifest a higher degree of freedom, prosperity and tolerance.

O Saint Germain, my body pure,
your violet flame for all is cure,
consume the cause of all disease,
and therefore I am all at ease.

> **O Saint Germain, what love you bring,**
> **it truly makes all matter sing,**
> **your violet flame does all restore,**
> **with you we are becoming more.**

7. Serapis Bey, radiate into the collective consciousness the awareness that when nations are faced with external challenges, such as terrorism or refugees, it is because there is something in the national consciousness that needs to be resolved.

> O Saint Germain, I'm karma-free,
> the past no longer burdens me,
> a brand new opportunity,
> I am in Christic unity.

> **O Saint Germain, what love you bring,**
> **it truly makes all matter sing,**
> **your violet flame does all restore,**
> **with you we are becoming more.**

8. Serapis Bey, radiate into the collective consciousness the awareness that instead of focusing exclusively on the outer crisis, nations can focus on the element of the national and even international psyche and thereby transcend the problem rather than solving the problem or destroying the cause of the problem.

> O Saint Germain, we are now one,
> I am for you a violet sun,
> as we transform this planet earth,
> your Golden Age is given birth.

**O Saint Germain, what love you bring,
it truly makes all matter sing,
your violet flame does all restore,
with you we are becoming more.**

9. Serapis Bey, radiate into the collective consciousness the awareness that the fallen beings can see no other solution than to destroy the cause of the problem or to find a solution that is in the material world where the problem is. There is no solution to material problems in the material world. The only solution is the transcendence of consciousness.

O Saint Germain, the earth is free,
from burden of duality,
in oneness we bring what is best,
your Golden Age is manifest.

**O Saint Germain, what love you bring,
it truly makes all matter sing,
your violet flame does all restore,
with you we are becoming more.**

Sealing

In the name of the Divine Mother, I call to all ascended masters for the sealing of myself and all people in my circle of influence in the creative flow of the Divine Mother, the River of Life. I call for the multiplication of my calls by all ascended masters, so that we form the perfect figure-eight flow of "As Above, so below." Thus, I accept that this is fully manifest, because the mouth of the Lord, the Divine Mother that I AM, has spoken it. Amen.

11 | MAKING THE IMPOSSIBLE POSSIBLE

I AM the Ascended Master Hilarion, Chohan of the Fifth Ray, which has often been called the Ray of Vision. Obviously, one of the most important things that could happen in terms of bringing a Golden Age in Europe, and elsewhere, is a raising of the people's vision.

It is a simple fact that you cannot manifest in the physical, that which you cannot visualize in the mind. If you have no higher vision, you cannot manifest anything higher and this is where the material universe can become a closed loop that traps people for a very long time.

The Alpha and Omega of vision

You grow up as a child seeing what is around you, seeing what you perceive through the physical senses. More than that, you are brought up – programmed – to perceive through the collective mindset that looks at life a certain way. This mindset goes all the way from the physical through the emotional, mental and into the identity realm. You will, of course, see that most people on earth think they are *human* beings. They may think they are somehow created by a deity, but they see that they are separated from that deity. They are brought up to believe (especially in the Catholic tradition) that they are sinners or fundamentally flawed or limited beings. Or they may have been brought up to believe that they are a product of the process of evolution and therefore have no capabilities beyond those of the physical body and whatever technologies can be created.

Of course, if you identify yourself as such, you already have set limitations for what you *can* and what you *dare* envision. There is a dual effect of vision. First of all, you have to be able to actually visualize in your mind that it is possible to create something that you do not already see on this planet. This is the Alpha aspect of vision. You have to be able to see something that no one has seen before; you have to be able to see in your mind's eye what you do not see with your physical eye. The Omega aspect of this is that you have to be able to not only *believe* but actually *accept* and *know* that it is possible to build or manifest this physically.

There are many, many people throughout the ages who have had grandiose visions in their minds. They have been enamored with these visions, but they have not truly believed and accepted that they could be made physical. This is where people need to wake up and realize that there are forces and beings in this world who are doing everything they can to limit your vision, by limiting what people can see but also limiting what they believe and accept can be manifest.

How to communicate a higher vision

In the modern age, we have – due to Saint Germain's release of certain communication technology – made tremendous progress in terms of being able to communicate a higher vision from one person to another. If you go back just a few decades, or a few hundred years, you will see that there may have been one or two people on earth who could grasp a higher vision, but how could we get that vision communicated from that person to others so that more than one person could begin to believe that there was a higher reality somewhere? This really did not become practical until the printing press was invented.

With more and more modern communication technology it has become easier and easier. We now have a situation where there is indeed a number of people on the planet who have their minds opened and attuned to the ascended realm. They can receive a higher vision of some aspect of society that could be improved. We actually have enough people in embodiment that are able to receive a higher vision. Those people do not all know about ascended masters, they do not understand or acknowledge where their visions are coming from.

We actually have enough people who have enough of a vision to receive the major blueprint for the Golden Age. This is a development that has taken a very long time to build. In fact, if we go back just to Jesus' mission, we can say that from his mission forward, there has been a very slow growth in the number of people who have been able to manifest a higher degree of Christhood. Of course, the Christian tradition is not the only one that has raised people's consciousness, for there are also other traditions that have raised people's consciousness over many lifetimes, to the point where they can receive a higher vision.

How fallen beings limit communication

The fallen beings have, of course, all along tried to limit this. They have in many ways tried to limit communication, to restrict communication, to censure communication. For example, during the Catholic era there was a censorship of books. Books were burned, people were executed or hauled in front of the inquisition for spreading heretical views. You saw the same in the Soviet Union, you see it today even in Russia, you see a similar development in Turkey, you see it in China, North Korea and many other nations.

The fallen ones have not been able to stop the growth in the number of people who could receive a higher vision. What have they done instead? Well, there is one thing you can always count on from the fallen beings: They don't stand still. Some of them do, some of them do become trapped and become attached to maintaining a certain state of privilege. That is why they become the established power elite that are overthrown by the aspiring power elite. In general, the fallen ones never stand still as a group. There will always be someone who is looking ahead, looking to what the ascended masters are doing and seeing how they can counteract it.

Given that they could see that they could not stop the spread of new ideas, the communication of new ideas, what did they do to counteract this? Well, they took over the minds of a number of people who were willing to let their minds be taken over by the lower forces. Then, they gave their own versions of different visions, very fanciful, very complicated, very complex—some of them seemingly very benign. Then they have used the same technology that is used to spread genuine ideas, to spread their false ideas. The result is that there are now so many ideas out there that most people feel completely overwhelmed. They don't know what to look at, they don't know what to believe.

Destroying people's faith

You have seen a very interesting phenomenon that has been recognized by very few people, namely, that as the number and complexity of alternative visions has grown, more and more people have started looking at this as complete fantasy. The people who are into this mindset lump it all together and say: "This is all fiction, this is all fantasy, we don't need to take any of it seriously." What is the result of this? It is that the fallen beings have blocked the Omega aspect of vision, namely people's ability to accept that a certain vision could be made manifest.

They have also been very clever at using science and technology to promote a mindset that the only solution to humankind's problems is a technological, mechanical solution. This you see promoted especially through materialism, but also through many aspects of business and the scientific research community, people who are making their living, or making their profits, off of researching mechanical technology.

This means that there is also a large group of people who believe that if any vision is presented that something could be brought forth in a way that is not technological or mechanical, then that vision is just fantasy. It is completely unrealistic, it is something that can be fun and entertaining to read about but it could never be manifest. People write it off as mere flight of fancy when, in reality, it in some cases is the vision of the

Golden Age. You have this very difficult situation right now in terms of vision. It is not a lack of ideas that is the problem anymore, as it was in past ages. It is the over-abundance of ideas and the lack of belief that ideas could be made reality, that thoughts could become things.

If there was one thing that, from the perspective of the Fifth Ray, we could see as bringing a contribution to this, it would therefore be that people would change their view of new ideas and that they would come to actually acknowledge that not all new ideas should be written off as fantasy. It is necessary for them to develop a certain discernment so they can see, so they can *know* within themselves, which ideas are realistic and which are not.

Writing off new ideas

You, who are the spiritual people, you can much more quickly develop this discernment. We are, of course, looking for you to do this so that you can again be the forerunners and help raise the collective consciousness. The way you can increase your discernment about ideas is to realize that you cannot truly discern the validity of a vision or idea by using the intellectual, analytical mind. In fact, in order to truly know the validity of an idea, you need to neutralize the intellectual mind.

The intellectual mind will immediately look at a certain vision in a specific way. Say you present a new type of democracy that is a more direct democracy, as we have talked about. The intellectual mind will immediately look at the idea and it will compare it to current conditions. It might say: "This idea is too far beyond current conditions, it is not realistic that it could be manifested." It may also be that the intellect will say:

"Well, if this idea was to be manifested, then we of course need to start at current conditions and we then need to create a linear sequential process that, in a mechanical step-by-step way, leads from where we are right now to where this vision says we could be."

This is the only way the linear, analytical mind can think; it can only think in linear cause and effect. Of course, the linear mind is also very focused on the physical; what changes need to be manifest in the physical for this vision to come about. If the linear mind cannot see a way to do this – perhaps because the technology has not yet been invented – it will reject the idea as unrealistic. In other words, the analytical mind starts with current conditions and then it thinks: "Is the vision realistic based on current conditions?"

My beloved, if your starting point was the technology and the living conditions that existed in the iron age over a thousand years ago, how could anyone believe that a modern jet airplane was a realistic manifestation? How would you ever breach the gap – if you had only seen what people could see in the iron age – and think it was possible to create a machine that would fly through the air?

If you had presented the vision of an airplane to people a thousand years ago, they would obviously have written it off as completely unrealistic. It is the same today. There is a mechanism in the linear mind that says: "If we cannot see a linear, sequential process that leads to the fulfillment of the vision in a mechanical way, then the vision is unrealistic and we write it off without even considering it as a possibility." It is the writing off of ideas without considering them as a possibility that truly is the single mechanism that is the greatest hindrance to progress and has been the greatest hindrance to progress, throughout the history of humankind.

Believing the impossible

You always look at what is there and then you think that what might be should somehow conform to what is there. As we have mentioned, this is the satanic consciousness that wants Spirit to conform to matter. What have we been telling you now for a very long time through ascended master teachings? We have told you that the physical universe is not an isolated unit. The physical universe is created as a projection of images that exists in the emotional, mental and identity levels. We have even given the comparison that what you see in the physical universe is like a movie that is projected onto the screen of the Mat-er light. Therefore, if you change what exists at the three higher levels of the mind, you *will* change what manifests in the physical.

This means that you can bring forth a vision that does not conform to what is currently manifest in the physical. You will see, for example, that a thousand years ago (when people in Northern Europe were running around in iron helmets, swinging axes and acting like the Vikings) the vision of a modern airplane was, of course, in existence in the etheric realm. All of the plans, all of the blueprints, were there. You can see, of course, that they did not have the technology to build an airplane back then. Did it really have to take 900 years for the idea, that was in the etheric, to be lowered into the physical? The answer is: "Not necessarily." It could have been brought forth earlier, not in a very short period of time given the state of the iron age, but certainly, it could have been brought forth in the 1500s, 1600s, 1700s—if there had been greater openness to new ideas.

It is not a matter of looking at a new idea and evaluating it based on what is currently manifest. It is a matter of realizing that there is the potential to bring forth something that is completely beyond what is currently manifest. This only requires the mind to be open to receive the idea from the ascended realm. It also requires the mind's ability to believe that this can be manifest.

If you take an honest look at the world today and look at the technology that exists in the modern age, you will see that there has been an incredible amount of progress compared to a thousand years ago. If you took a Viking from those days and brought him into the modern world, he would be in a state of total shock. In fact, his mind would simply shut down and he would refuse to accept what he is seeing in the modern world. You have heard that there are some times that people can see something that is so far beyond what they know that their minds cannot accept it. If you had taken an airplane and brought it back to the time of a thousand years ago, people would have refused to accept what they are seeing—their minds would simply have shut down.

The cause of technological progress

With that, I want you to realize how much progress has been made. Look at the last hundred years and how much technological progress has been made. Part of the reason for this progress is that we of the ascended masters have created blueprints of technological inventions in the etheric realm. We are releasing them to those minds who are open and capable of receiving them and who are also in a position where they can bring them into physical manifestation.

We have done this because we saw that, realistically, it was not possible to raise the awareness of humankind to realizing and accepting the powers of the mind to create. We had to first give people a way to create and manifest new visions that was more mechanical, more technological, so that they were able to believe that this was possible. Then, the hope is that (as they have now seen how much change can be brought about through mechanical technology) more and more people will begin to open up to the possibility that you can create directly through the mind.

Many of the changes that need to happen for the Golden Age to be manifest will not be the result of a linear, gradual cause-effect process where there is a gradual evolution. One new idea leads to another, to another invention and another invention—and pretty soon you have (through separate processes) invented all of the single technologies that are combined into a modern airplane. This is one way to bring forth something new, but it is the slow way. There are certain things that pertain to society as a whole that cannot be manifested this way and the reason for this is quite simple.

Force-based technology

Much of the technology you have seen so far has been what we call force-based technology. It has been technology that is a reaction to the density of matter, as it currently is on this planet. As we have explained, the density of matter is a product of the density of the collective consciousness. The collective consciousness has become so dense that people cannot consciously create through the mind. They need to compensate for the density they have created through a mechanical process. It is not a matter of the mind having mastery over matter; you are using matter itself to circumvent some of the limitations that are a product of the density of matter.

This is a mechanical process. There is a limit to how far you can go with this process and it is illustrated very clearly in

11 | Making the impossible possible

the current belief in science that nothing can move faster than the speed of light. You know the theory, I assume, that if you take an object, it takes a certain amount of energy to accelerate its speed. Say it is a spacecraft. It takes a certain amount of energy to accelerate its speed, and the closer the spacecraft comes to the speed of light, the more energy it takes. As you come very close to the speed of light, you reach a limit where there simply is not enough energy. There is no energy source in the material universe that can provide the extra boost that brings the spaceship up to the speed of light.

This is perfectly true, but it illustrates exactly what I have been saying. There is a limit to how far you can go when you are using only mechanical technology that is based on matter. You cannot use technology that is based on the current density of matter to transcend the current density of matter. In order for a Golden Age to be manifest, we do need to transcend the current density of matter. We do need to raise the vibration of the entire planet so that there are certain things that can suddenly be manifest that people today believe are impossible.

Free energy

Take the other obvious example, the debate around free energy. Is there an energy source that can give you energy for free where you have more energy coming out of it than you put into it? You know that with your traditional energy sources, for example a steam engine, you need to put some combustible material in there to free the energy. You need to put coal or wood into the steam boiler in order to generate the energy that heats the water, which turns it into steam and then you use the steam to drive a mechanical device. In a combustion engine (such as many of you have in your cars) the energy source is more concentrated, the fuel is more concentrated. Of course, you can go to a nuclear power station where it requires even less fuel to power the plant. Still, you have to put energy in to get something *out,* and there are scientists who are extremely insistent that it will never be possible to create a device where you get energy out without putting anything in.

My beloved, how will you fuel the progress of the Golden Age unless you get access to an energy source that is virtually unlimited compared to the current sources of energy? It simply cannot be done, my beloved. Again, as Mother Mary said: "Just take what you currently believe and take it to its ultimate conclusion to see whether it is realistic." You can look at yourselves in the modern developed world and you can look at why you have the amount of progress, why you have the living standard, why you have the amount of affluence that you have. You can see that you owe this in large part to technology and this technology requires energy. It requires either oil, it requires solar, wind, nuclear, but some kind of material, physical energy source.

Then you can look at the fact that there are a few hundred million people who live in this state of affluence. In order to have raised that amount of people up to this state of living, you have expended this amount of fossil fuels or other fuels. These fuels all have a limited supply. Now, you project out and say: "How much has it taken to raise half a billion people to this standard of living? Now we want to raise the other six and a half billion to that standard of living, how can we do this with current energy sources?" You can see that it simply cannot be done with fossil fuels. It cannot even be done by nuclear power because it would be so complicated and the risk of pollution would be so great that it simply would not be realistic to do this. You can look at yourselves and you can say: "Yes, but we have compassion for all of the people living in poverty, we want to raise them up to the same standard of living. We know in our hearts that it is not right that some people have a good standard of living and others don't know how to feed their children or themselves." That is why you have all of these scientists, many of them attuned to the fallen beings in the mental and identity realms, who are projecting these prognoses of the future and saying: "This simply cannot be done."

The lie of overpopulation

I am in agreement that this simply cannot be done, but that is not where the sentence ends. This simply cannot be done with the current approach to life. With a mechanical, materialistic approach, it cannot be done. It cannot be done with force-based technology, it cannot be done with the present energy sources that are available. It cannot be done. That is why you see many people, even many spiritual people, who have begun to believe in one of the most insidious lies that the fallen beings have ever put out on this planet, namely the belief that there are too many people in embodiment on earth and that we should do something to limit the size of the population.

It is absolutely necessary that you, who are the spiritual people, become completely clear in your minds that this is a lie produced by the fallen beings. It is necessary that you make the calls for the exposure of this lie so that more and more people can come to see it for what it is. There are so many, not only spiritual people, but other people who are well-meaning, who are attuned to some new ideas and new ways of thinking. They have been sucked into the downward spiral of believing that the planet is already overpopulated and that active, drastic measures need to be taken in order to reduce the size of the population. It is absolutely necessary to shatter this matrix in the collective consciousness, to shatter it and to awaken people to the reality that the purpose of life on this planet is not that a few hundred million people live a comfortable life in an affluent state.

The absolute purpose of earth, the only justification for the existence of the earth, is that ten billion people are given an opportunity to be in embodiment on this planet. You have been programmed by the dark forces to believe that ten billion people simply could not be supported by the amount of resources on the planet. I will say to you: "This is another lie!" Number one: Ten billion people cannot be supported by the resources that are currently in use. Secondly: Ten billion people cannot be supported with the current unequal distribution of resources where a few hundred million are hoarding resources, at the cost of keeping many more millions of people below the poverty level.

The privileged elite

The fallen beings have always wanted to set themselves up in positions of privilege. They have had to concede that they could not maintain, what was in many ways for them the ideal society, namely the society you saw in Europe during the feudal age. You had a very small noble class that lived comfortable, affluent lives because the majority of the population were the slaves of the noble class. They would love to maintain some kind of society like that, but they have not been able to do so in the developed nations because the people started to revolt against it and they started becoming too educated and aware.

The fallen beings have had to allow the creation of a situation where you now have a number of nations where the population at large has been raised up to a comfortable lifestyle.

11 | Making the impossible possible

They have still managed to maintain this unequal distribution of resources that keeps hundreds of millions of people in poverty. They know this is not sustainable in the long run because the people in the richer nations are already beginning to revolt against it. They know in their hearts it is not right. The fallen beings are desperately trying to maintain this state by putting out the ideas that the planet simply cannot support it, that there are not enough resources and that therefore the population should be limited.

This is a complete lie, my beloved! You need to be aware that it is a lie. You need to accept that if the fallen beings were successful in drastically reducing the population of this planet, then planet earth would actually cease to have justification for its existence. This would be based on the evaluation of what helps the entire universe progress, and this means that the planet would actually disintegrate. If the population was reduced to the level that some fallen beings propose, the planet would simply fall apart because it would have no justification for existing as a platform for the growth of souls.

The only way the planet can actually justify its existence is that the population continues to rise until it will stabilize around ten billion people. This is the number that the planet is designed to sustain, and unless some completely ungodly measures are taken, the population will continue to increase until that number is reached. It is the only practical way to force people to reconsider the current distribution of resources and the current use of technology.

Sustaining ten billion people

Can the planet sustain ten billion people? Yes, it can, but not in its present state. If you look at current conditions and project into the future how much of existing resources will be required to sustain ten billion people, then you are perfectly right that this cannot be done. But you see, you are using the analytical mind to create a linear, cause-effect progression that says: "Only the current limited resources exist and only the current amount of resources that we are aware of is available to us." You are creating an unrealistic linear projection. What we are calling you to see is that it is possible to raise society to an entirely higher level where all of these linear projections are completely circumvented. They are transcended because new things come into being.

My beloved, just go back 100 years, to the early 1900s. Look at what the population was at the time, look at the technology that was available at the time. Then imagine that a scientist had made the same calculations and had said: "How can the planet sustain six and a half billion people or seven billion people?" You would have seen that, again, the calculations would have shown it was impossible.

When you look at what technology has been invented in the last hundred years, how agricultural methods have been improved, then you can see that the planet can actually sustain six and a half, seven billion people. It does not sustain them in a sufficient degree of affluence, but that is partly because there has not been the equivalent of a sociological, political evolution to what you have seen at the technological level. You have actually seen the arriving of technology that has made it possible that people can survive, but you have not seen the development in society that has redistributed resources so that they can all survive in an acceptable degree of affluence.

What I am talking about is that it is possible to go even higher and bring forth new technology. I want you to be absolutely sure and absolutely clear that the vision that Saint Germain has for the manifestation of the Golden Age does not require a reduction of the size of the human population. Saint Germain's vision is calculated to be completely realistic and to sustain ten billion people in a golden age society. As we have said, not all of the ten billion people will be in the golden age consciousness and some will live in pockets that are at a lower level of development. But the majority of the people in Saint Germain's plan for the Golden Age can be sustained in a very high degree of affluence.

The connecting field

How is this possible? It is not possible through force-based technology and force-based sources of energy. It is possible only by bringing forth the awareness that there are ways to extract energy that do not require you to burn any fuel or to split any atoms. There are researchers who have already realized that beyond the material frequency spectrum, is a field that they may call the Zero Point field or other names, but it is a field that has unlimited energy. What they call the Zero Point field is what we call the emotional, mental and identity realm, plus the spiritual realm.

What scientists are beginning to realize is that the current vision, where everything is seen as separate objects existing in a spatial dimension, is unrealistic. There are no separate objects because every object you see on earth or in the material universe is actually manifested out of the field. It is a densification of the field where the unlimited energy of the field has taken on a finite form. It is a temporary form but it can be sustained over time (as *you* see time).

What these scientists have already realized is that each object is connected to the field. It is not that an object becomes separated from the field; it is still connected to the field. This means that, although the earth may seem to be an object floating in space and Venus may be seen to be another planet floating in space, they are not separated. Earth is a manifestation of the field, and it is connected to the field. Venus is a manifestation of the field, and it is connected to the field. In order for beings on earth to communicate with beings on Venus, they do not have to send a physical signal, such as a radio signal, from earth to Venus. There needs to be no physical signal that is traveling below the speed of light sent to Venus, interpreted there and sent back—which takes time.

Instead, it is possible for human beings on earth to connect to the field and for beings on Venus to connect to the field. Through the field, which is beyond the limitations of the physical octave, you can have instant communication. This is completely possible! You just don't believe it is possible because you are evaluating what is possible based on what is currently manifest.

That is the one thing that needs to be put out there in the collective consciousness. Those who will create a better future on this planet will never allow their vision of what is possible to be limited by what is present. *"Never allow your vision of the possible to be limited by the present."* This is the essence of how you step up to the vision of the Golden Age.

New sources of energy

It is, of course, the same with energy. There are scientists who have already conducted experiments that show that you can extract energy directly from the field and use it for practical purposes on earth. They have been ridiculed and put down, they have had their research grants taken away and they have been labeled as kooks. Some of them do not have technology

11 | Making the impossible possible

that is viable, but the fact of the matter is that all of the people who are researching free energy have grasped onto the possibility and they believe it is possible.

You can look at a person and say that he has created a device that he claims works and it doesn't work and therefore the person is crazy. Or you can look at the person and say: "But the fact that he hasn't found out *how* it can be done, does not mean that he has a wrong vision of *what* can be done." Did not the Wright brothers have to experiment with several things before they had an airplane that could actually fly for a few seconds?

Have you not had to improve technology many, many times to create the modern airplane, compared to those first planes of the Wright brothers? You can see that whenever someone is quick to put down new ideas as impossible or unrealistic, you know they are either fallen beings in embodiment, or their minds are taken over by fallen beings in other realms. It is that simple.

It doesn't mean that any new idea is valid because, as I have said, there are those whose minds have been taken over by the fallen beings who are putting out unrealistic ideas. What I am pointing out to you is this: "The blanket rejection of a new idea based on the evaluation that it is too far beyond what is currently manifest, is the hallmark of the fallen beings."

They want to maintain the status quo where they are in control. What has caused them to lose control, time and time again over millions of years, is that a new idea was brought forth that either brought forth new technology, or a new idea in society that people grasped onto and demanded change. They are mortally afraid of new ideas. Their greatest enemy is new ideas. The greatest threat they can see is this: One person brings forth an idea that they could not foresee, they could not stop, and it starts to spread.

How fallen beings stop new ideas

Now my beloved, why is it that so many times the fallen beings are shocked over a new idea? Why is it that they could not even prevent it from coming into the physical? It is because they have closed their minds to attunement with the ascended masters. They may see certain trends. As I said, they could see that more and more new ideas were coming in, and they were therefore seeking to counteract it by bringing out false ideas. They could not predict which idea we were going to release next, for they do not have the ability.

They have shut themselves off from the ability to look beyond what is currently manifest. That is why the fallen beings are always behind the creative growth in society. They are always trying to maintain their power and privilege, based on what is in existence now. This is how they got their current positions and they think this is the only way to maintain it. They are always afraid that something new will come up that will, so to speak, pull the rug from under them. Suddenly, their great thrones fall apart and they have lost the grip on society that they thought they would have forever.

You who are the spiritual people, we look to you to raise your consciousness so you can grasp new ideas. We are not looking at you, not all of you at least, to go out in society and become scientists, inventors or this or that. We are looking for you to open your minds to the research that is being done in the most advanced fields of science. Select one or two ideas that is dear to your heart and then make the calls. Make the calls that these ideas will be implemented, that there will be people who will be able to receive more and more sophisticated blueprints of how to implement these ideas, for example a new form of energy. Make the calls, hold the vision, hold the spiritual balance for this to happen and be perfectly happy, my beloved, that it is someone else who will bring forth the invention, receive the patent, make the money and receive the glory or the Nobel prize. I assure you that your prize will be received in heaven and it will be of far greater value to you than any honor you could receive on earth.

Attuning to a specific master

How do you build your own discernment so you can look at the confusing array of new ideas and claims that are on the Internet and see what is valid and what is not? Well, the only way to do this is to learn what I have already said, namely that everything that is manifest in the physical has come out of the field. This means that for everything that is physical, there is an energy field in the emotional, mental, and identity realms. Just as we have talked to you about your physical body that is actually a manifestation of the three higher bodies, so is anything that is physical.

Even the physical thing is, of course, not physical. It is still an energy field, but it is easier for you to read the vibration of the energy fields in the higher realms. When you learn to do this, you can simply look at an idea, you can tune in to the energy field behind it and then you can know in your heart whether this is valid or not. You can come to the point where you can do this instantly when you have sharpened your ability.

How do you sharpen your ability? Well, our teachings and tools are given for that purpose, but I suggest especially that you sharpen your ability to discern by attuning to the master who is closest to your heart and seeing what is the vibration of the master. The vibration of the master becomes your frame of reference for everything else, and then you can use that to evaluate anything else.

You may have an idea that was brought forth by say Saint Germain, but you are attuned to Mother Mary. Of course, Mother Mary is attuned to Saint Germain. If you can attune to Mother Mary, you can also know whether that idea is valid or not. You can know whether an idea was brought forth from the ascended masters, from the etheric octave or whether it was brought forth from a lower realm, be it the lower identity, the mental, or even the emotional realm.

You can read vibration, and you can learn to read vibration instantly and that is one of the gifts of the Fifth Ray. One of the gifts of vision is that it is not your physical vision that is increased; it is the vision of the heart, your intuitive faculties, your ability to instantly sense: "Is this valid or is it not?" This is also how you can evaluate everything, including spiritual ideas. Are they from the ascended realm or are they from a lower source?

You do not have to label them as false, you just need to decide: "Where do I choose to focus my attention? Is it on the ascended masters, is it on a lower force?" You have free will, you should attune to whatever you feel you should attune to. We are only here offering our services, but of course we suggest that if you can attune to us, you will indeed find that we can give you everything you need for the fulfillment of your Divine plan.

Exposing the power elite

My beloved, I have given you much food for thought here, and I have given you a somewhat heavy teaching that requires perhaps a mental retooling before you can accept the manifestation of this higher vision of the Golden Age. I can assure you that there are many other areas of society that need to change

11 | Making the impossible possible

for the Golden Age to be manifest. It is not just a matter of having unlimited energy, it is, of course, also necessary that the awareness of the population shifts so that you do not allow a small elite to hold back new technology because they want to maintain the control they have, by controlling current technology and current resources.

You do realize, I am sure, that there is a power elite that has control over, for example, oil. They are not very anxious to give up that control and, therefore, would do whatever they could to hold back a new technology, especially a technology that is not force-based. Do you realize that a technology that is not force-based, cannot be patented or monopolized by a single entity on earth? It will not be possible for the fallen beings to monopolize and manipulate free energy—it is free. It is freely available to all everywhere and there is not just one technology that can make use of it.

You also need to hold the vision and make the calls that the people are awakened to the existence of the power elite and how they are seeking to manipulate every aspect of life on earth and how the people simply cannot allow this to continue to happen. The way to go about making a change is that the people educate themselves, speak out and demand a change. There is no violent revolution needed. There is no need to create concentration camps and put the fallen beings there. It is simply a matter of the people raising their awareness, and they will lose their grip on society, as they have done before.

I continually see people, my beloved, who get caught up in some conspiracy theory that claims that there is a power elite that is about to shut down life on earth and take control over everything. Ask yourself this simple question: "There has always been a power elite that wanted to stop progress, how come that power elite allowed the emergence of democracy?" They did not allow it, *they could not stop it*. That is why when the collective consciousness is raised to a certain level, the power elite can never stop progress. They can delay it for some time, but they cannot stop it when enough people awaken from the illusion.

Do not be caught up in this sense of hopelessness or despair, the sense that things are so bad and that there is such a control by the power elite that there is nothing you can do about it. There *is* something you can do about it and we have given you the knowledge and the tools of what you can do. *So do it! Do it!*

Shift the collective consciousness so that the physical manifestation must follow the shift in consciousness. The physical world will *always* follow a shift in consciousness. Accept that it is possible to shift consciousness. Believe it! Accept it! Know that it is not only possible, *it is happening!* Be part of what is happening instead of being part of those who are standing by watching what is happening. Therefore, I say to you: "*Join us* in the upward movement of manifesting Saint Germain's Golden Age!"

12 | INVOKING A NEW VISION OF WHAT IS POSSIBLE

In the name I AM THAT I AM, Jesus Christ, I call to all ascended masters working on manifesting the Golden Age, especially Archangel Raphael, Elohim Cyclopea, Hilarion, Great Divine Director and Saint Germain, to radiate into the collective consciousness a new awareness of what is possible when we go beyond duality. Help people see that we can build a new future by working with the ascended masters and letting go of the old way of looking at life, including…

[Make personal calls.]

Part 1

1. Master Hilarion, radiate into the collective consciousness the awareness that we cannot manifest in the physical what we cannot visualize in the mind. If we have no higher vision, the material universe becomes a closed loop that traps people for a very long time.

> Raphael Archangel, your light so intense,
> raise us beyond all human pretense.
> Mother Mary and you have a vision so bold,
> to see that our highest potential unfold.
>
> **Raphael Archangel, for vision we pray,**
> **Raphael Archangel, show us the way,**
> **Raphael Archangel, your emerald ray,**
> **Raphael Archangel, our lives a new day.**

2. Master Hilarion, radiate into the collective consciousness the awareness that we are programmed to perceive through the collective mindset and think we are human beings and either separated from God or a product of evolution. Either way, we have no capabilities beyond the physical body and material technology.

> Raphael Archangel, in emerald sphere,
> to immaculate vision we always adhere.
> Mother Mary enfolds us in her Sacred Heart,
> from Mother's true love, we're never apart.

**Raphael Archangel, for vision we pray,
Raphael Archangel, show us the way,
Raphael Archangel, your emerald ray,
Raphael Archangel, our lives a new day.**

3. Master Hilarion, radiate into the collective consciousness the awareness that the Alpha aspect of vision is that we can visualize in our minds that it is possible to create something that we do not already see on this planet. The Omega aspect is that we accept and know that it is possible to manifest this physically.

Raphael Archangel, all ailments you heal,
each cell in our bodies in light now you seal.
Mother Mary's immaculate concept we see,
perfection of health our new reality.

**Raphael Archangel, for vision we pray,
Raphael Archangel, show us the way,
Raphael Archangel, your emerald ray,
Raphael Archangel, our lives a new day.**

4. Master Hilarion, radiate into the collective consciousness the awareness that there are forces and beings in this world who are doing everything they can to limit our vision, by limiting what people can see but also limiting what they believe and accept can be manifest.

Raphael Archangel, your light is so real,
the vision of Christ in us you reveal.
Mother Mary now helps us to truly transcend,
in emerald light with you we ascend.

> **Raphael Archangel, for vision we pray,**
> **Raphael Archangel, show us the way,**
> **Raphael Archangel, your emerald ray,**
> **Raphael Archangel, our lives a new day.**

5. Master Hilarion, radiate into the collective consciousness the awareness that these forces also seek to restrict our ability to communicate a higher vision to large numbers of people. They have used the same technology that is used to spread genuine ideas, to spread their false ideas.

> Raphael Archangel, diseases are done,
> as you help us see that all life is One,
> we no longer do your true love reject,
> immaculate vision on all we project.

> **Raphael Archangel, for vision we pray,**
> **Raphael Archangel, show us the way,**
> **Raphael Archangel, your emerald ray,**
> **Raphael Archangel, our lives a new day.**

6. Master Hilarion, radiate into the collective consciousness the awareness that there are now so many ideas out there that most people feel completely overwhelmed. As the number and complexity of alternative visions has grown, more and more people look at it as fantasy. The fallen beings have blocked the Omega aspect of vision, namely people's ability to accept that a certain vision could be made manifest.

> Raphael Archangel, we're healing the earth,
> in immaculate vision we give her rebirth,
> a new era has on this day begun,
> your emerald light now shines like a sun.

> **Raphael Archangel, for vision we pray,**
> **Raphael Archangel, show us the way,**
> **Raphael Archangel, your emerald ray,**
> **Raphael Archangel, our lives a new day.**

7. Master Hilarion, radiate into the collective consciousness the awareness that dark forces are using science and technology to promote the mindset that the only solution to humankind's problems is a technological, mechanical solution.

> Raphael Archangel, the fall is behind,
> as all of earth's people the Christ path do find,
> we call now to you all people to heal,
> as four lower bodies in love you do seal.

> **Raphael Archangel, for vision we pray,**
> **Raphael Archangel, show us the way,**
> **Raphael Archangel, your emerald ray,**
> **Raphael Archangel, our lives a new day.**

8. Master Hilarion, radiate into the collective consciousness the awareness that the problem limiting progress today is not a lack of ideas but an over-abundance of ideas and the lack of belief that ideas could be made reality, that thoughts could become things.

> Raphael Archangel, as you bring the light,
> the forces of darkness swiftly take flight,
> their day is now done as we claim the earth,
> spreading to all an innocent mirth.

Raphael Archangel, for vision we pray,
Raphael Archangel, show us the way,
Raphael Archangel, your emerald ray,
Raphael Archangel, our lives a new day.

9. Master Hilarion, radiate into the collective consciousness the awareness that people need to change their view of new ideas and acknowledge that not all new ideas should be written off as fantasy. It is necessary to develop discernment so we can know within themselves which ideas are realistic and which are not.

Raphael Archangel, our vision set free,
as we can now see God's reality,
as Saint Germain's vision is manifest here,
the earth is now sealed in immaculate sphere.

Raphael Archangel, for vision we pray,
Raphael Archangel, show us the way,
Raphael Archangel, your emerald ray,
Raphael Archangel, our lives a new day.

Part 2

1. Master Hilarion, radiate into the collective consciousness the awareness that we cannot discern the validity of a vision or idea by using the intellectual, analytical mind. In order to truly know the validity of an idea, we need to neutralize the intellectual mind.

Cyclopea so dear, the truth you reveal,
the truth that duality's ailments will heal,
your Emerald Light is like a great balm,
our emotional bodies are perfectly calm.

**Cyclopea so dear, in Emerald Sphere,
in raising perception we shall persevere,
as deep in our hearts your truth we revere,
to immaculate vision the earth does adhere.**

2. Master Hilarion, radiate into the collective consciousness the awareness that the intellect compares any vision to existing conditions, and this prevents us from accepting a vision that is too far beyond what exists today. If we cannot see a linear, sequential process that leads to the fulfillment of a vision in a mechanical way, then the vision will be rejected.

Cyclopea so dear, with you we unwind,
all negative spirals clouding the mind,
we know pure awareness is truly our core,
the key to becoming the wide-open door.

**Cyclopea so dear, in Emerald Sphere,
in raising perception we shall persevere,
as deep in our hearts your truth we revere,
to immaculate vision the earth does adhere.**

3. Master Hilarion, radiate into the collective consciousness the awareness that it is the writing off of ideas without considering them as a possibility that has been the greatest hindrance to progress throughout the history of humankind.

> Cyclopea so dear, clear our inner sight,
> empowered, we pierce the soul's fearful night,
> we now see our life through your single eye,
> beyond all disease we're ready to fly.
>
> **Cyclopea so dear, in Emerald Sphere,**
> **in raising perception we shall persevere,**
> **as deep in our hearts your truth we revere,**
> **to immaculate vision the earth does adhere.**

4. Master Hilarion, radiate into the collective consciousness the awareness that when we look at what is there and then think that what might be should conform to what is there, this is the satanic consciousness that wants Spirit to conform to matter.

> Cyclopea so dear, life can only reflect,
> the images that the mind does project,
> the key to our healing is clearing the mind,
> from the images the ego is hiding behind.
>
> **Cyclopea so dear, in Emerald Sphere,**
> **in raising perception we shall persevere,**
> **as deep in our hearts your truth we revere,**
> **to immaculate vision the earth does adhere.**

5. Master Hilarion, radiate into the collective consciousness the awareness that the physical universe is not an isolated unit. It is created as a projection of images that exist in the emotional, mental and identity levels. If we change what exists at the three higher levels, we *will* change what manifests in the physical.

12 | Invoking a new vision of what is possible

> Cyclopea so dear, we want to aim high,
> to your healing flame we ever draw nigh,
> through veils of duality we now take flight,
> bathed in your penetrating Emerald Light.
>
> **Cyclopea so dear, in Emerald Sphere,**
> **in raising perception we shall persevere,**
> **as deep in our hearts your truth we revere,**
> **to immaculate vision the earth does adhere.**

6. Master Hilarion, radiate into the collective consciousness the awareness that bringing forth something that is completely beyond what is currently manifest requires the mind to receive ideas from the ascended realm. It also requires the mind's ability to believe that this can be manifest.

> Cyclopea so dear, your Emerald Flame,
> exposes every subtle, dualistic power game,
> including the game of wanting to say,
> that truth is defined in only one way.
>
> **Cyclopea so dear, in Emerald Sphere,**
> **in raising perception we shall persevere,**
> **as deep in our hearts your truth we revere,**
> **to immaculate vision the earth does adhere.**

7. Master Hilarion, radiate into the collective consciousness the awareness that the technological progress has happened because the ascended masters have created blueprints of technological inventions in the etheric realm. The masters are releasing them to those minds who can bring them into physical manifestation.

> Cyclopea so dear, we're feeling the flow,
> as your Living Truth upon us you bestow,
> from all dual vision we are now set free,
> planet earth in immaculate matrix will be.
>
> **Cyclopea so dear, in Emerald Sphere,**
> **in raising perception we shall persevere,**
> **as deep in our hearts your truth we revere,**
> **to immaculate vision the earth does adhere.**

8. Master Hilarion, radiate into the collective consciousness the awareness that technology is needed only because it has not been possible to raise the awareness of humankind to realizing and accepting the creative powers of the mind.

> Cyclopea so dear, the truth is now clear,
> we see higher purpose for which we are here
> we know truth transcends all systems below,
> immersed in your light, we continue to grow.
>
> **Cyclopea so dear, in Emerald Sphere,**
> **in raising perception we shall persevere,**
> **as deep in our hearts your truth we revere,**
> **to immaculate vision the earth does adhere.**

9. Master Hilarion, radiate into the collective consciousness the awareness that the masters first gave us a way to manifest new visions that was mechanical. Then, the hope is that we will begin to accept the possibility that we can create directly through the mind.

> Cyclopea so dear, we're feeling your joy,
> as creative vision we now do employ,
> in lifting earth out of serpentine cage,
> to manifest Saint Germain's Golden Age.
>
> **Cyclopea so dear, in Emerald Sphere,**
> **in raising perception we shall persevere,**
> **as deep in our hearts your truth we revere,**
> **to immaculate vision the earth does adhere.**

Part 3

1. Master Hilarion, radiate into the collective consciousness the awareness that many of the changes for the Golden Age will not be the result of a linear, gradual cause-effect process where there is a gradual evolution. This is too slow for bringing the Golden Age.

> Hilarion, on emerald shore,
> we're free from all that's gone before.
> Hilarion, we let all go,
> that keeps us out of sacred flow.
>
> **Hilarion, with light so green,**
> **we see behind the matter screen,**
> **immaculate our inner sight,**
> **we see the earth is taking flight.**

2. Master Hilarion, radiate into the collective consciousness the awareness that most technology is force-based technology. It is a reaction to the density of matter, as it currently is on this planet. The density of matter is a product of the density of the collective consciousness.

> Hilarion, the secret key,
> is wisdom's own reality.
> Hilarion, all life is healed,
> the ego's face no more concealed.
>
> **Hilarion, with light so green,**
> **we see behind the matter screen,**
> **immaculate our inner sight,**
> **we see the earth is taking flight.**

3. Master Hilarion, radiate into the collective consciousness the awareness that our consciousness has become so dense that we cannot consciously create through the mind. We need to compensate for the density we have created through a mechanical process.

> Hilarion, your love for life,
> helps us surrender inner strife.
> Hilarion, your loving words,
> thrill our hearts like song of birds.
>
> **Hilarion, with light so green,**
> **we see behind the matter screen,**
> **immaculate our inner sight,**
> **we see the earth is taking flight.**

12 | Invoking a new vision of what is possible

4. Master Hilarion, radiate into the collective consciousness the awareness that technology uses matter to circumvent some of the limitations that are a product of the density of matter, but there is a limit to how far this can go.

> Hilarion, invoke the light,
> your sacred formulas recite.
> Hilarion, your secret tone,
> philosopher's most sacred stone.
>
> **Hilarion, with light so green,**
> **we see behind the matter screen,**
> **immaculate our inner sight,**
> **we see the earth is taking flight.**

5. Master Hilarion, radiate into the collective consciousness the awareness that we cannot use technology that is based on the current density of matter to transcend the current density of matter. In order for a Golden Age to be manifest, we need to raise the vibration of the entire planet.

> Hilarion, with love you greet,
> us in your temple over Crete.
> Hilarion, your emerald light,
> the third eye sees with Christic sight.
>
> **Hilarion, with light so green,**
> **we see behind the matter screen,**
> **immaculate our inner sight,**
> **we see the earth is taking flight.**

6. Master Hilarion, radiate into the collective consciousness the awareness that we cannot fuel the progress of the Golden Age unless we get access to an energy source that is virtually unlimited compared to current sources of energy.

> Hilarion, you give us fruit,
> of truth that is so absolute.
> Hilarion, all stress decrease,
> as our ambitions we release.
>
> **Hilarion, with light so green,**
> **we see behind the matter screen,**
> **immaculate our inner sight,**
> **we see the earth is taking flight.**

7. Master Hilarion, radiate into the collective consciousness the awareness that raising all people on earth to a high standard of living cannot be done with a mechanical, materialistic approach. It cannot be done with force-based technology, it cannot be done with the energy sources currently available.

> Hilarion, our chakras clear,
> as we let go of subtlest fear.
> Hilarion, we are sincere,
> as freedom's truth we do revere.
>
> **Hilarion, with light so green,**
> **we see behind the matter screen,**
> **immaculate our inner sight,**
> **we see the earth is taking flight.**

8. Master Hilarion, radiate into the collective consciousness the awareness that one of the most insidious lies that the fallen beings have ever put out on this planet is the belief that there are too many people in embodiment on earth and that we should do something to limit the size of the population.

> Hilarion, you balance all,
> the seven rays upon our call.
> Hilarion, you keep us true,
> as we remain all one with you.

> **Hilarion, with light so green,**
> **we see behind the matter screen,**
> **immaculate our inner sight,**
> **we see the earth is taking flight.**

9. Master Hilarion, radiate into the collective consciousness the awareness that overpopulation is a lie and that many well-meaning people have been sucked into the downward spiral of believing that the planet is already overpopulated and that active, drastic measures need to be taken in order to reduce the size of the population.

> Hilarion, your Presence here,
> filling up the inner sphere.
> Life is now a sacred flow,
> God Vision we on all bestow.

> **Hilarion, with light so green,**
> **we see behind the matter screen,**
> **immaculate our inner sight,**
> **we see the earth is taking flight.**

Part 4

1. Master Hilarion, radiate into the collective consciousness the awareness that it is absolutely necessary to shatter this matrix and awaken people to the reality that the purpose of life on this planet is not that a few hundred million people live a comfortable life in an affluent state.

> Divine Director, I now see,
> the world is unreality,
> in my heart I now truly feel,
> the Spirit is all that is real.
>
> **Divine Director, send the light,**
> **from blindness clear my inner sight,**
> **my vision free, my vision clear,**
> **your guidance is forever here.**

2. Master Hilarion, radiate into the collective consciousness the awareness that the absolute purpose of earth, the only justification for the existence of the earth, is that ten billion people are given an opportunity to be in embodiment on this planet.

> Divine Director, vision give,
> in clarity I want to live,
> I now behold my plan Divine,
> the plan that is uniquely mine.
>
> **Divine Director, send the light,**
> **from blindness clear my inner sight,**
> **my vision free, my vision clear,**
> **your guidance is forever here.**

3. Master Hilarion, radiate into the collective consciousness the awareness that ten billion people cannot be supported by the resources that are currently in use. They cannot be supported with the current unequal distribution of resources where a few hundred million are hoarding resources at the cost of keeping many more millions below the poverty level.

> Divine Director, show in me,
> the ego games, and set me free,
> help me escape the ego's cage,
> to help bring in the Golden Age.
>
> **Divine Director, send the light,**
> **from blindness clear my inner sight,**
> **my vision free, my vision clear,**
> **your guidance is forever here.**

4. Master Hilarion, radiate into the collective consciousness the awareness that the fallen beings have always wanted to set themselves up in positions of privilege. Their ideal society is what we saw in Europe during the feudal age.

> Divine Director, I'm with you,
> my vision one, no longer two,
> as karma's veil you do disperse,
> I see a whole new universe.
>
> **Divine Director, send the light,**
> **from blindness clear my inner sight,**
> **my vision free, my vision clear,**
> **your guidance is forever here.**

5. Master Hilarion, radiate into the collective consciousness the awareness that the fallen beings are desperately trying to maintain their privileges by putting out the ideas that the planet cannot support it, that there are not enough resources and that therefore the population should be limited.

> Divine Director, I go up,
> electric light now fills my cup,
> consume in me all shadows old,
> bestow on me a vision bold.
>
> **Divine Director, send the light,**
> **from blindness clear my inner sight,**
> **my vision free, my vision clear,**
> **your guidance is forever here.**

6. Master Hilarion, radiate into the collective consciousness the awareness that if the fallen beings were successful in drastically reducing the population, then planet earth would actually cease to have justification for its existence and the planet would disintegrate.

> Divine Director, heart of gold,
> my sacred labor I unfold,
> o blessed Guru, I now see,
> where my own plan is taking me.
>
> **Divine Director, send the light,**
> **from blindness clear my inner sight,**
> **my vision free, my vision clear,**
> **your guidance is forever here.**

7. Master Hilarion, radiate into the collective consciousness the awareness that earth can sustain ten billion people, but not in its present state. It is possible to raise society to a higher level where all of the linear projections are circumvented. They are transcended because new things come into being.

> Divine Director, by your grace,
> in grander scheme I find my place,
> my individual flame I see,
> uniqueness God has given me.
>
> **Divine Director, send the light,**
> **from blindness clear my inner sight,**
> **my vision free, my vision clear,**
> **your guidance is forever here.**

8. Master Hilarion, radiate into the collective consciousness the awareness that technology has made it possible for the current population to survive, but there has not been the equivalent sociological, political evolution that has redistributed resources so that they can all survive in an acceptable degree of affluence.

> Divine Director, vision one,
> I see that I AM God's own Sun,
> with your direction so Divine,
> I am now letting my light shine.
>
> **Divine Director, send the light,**
> **from blindness clear my inner sight,**
> **my vision free, my vision clear,**
> **your guidance is forever here.**

9. Master Hilarion, radiate into the collective consciousness the awareness that it is possible to go even higher and bring forth new technology. The vision that Saint Germain has for the manifestation of the Golden Age does not require a reduction of the size of the population. Instead, the majority of the people can be sustained at a very high degree of affluence.

> Divine Director, what a gift,
> to be a part of Spirit's lift,
> to raise mankind out of the night,
> to bask in Spirit's loving sight.
>
> **Divine Director, send the light,**
> **from blindness clear my inner sight,**
> **my vision free, my vision clear,**
> **your guidance is forever here.**

Part 5

1. Master Hilarion, radiate into the collective consciousness the awareness that this is not possible through force-based technology and force-based sources of energy. It is possible only by bringing forth the awareness that there are ways to extract energy from the emotional, mental and identity realm, plus the spiritual realm.

> O Saint Germain, you do inspire,
> my vision raised forever higher,
> with you I form a figure-eight,
> your Golden Age I co-create.

> **O Saint Germain, what love you bring,**
> **it truly makes all matter sing,**
> **your violet flame does all restore,**
> **with you we are becoming more.**

2. Master Hilarion, radiate into the collective consciousness the awareness that everything is connected to a non-physical field that has unlimited energy resources and can take humankind to an entirely new level.

> O Saint Germain, what Freedom Flame,
> released when we recite your name,
> acceleration is your gift,
> our planet it will surely lift.

> **O Saint Germain, what love you bring,**
> **it truly makes all matter sing,**
> **your violet flame does all restore,**
> **with you we are becoming more.**

3. Master Hilarion, radiate into the collective consciousness the awareness that those who will create a better future on this planet will never allow their vision of what is possible to be limited by what is present.

> O Saint Germain, in love we claim,
> our right to bring your violet flame,
> from you Above, to us below,
> it is an all-transforming flow.

> **O Saint Germain, what love you bring,**
> **it truly makes all matter sing,**
> **your violet flame does all restore,**
> **with you we are becoming more.**

4. Master Hilarion, radiate into the collective consciousness the awareness that the blanket rejection of a new idea based on the evaluation that it is too far beyond what is currently manifest, is the hallmark of the fallen beings.

> O Saint Germain, I love you so,
> my aura filled with violet glow,
> my chakras filled with violet fire,
> I am your cosmic amplifier.

> **O Saint Germain, what love you bring,**
> **it truly makes all matter sing,**
> **your violet flame does all restore,**
> **with you we are becoming more.**

5. Master Hilarion, radiate into the collective consciousness the awareness that the fallen beings want to maintain the status quo where they are in control. What has caused them to lose control is that a new idea was brought forth that changed the status quo.

> O Saint Germain, I am now free,
> your violet flame is therapy,
> transform all hang-ups in my mind,
> as inner peace I surely find.

> **O Saint Germain, what love you bring,**
> **it truly makes all matter sing,**
> **your violet flame does all restore,**
> **with you we are becoming more.**

6. Master Hilarion, radiate into the collective consciousness the awareness that we can no longer allow a small elite to hold back new technology because they want to maintain the control they have, by controlling current technology and current resources.

> O Saint Germain, my body pure,
> your violet flame for all is cure,
> consume the cause of all disease,
> and therefore I am all at ease.

> **O Saint Germain, what love you bring,**
> **it truly makes all matter sing,**
> **your violet flame does all restore,**
> **with you we are becoming more.**

7. Master Hilarion, radiate into the collective consciousness the awareness that there is a power elite and that they are seeking to manipulate every aspect of life on earth and that we simply cannot allow this to continue to happen.

> O Saint Germain, I'm karma-free,
> the past no longer burdens me,
> a brand new opportunity,
> I am in Christic unity.

**O Saint Germain, what love you bring,
it truly makes all matter sing,
your violet flame does all restore,
with you we are becoming more.**

8. Master Hilarion, radiate into the collective consciousness the awareness that there is no violent revolution needed. When people raise their awareness, the power elite will lose their grip on society, as they have done before.

O Saint Germain, we are now one,
I am for you a violet sun,
as we transform this planet earth,
your Golden Age is given birth.

**O Saint Germain, what love you bring,
it truly makes all matter sing,
your violet flame does all restore,
with you we are becoming more.**

9. Master Hilarion, radiate into the collective consciousness the awareness that when consciousness is raised to a certain level, the power elite can never stop progress. They can delay it for some time, but they cannot stop it when enough people awaken from the illusion.

O Saint Germain, the earth is free,
from burden of duality,
in oneness we bring what is best,
your Golden Age is manifest.

**O Saint Germain, what love you bring,
it truly makes all matter sing,
your violet flame does all restore,
with you we are becoming more.**

Sealing

In the name of the Divine Mother, I call to all ascended masters for the sealing of myself and all people in my circle of influence in the creative flow of the Divine Mother, the River of Life. I call for the multiplication of my calls by all ascended masters, so that we form the perfect figure-eight flow of "As Above, so below." Thus, I accept that this is fully manifest, because the mouth of the Lord, the Divine Mother that I AM, has spoken it. Amen.

13 | THE POWER OF COLLECTIVE DECISIONS

I AM the Ascended Master Nada, the Chohan of the Sixth Ray. The Sixth Ray has been seen as peace and service. What does it take to give service to life? It takes that you are at peace with yourself. You can look upon yourself as an individual, and you can see that if you are not at peace with other people around you, over the circumstances you find yourself in or with the planet on which you live, then it is because you are not at peace with yourself.

Internal cause of terrorism

You can transfer this to a nation and say that if a nation is not at peace with other nations, then it is because it does not have peace within itself. This is an important idea to send into the collective consciousness so that the nations of Europe (and around the world) can take an honest look at themselves and see whether they are at peace with their neighbors, at peace with the world. If they find that they are not at peace with the world, then they need to stop doing what they have been doing in these later years where there have been certain terrorist attacks on the European continent.

They need to *not* do what the United States has been doing since the terrorist attacks there in 2001. You need to recognize that when you are being attacked by an outside force, the worst thing you can do is to strengthen the fortifications around your mind. It is precisely the fortifications you have built around your mind that attracted the attack. If you had not built the fortifications, you would have sent a different signal to the cosmic mirror. When you build fortifications, what is the signal you are sending? You want to live in a world where there is a need for the fortifications. How will you know there is a need unless there once in a while is an attack?

Of course, there are many nations in the world that are not at the level where they are able to see this. The Arab nations, for example, where many of the attacks have come from, would not right now be able to see that it is their own attitude that creates the external enemy. I am giving this message here in Europe because there are a number of European nations that are at the level where, at inner levels, they are ready to acknowledge this. Therefore, this is just a matter of making it break through at the outer, conscious level where they acknowledge fully that it is your own internal strife that creates the external enemy, or that at least attracts the external enemy and makes you a target of that enemy.

Self-defense

I know well that there are many people who will object to this statement, and they will point to all kinds of examples from history. They will say: "What should the people have done about

Hitler? Should they have not defended themselves? Should they have let Hitler overtake the whole world? Should they have let the Soviet Union overtake the whole world? Should they have let Attila overtake the whole world?" My beloved, it is possible (and we have spoken about this before) to take certain physical measures that are aimed at defending yourself in a practical situation but you are still doing it with a mindset that is at peace.

This may seem like a contradiction, but it is not a contradiction when you step up to a higher understanding. It is possible to recognize that you may have nations in the world that have an aggressive intent and that the only way to deter them from attacking you is that they fear the consequences because you have a capable defense. Saint Germain has said before that he is not asking all nations at this point to abandon their military. He has asked that some nations do so because they are ready to set forth that example. It is still possible to maintain a certain defense that can deter an attack, though you are not in a state of mind that encourages the attack.

There were, in fact, nations in Europe that had attained some degree of this consciousness before the terrorist attack in 2001. After that attack, many nations in Europe went along with the United States' reaction to that attack. This has created a new consciousness in Europe where the nations of Europe have also felt threatened. It is this awareness that has precipitated the terrorist attacks on this continent and will continue to precipitate such attacks until it is again abandoned.

Terrorism is insignificant

My beloved, it is easy to be at peace when there seems to be no threat and all seems to be peace. The challenge is to also be at peace within even when there seems to be some concern, some outer force that may be looking to attack you. The real challenge is, of course, to respond to an attack by staying in peace. This test, the European nations have clearly not passed with flying colors in these last several years. Yet I tell you again that at inner levels there are now a number of nations that are ready to pass this test and say: "We cannot allow these external attacks, these external threats, to force us back into the state of consciousness we abandoned after the end of the Cold War. We cannot allow them to force us to go backwards in our national growth."

It is important to make calls for the nations of Europe to realize that they first need to manifest peace within in order to avoid the outer enemy, in order to avoid the reaction from the universe that validates their view that they are under threat. I am not saying here that the nations of Europe should not take precautions to prevent further attacks. Again, there is an interplay of the Wisdom of the Mother where you accept current conditions for what they are and take the necessary steps to live with those conditions in the best possible way, without letting them deter you from your progress, from manifesting your greater goals.

These terrorist attacks are just a very insignificant incident in the long history of Europe. When you see that there is a vision of what Europe can become, you will not allow such attacks to deter you from moving forward towards that vision.

The long-term vision for Europe

How then can you be at peace with yourself? Well, as some of my beloved brothers have talked about, you must go within and accept that you are loved by a higher source, that you came from a higher source. It is more important for you to be attuned to that higher source than to be engaged in all these outer struggles, or to win a struggle, or to be proven right compared to others.

So many times we see how people and nations are pulled into a struggle, a reactionary pattern, because they lack the vision where they can say, as Jesus said 2000 years ago: "What is that to thee? Follow thou me." This may not even have to be a religious or spiritual recognition. It can be that the nations of Europe realize: "We have a vision of what kind of nation we want to be, what kind of nation we can become. We have a goal. We are moving towards that goal and we will not let anything detract us from that goal. We will not make something in this world more important than attaining the goal of manifesting a higher state in our nation."

It is more difficult to do this in a completely secular way, but it is not that progress cannot be made. However, it should also be said that you cannot manifest a truly Golden Age through entirely secular means and an entirely secular approach. The reason for this is very simple, as we have said. You human beings on earth simply do not have the energy to manifest a Golden Age.

Hilarion was talking about the need to raise the vibration of matter, to reduce the density of matter, and the only way to accomplish this is an influx of energy from the ascended realm. There is no way that human beings in embodiment could raise the vibration of matter sufficiently by their own powers. They could have some impact, but they could not raise it to the level necessary for the Golden Age. That is why there needs to be this figure-eight flow, this symbiotic relationship between us and you. You act for the good of the All, thereby multiplying what you have received from us so that we can multiply what you send back to us and give you even more. When this figure-eight flow is accelerated to a certain level, then we are allowed by the law to release sufficient energy from the ascended realm that it will actually raise the vibration of the matter realm. This will mean many, many things, but it will, among other things, mean that free energy becomes more of a practical reality than a vision.

It will mean that many diseases will begin to disappear. It will mean that natural disasters will drop in frequency. It will mean that new resources will be discovered around the earth. As we have said many times, there are resources that today are driving technological progress that were not even considered resources five hundred years ago because there was not the knowledge of how to apply them in practical terms.

As you raise the collective consciousness, as you raise the vibration of matter, suddenly matter stops being so much of a veil to people's vision. They will suddenly discover plenty of resources that will make it possible to sustain ten billion people at a high level of affluence. You simply cannot look at current conditions and even believe that it is possible to sustain so many people at this level. I can assure you that once you raise your vision and raise the vibration of matter, it is indeed possible.

How to increase resources

You could scarcely believe what this planet is capable of bringing forth in terms of resources when the vibration is raised, when there is the figure-eight flow from us Above to you below. It is not just that the planet itself brings forth resources. It is also that we accelerate the planet to a higher level by releasing energy, and therefore there are more resources available. After all, what have we said time and time again? All matter is truly energy. The more energy is released into the energy system of earth from the ascended realm, the more matter resources there will suddenly be for practical application.

When you begin to realize that you can achieve much more by working with the ascended masters, by working with the Source, by working with the spiritual realm, then you can suddenly begin to find peace in yourself. You begin to realize as an individual that you are not completely dependent on material, physical resources, that your growth can never be stopped by the conditions on earth. It is also possible for a nation to begin to realize that it is not so dependent on the cooperation of other nations. You do not need to feel as a nation that you absolutely need something from other nations, and therefore you feel threatened if they do not give you what you think you need.

You realize that as a nation you have an inherent creativity and through that you can bring forth what you need, and then you no longer feel threatened by others. You no longer need to take by force from others. Why would you bother taking by force when it is much easier to get it from within, to get it from Above? When a nation begins to become aware of this and does not feel so threatened, then that nation can become truly peaceful with its neighbors. It has the peace within of not feeling threatened, ultimately threatened, by anything on earth.

The information age

There are nations in Europe that have begun to realize that the world, or at least the more evolved part of the world, is moving into an era that has by some been called the information society. The basic resource of the nation is not coal or iron or even land, but it is information, know-how, creativity. This makes you much less threatened by those nations that have physical resources you do not have. Suddenly, you see that you need less and less from other nations in order to maintain your standard of living. This, of course, ties in with what we have previously talked about, namely how things are connected. Everything that you see on earth is connected to this field. You have an underlying field of unlimited energy that has the potential to manifest many physical things. When a physical thing is manifest, it is manifest out of the field of energy.

What is it that makes the energy take on that particular form? Well, it is information—information applied by a conscious mind to basic energy. Source energy is what manifests form. When you begin to realize this on an individual level, you can see the need to shift your consciousness, to purify your consciousness of information that does not help you manifest a higher vision. You also need to fill your mind with information that does help you. Get your mind *off* what you don't want and put your mind *on* what you do want, as the old saying goes.

Even nations can come to realize that it is a growth in awareness that has been the driving force of all the progress you have seen in society. Even technology has been driven by a growth in awareness. There is a possibility to step up to an even higher awareness where you are not looking for mechanical solutions. You are looking for *creative* solutions.

Again, you may think this is fanciful and too far beyond what the nations are ready to accept. I tell you that if you look at some of the more developed nations of Europe – Holland among them, the Scandinavian countries, to some degree Germany – you can see that they have manifested a higher level of abundance. They have manifested a higher level of equality through a raising of the collective awareness in that nation.

You can manifest what you can envision

You can look at the United States and see that it prides itself on being the richest country in the world, yet it is not able to provide free health care for all of its citizens. Many countries in Europe are able to do this, and how is this possible? There are people in America who would say that it would bankrupt the country if they enacted universal health care, but it has not done so in the European countries.

Why has it not done so? Is it because those countries have found some magical, mechanical formula? Nay, it is because the collective consciousness was raised to such a level where it was determined by a majority of the people that everyone should have access to health care. Everyone should have equal access to health care. Nobody should be forced to go bankrupt because they had a health problem. Nobody should be forced to not go to the doctor because they were afraid of the cost so that the health problem would become worse or they would die from a curable disease because they could not afford to see a doctor. This was a growth in compassion, in sensitivity towards life. By a nation collectively making this decision, the resources were manifested.

If you are truly honest and analyze some of the nations that have gone through this process, you would be able to see that it simply should not be possible that they would have the money to do this. Certainly, some of them have had to go into debt for a time. Nevertheless, I can assure you that it is the raising of the collective consciousness that simply brought forth more resources than were physically available. Suddenly, the country found that what they had collectively decided to manifest, somehow the money was there to implement it.

Collective decisions raise the economy

I know there are issues about health care, as we have talked about with mental illness, that are threatening to overwhelm the health care systems of some nations. Nevertheless, this can be transferred to many other things. There has been a decision collectively made to raise the standard of living, to raise wages, so that no one is truly poor in a nation because all should share in the abundance and have a decent life. When a nation makes that decision collectively, then the resources will be there. They will be brought forward because we, then, through the collective decision, can release more energy to that nation. This makes it possible that somehow people find a way to make more money, to bring forth more abundance so they can pay more taxes. The entire economy of a nation is raised to a higher level.

Look at some of the nations – Holland, the Scandinavian nations – look at how their economy was right after the Second World War, and then look at how much more wealth there is in those nations today. This is not brought about only by physical changes. It is brought about by a series of collective decisions that opened up for the possibility that we in the ascended realm could release energy to those nations. This provided the increase that somehow made it physically possible, often through many different means, but it raised the entire economy to a different level.

Raising Eastern Europe

You can look at the nations that have been liberated from the Communist yoke and whose abundance has not yet come up to the level in Western Europe. You can see that the nations

13 | The power of collective decisions

of Western Europe missed a historic opportunity to help those nations to a greater degree, although they have helped to some degree. Nevertheless, it needs to be recognized that it is necessary to raise all nations of Europe, and it is *possible* to raise all nations of Europe to a much higher level. This requires a collective decision. It is a collective decision that cannot only be made by the Western nations.

It also needs to be made by other nations where they simply need to decide: "We want the same level of affluence that we see in the Western nations. Why should our best workers have to go abroad in order to receive a decent wage when all that is really required for them to get that wage at home is that the entire level of abundance is raised, the economy is raised to a higher level?" This is possible. I recognize it is difficult for nations that have been under the yoke of Communism for so long, but *is* possible. There are certainly nations that are ready for this breakthrough and that have already started breaking through and have already started raising their economies.

What I am saying here is that one of the greatest incidents of progress that could be envisioned from the perspective of the Sixth Ray is that nations would recognize the value of making collective decisions. They would begin to realize that they have so far done this unconsciously, without really being aware of what they were doing. There is no limit to how far they can take this if they do it more consciously and actually come to the point of having a public debate, having those who have a vision, and then they collectively decide that this is what we want.

They, of course, take practical measures, as you have seen in the more developed nations that they have taken practical measures. It has taken them some time to implement it, but I tell you that once the decision is made, the clearer it is, the shorter will be the time span before the condition is manifest.

This would be a tremendous step up for Europe. It would be a step up in the European nations' ability to serve in the further progress of life on earth and in the manifestation of the Golden Age.

As we have said, there are nations in Western Europe that have reached the point where they cannot really grow further until they begin to selflessly serve others. There are nations in Eastern Europe that could use that kind of cooperation and service from the Western nations so that they could be raised up, so that all of Europe could come to a point where they could now truly begin to serve outside the borders of Europe. They could show that it is possible for nations to raise each other up, to raise their economies to an entirely different level. There is a model that can work. Therefore, Europe can be an example that can be adapted to other parts of the world.

No outer religion needed

This requires also that the nations begin to realize that you can never get beyond a certain level of abundance by human, physical, material power. You can only do so by the combined power of the minds of the citizens, which then opens up for a connection to the ascended masters. Do you understand why Jesus said: "Where two or three are gathered in my name, there I am in the midst of them" What he meant was very simple. If you are not at peace with yourself and cannot get along with anyone else, you cannot magnetize the Living Christ.

You can, of course, magnetize the Living Christ as an individual, but what he was saying is that if two people can get together in some state of harmony and cooperation, then the Christ is there to multiply their efforts. This does not mean that those two people have to have the fullness of Christhood.

13 | The power of collective decisions

What he is saying is that if people – at whatever level of consciousness they are – can set aside their differences, their conflicts, and come together behind some goal, then there will be the multiplication from the Christ mind and from Source energy.

When all people in a nation (even if they do not have a particularly spiritual awareness) come together and stand behind a certain decision, such as: "We want universal health care for all people," then the Christ mind will provide the insights necessary and the multiplication of the energy that makes it possible. Of course, the higher the awareness that the people have, the more the multiplication factor can be increased and the more can then be manifest.

It is not necessary that a nation has a particular religion or follows a specific spiritual teaching. It can be done by people having a vision of certain principles, a vision of certain conditions, having compassion for others, respect for other people, and desiring to manifest a better standard of living. We are not here saying that first the nations of Europe need to accept the ascended masters' teachings and then we can multiply their effort. We have already multiplied the efforts – that is why you are seeing progress – and we are continuing to do so. The more people can become aware of a higher vision, a higher goal, and unite around that higher goal, the more we can multiply their efforts.

It is not necessary that they have the spiritual understanding we are giving you. It is necessary that some people have that understanding and can therefore pull up on the collective consciousness, but there are many that can be motivated towards a higher vision without having the fullness of this understanding, without having the recognition of the ascended masters. There is something that motivates them. Some people are motivated by compassion, motivated by equality, motivated by giving other people an opportunity, motivated by a higher principle, by a dream of a better society. Whatever the motivation is, if people can come together behind it, there will be the multiplication.

We are not putting conditions that they need to recognize us, that they need to know where the multiplication comes from. We are not putting any of these conditions on it. We are ready to multiply whenever people fulfill the condition that they set aside their differences to some degree and unite behind a higher vision. They do what Jesus said: "What is that to us? What are these outer things, these conflicts? They are no longer as important to us as moving towards our higher vision, our higher goal. And therefore we set them aside. We walk away from them." Then, there is the opening for the multiplication. Whenever people can find some motivation that opens them up to giving service to life, then there is multiplication. *Then* things can happen.

The desire to serve life

That is also the absolute necessity for bringing forth some of these changes that we have talked about. How should free energy ever become a physical reality if it was monopolized by some multinational corporation that wants to use it to control the world and blackmail all nations of the world? How could this ever be free energy? Free energy cannot be monopolized, cannot be forced. What would it take for people to be able to receive the knowledge of how to use this unlimited energy? It would take that they step up to the attitude of simply wanting to serve life. They are not doing it for personal gain, for personal recognition. They are not doing it for fame or fortune, for the Nobel Prize or whatever. They are doing it because they desire to serve life. This is a very delicate process where you see so many people in the world who are scientists, who are inventors, who are visionaries.

They are to some degree open to new ideas, new ways of looking at things, but they still have a motivation that is ego-based. They have some motivation of gaining for themselves, or even gaining for their nation or proving a certain ideology or certain thought system. This is not going to allow them to receive these new ideas and this new technology. It takes this completely selfless service where you are not motivated by any earthly desires. You actually realize that you can have your reward on earth if you want or you can have your reward in heaven.

The reward you can have on earth will always be limited, but the reward you have in heaven is much greater. You can come to the point where you say: "I am going to focus the rest of my time in embodiment on serving life, and I will have my reward after I ascend." That is the attitude that is truly selfless service. You can have it only when you are at peace with yourself because you realize there is nothing on earth that is ultimately important to you. There is something you want much more. You want to ascend, but you also want to fulfill your Divine plan while you are in embodiment and make the most of the incredible opportunity that it is to be in embodiment.

Being in embodiment is a unique opportunity

I know very well, my beloved, that it is difficult to be in embodiment on earth, that it is a very heavy planet. I know also, as we said last year, that you are in embodiment at a time that is a transition period between Pisces and Aquarius and there is much upheaval. This makes it even heavier for you to be in embodiment. Nevertheless, I can tell you that it is also an incredible opportunity to be in embodiment at this time because there is such potential to make personal progress and to give service that lays up your treasure in heaven. There has not for a very, very long time on earth been a period where the potential for personal growth and the potential for giving service has been greater than it is right now.

If I could, I would gladly help you treasure the opportunity that it is to be in physical embodiment on this planet at this particular, unique time. If you will apply to me individually, spend a little time each day tuning in to me, I will seek to help you, as I can give you that appreciation. Truly, it is such an opportunity that if an ascended master was capable of regretting ascending, you would almost wish you had postponed your ascension so you could be in embodiment at this time. I said *almost,* for, of course, once you ascend, there is no regret possible. I can tell you that it is a privilege to be in embodiment at this time. It is a privilege to be part of this process of manifesting the Golden Age.

My beloved, if you were to step back now and consider the dictations we have given so far, I would like to ask you this: "Have we ever in any of our dictations expressed that it is a question of *whether* the Golden Age will be manifest or will not be manifest? Have we ever expressed any doubt about whether the Golden Age *will* be manifest?" We have not, for there is no doubt that the Golden Age *is* already being manifest in increment by increment. Step up to accepting that, and then focus the rest of your time in embodiment on how you can be a part of manifesting the Golden Age that is already descending into physical manifestation.

I am not asking you to ignore every problem on earth, but I am asking you not to let them distract you from the positive aspect that you defined in your Divine plan when you chose to descend into embodiment at this time. You did see the opportunity before you came into this lifetime, I can assure you. Try to reconnect to that, the joy, the sense of excitement that you wanted to be in embodiment at this time because there is a unique opportunity and you wanted to serve. You love Saint Germain, and you want to see him have the victory of the manifestation of his Golden Age. By you being in embodiment, by Saint Germain being in the ascended realm, and by you connecting to Saint Germain and to your desire for being in embodiment, there is no doubt that the Golden Age will be and is being manifest. It is not a matter of *if*. It is only a matter of *when*.

The Golden Age is now

When will the Golden Age be manifest? *Now,* my beloved. When you accept that it is manifest *now,* then it *is* manifest for you. Then you have made your contribution, and you can become an example for others so that they can also begin to accept that, regardless of what things look like right now, it is possible to manifest a Golden Age. Do not let the problems you see right now detract you from accepting that a Golden Age is possible. We are not giving you a Utopian pipe dream. We are giving you an absolute reality. It is manifest in the etheric, to a large degree in the mental, to a large degree in the emotional and to some degree in the physical already. Accept that. Flow with it. Be at peace in knowing that you are part of manifesting reality, a new and better age on this planet. Let not anything that happens cause you to go into a spiral of fear or discouragement, but always see that whatever happens is simply an outplaying of a certain state of consciousness. It has only the purpose of making it more visible so that people can come to the point of saying: "Enough is enough. It is time to move on."

You move on from all the negativity, all the burdens, all the problems. You focus on the positive. What was it that you decided that you loved so much that you wanted to be a part of bringing that manifestation into the physical realm? What was that, my beloved, for each one of you? Then focus all your energy and attention on manifesting that, making the calls for it, doing whatever you can in the physical. Focus on that as a living reality and be not detracted from it by any negativity. Do not let what is present on earth prevent you from accepting what is not only possible but is already being lowered into physical manifestation.

There is a story that while I was in my last embodiment, I was holding the spiritual balance for my brothers and sisters who achieved high positions in society. You can hold the vision that those who are able to bring forth and implement certain golden age ideas will be able to do so. You may also be part of bringing forth those ideas. What you realize is that when I was doing this, I would not let anything that happened detract me from holding the highest vision for my brothers and sisters. It was not that everything went smoothly. It was that whatever happened, I held fast to the decision, and I remained at peace within myself.

I am the Chohan of the Sixth Ray of Peace. What I want from you is for you to be at peace, being who you are where you are at this time, being part of manifesting the Golden Age. Let go of your anxiety, let go of your fears, let go of your concerns, let go of your intellectualizing and focusing on this problem and that problem and the next problem. Be at peace and then serve from that state of peace, and *then* you will find true joy.

14 | INVOKING AWARENESS OF COLLECTIVE DECISIONS

In the name I AM THAT I AM, Jesus Christ, I call to all ascended masters working on manifesting the Golden Age, especially Archangel Uriel, Elohim Peace, Nada, Jesus and Saint Germain to radiate into the collective consciousness a new awareness of the power of making collective decisions in order to raise a nation to a higher level. Help people see that we can build a new future by working with the ascended masters and letting go of the old way of looking at life, including…

[Make personal calls.]

Part 1

1. Master Nada, radiate into the collective consciousness the awareness that if a nation is not at peace with other nations, then it is because it does not have peace within itself.

Uriel Archangel, immense is the power,
of angels of peace, all war to devour.
The demons of war, no match for your light,
consuming them all, with radiance so bright.

Uriel Archangel, use your great sword,
Uriel Archangel, consume all discord,
Uriel Archangel, we're of one accord,
Uriel Archangel, we walk with the Lord.

2. Master Nada, radiate into the collective consciousness the awareness that the developed nations need to find a new way to respond to the terrorist attacks.

Uriel Archangel, intense is the sound,
when millions of angels, their voices compound.
They build a crescendo, piercing the night,
life's glorious oneness revealed to our sight.

Uriel Archangel, use your great sword,
Uriel Archangel, consume all discord,
Uriel Archangel, we're of one accord,
Uriel Archangel, we walk with the Lord.

3. Master Nada, radiate into the collective consciousness the awareness that when nations are being attacked by an outside force, the worst thing they can do is to strengthen the fortifications around the collective mind.

Uriel Archangel, from out the Great Throne,
your millions of trumpets, sound the One Tone.
Consuming all discord with your harmony,
the sound of all sounds will set all life free.

**Uriel Archangel, use your great sword,
Uriel Archangel, consume all discord,
Uriel Archangel, we're of one accord,
Uriel Archangel, we walk with the Lord.**

4. Master Nada, radiate into the collective consciousness the awareness that it is the fortifications we have built around our minds that attracted the attacks. The signal we have sent to the cosmic mirror is that we want to live in a world where there is a need for the fortifications.

Uriel Archangel, all war is now done,
for you bring a message, from heart of the One.
The hearts of all men, now singing in peace,
the spirals of love, forever increase.

**Uriel Archangel, use your great sword,
Uriel Archangel, consume all discord,
Uriel Archangel, we're of one accord,
Uriel Archangel, we walk with the Lord.**

5. Master Nada, radiate into the collective consciousness the awareness that a number of developed nations are ready to acknowledge that it is our own internal strife that creates the external enemy, or that attracts the external enemy and makes us a target of that enemy.

Uriel Archangel, your infinite peace,
from all warring beings our planet release,
war is a prison from which we are free,
embracing the peace of true unity.

> **Uriel Archangel, use your great sword,**
> **Uriel Archangel, consume all discord,**
> **Uriel Archangel, we're of one accord,**
> **Uriel Archangel, we walk with the Lord.**

6. Master Nada, radiate into the collective consciousness the awareness that it is possible to take physical measures aimed at defending ourselves in a practical situation but we are doing it with a mindset that is at peace.

> Uriel Archangel, we send forth the call,
> reveal now the oneness that unifies all,
> help us the vision of peace now to see,
> so we from all conflicts and struggles are free.

> **Uriel Archangel, use your great sword,**
> **Uriel Archangel, consume all discord,**
> **Uriel Archangel, we're of one accord,**
> **Uriel Archangel, we walk with the Lord.**

7. Master Nada, radiate into the collective consciousness the awareness that it is possible to maintain a certain defense that can deter an attack, though we are not in a state of mind that encourages the attack.

> Uriel Archangel, in service to life,
> you give us release from struggle and strife,
> forgetting the self is truly the key,
> to living a life in true harmony.

**Uriel Archangel, use your great sword,
Uriel Archangel, consume all discord,
Uriel Archangel, we're of one accord,
Uriel Archangel, we walk with the Lord.**

8. Master Nada, radiate into the collective consciousness the awareness that after the terrorist attack in 2001, many nations went along with the United States' reaction to that attack.

Uriel Archangel, the earth now you raise,
out of duality's death-bringing haze,
we call now upon your great Flame of Peace,
commanding that all petty squabbles do cease.

**Uriel Archangel, use your great sword,
Uriel Archangel, consume all discord,
Uriel Archangel, we're of one accord,
Uriel Archangel, we walk with the Lord.**

9. Master Nada, radiate into the collective consciousness the awareness that this created a new consciousness where nations feel threatened. It is this awareness that has precipitated recent terrorist attacks and will continue to precipitate such attacks until it is abandoned.

Uriel Archangel, as peace is the norm,
to your higher vision the earth does conform,
as people have found your peace from within,
a Golden Age is the prize that we win.

> Uriel Archangel, use your great sword,
> Uriel Archangel, consume all discord,
> Uriel Archangel, we're of one accord,
> Uriel Archangel, we walk with the Lord.

Part 2

1. Master Nada, radiate into the collective consciousness the awareness that we cannot allow these external attacks to force us back into the state of consciousness we abandoned after the end of the Cold War. We cannot allow them to force us to go backwards in our national growth.

> O Elohim Peace, in Unity's Flame,
> there is no more room for duality's game,
> we know that all form is from the same source,
> empowering us to plot a new course.
>
> **O Elohim Peace, through your tranquility,**
> **we are free from the chaos of duality,**
> **in oneness with God a new identity,**
> **we are raising the earth into Infinity.**

2. Master Nada, radiate into the collective consciousness the awareness that the developed nations first need to manifest peace within in order to avoid the outer enemy, in order to avoid the reaction from the universe that validates their view that they are under threat.

14 | Invoking awareness of collective decisions

O Elohim Peace, the bell now you ring,
causing all atoms to vibrate and sing,
we give up the sense of a separate "me,"
we're crossing Samsara's turbulent sea.

**O Elohim Peace, through your tranquility,
we are free from the chaos of duality,
in oneness with God a new identity,
we are raising the earth into Infinity.**

3. Master Nada, radiate into the collective consciousness the awareness that these terrorist attacks are insignificant incidents in the long history of the world. Given the vision of what the Golden Age can become, we cannot allow such attacks to deter us from moving forward.

O Elohim Peace, you help us to know,
that Jesus has come your Flame to bestow,
upon all who are ready to give up the strife,
by following Christ into infinite life.

**O Elohim Peace, through your tranquility,
we are free from the chaos of duality,
in oneness with God a new identity,
we are raising the earth into Infinity.**

4. Master Nada, radiate into the collective consciousness the awareness that we cannot manifest a truly Golden Age through an entirely secular approach. We human beings do not have the energy to manifest a Golden Age.

> O Elohim Peace, through your eyes we see,
> that only in oneness will we ever be free,
> we now see that there is no separate thing,
> to the ego-based self we no longer cling.
>
> **O Elohim Peace, through your tranquility,**
> **we are free from the chaos of duality,**
> **in oneness with God a new identity,**
> **we are raising the earth into Infinity.**

5. Master Nada, radiate into the collective consciousness the awareness that there needs to be a figure-eight flow, a symbiotic relationship, between ourselves and the ascended masters.

> O Elohim Peace, you show us the way,
> for clearing the mind from duality's fray,
> you pierce the illusions of both time and space,
> separation consumed by your Infinite Grace.
>
> **O Elohim Peace, through your tranquility,**
> **we are free from the chaos of duality,**
> **in oneness with God a new identity,**
> **we are raising the earth into Infinity.**

6. Master Nada, radiate into the collective consciousness the awareness that when this figure-eight flow is accelerated to a certain level, then the masters will release sufficient energy from the ascended realm that it will raise the vibration of the matter realm.

O Elohim Peace, what beauty your name,
consuming within us duality's shame,
the earth is set free from burden of fear,
accepting your peace is now manifest here.

**O Elohim Peace, through your tranquility,
we are free from the chaos of duality,
in oneness with God a new identity,
we are raising the earth into Infinity.**

7. Master Nada, radiate into the collective consciousness the awareness that this will mean that free energy becomes a practical reality, that many diseases will disappear, that natural disasters will drop in frequency and that new resources will be discovered.

O Elohim Peace, with Christ at our side,
no force of duality can evermore hide,
It was through the vibration of your Golden Flame,
that Christ the illusion of death overcame.

**O Elohim Peace, through your tranquility,
we are free from the chaos of duality,
in oneness with God a new identity,
we are raising the earth into Infinity.**

8. Master Nada, radiate into the collective consciousness the awareness that as we raise our consciousness, we raise the vibration of matter. When matter stops being a veil to people's vision, we will discover new resources that will make it possible to sustain ten billion people at a high level of affluence.

O Elohim Peace, you bring now to earth,
the unstoppable flame of Cosmic Rebirth,
we give up the sense that something is "mine,"
allowing your Light through our beings to shine.

**O Elohim Peace, through your tranquility,
we are free from the chaos of duality,
in oneness with God a new identity,
we are raising the earth into Infinity.**

9. Master Nada, radiate into the collective consciousness the awareness that when there is a figure-eight flow from Above to below, it can accelerate the planet to a higher level and make more resources available.

O Elohim Peace, as peace now we feel,
all records of war you totally heal,
the earth is now free from forces of war,
restoring her purity known from before.

**O Elohim Peace, through your tranquility,
we are free from the chaos of duality,
in oneness with God a new identity,
we are raising the earth into Infinity.**

Part 3

1. Master Nada, radiate into the collective consciousness the awareness that by working with the Source, a nation is not so dependent on the cooperation of other nations.

14 | Invoking awareness of collective decisions

Master Nada, beauty's power,
unfolding like a sacred flower.
Master Nada, so sublime,
a will that conquers even time.

Master Nada, peace you give,
forevermore in peace we live,
our planet has a peaceful morn,
the Golden Age is hereby born.

2. Master Nada, radiate into the collective consciousness the awareness that when a nation no longer feels threatened, it no longer needs to take by force from others. Why take by force when it is much easier to get it from within, to get it from Above?

Master Nada, you bestow,
upon us wisdom's rushing flow.
Master Nada, mind so strong
rising on your wings of song.

Master Nada, peace you give,
forevermore in peace we live,
our planet has a peaceful morn,
the Golden Age is hereby born.

3. Master Nada, radiate into the collective consciousness the awareness that when a nation does not feel so threatened, then that nation can become truly peaceful with its neighbors.

> Master Nada, precious scent,
> your love is truly heaven-sent.
> Master Nada, kind and soft
> on wings of love we rise aloft.
>
> **Master Nada, peace you give,**
> **forevermore in peace we live,**
> **our planet has a peaceful morn,**
> **the Golden Age is hereby born.**

4. Master Nada, radiate into the collective consciousness the awareness that the world is moving into the information society. The basic resource of a nation is information, know-how, creativity. This makes a nation much less threatened by other nations.

> Master Nada, mother light,
> our hearts are rising like a kite.
> Master Nada, from your view,
> all life is pure as morning dew.
>
> **Master Nada, peace you give,**
> **forevermore in peace we live,**
> **our planet has a peaceful morn,**
> **the Golden Age is hereby born.**

5. Master Nada, radiate into the collective consciousness the awareness that it is a growth in awareness that has been the driving force of all progress. Even technology has been driven by a growth in awareness.

Master Nada, truth you bring,
as morning birds in love do sing.
Master Nada, we now feel,
your love that all four bodies heal.

**Master Nada, peace you give,
forevermore in peace we live,
our planet has a peaceful morn,
the Golden Age is hereby born.**

6. Master Nada, radiate into the collective consciousness the awareness that there is a possibility to step up to a higher awareness where we are not looking for mechanical solutions but for creative solutions.

Master Nada, serve in peace,
as all emotions we release.
Master Nada, life is fun,
the solar plexus is a sun.

**Master Nada, peace you give,
forevermore in peace we live,
our planet has a peaceful morn,
the Golden Age is hereby born.**

7. Master Nada, radiate into the collective consciousness the awareness that in some nations the consciousness has been raised so that a majority of the people decided that everyone should have equal access to health care. By a nation collectively making this decision, the resources were manifested.

Master Nada, love is free,
conditions we no longer see.
Master Nada, rise above,
all human forms of lesser love.

Master Nada, peace you give,
forevermore in peace we live,
our planet has a peaceful morn,
the Golden Age is hereby born.

8. Master Nada, radiate into the collective consciousness the awareness that these nations did not have the money to do this. It was the raising of the collective consciousness that brought forth more resources than were physically available. The money was there to implement what they had collectively decided to manifest.

Master Nada, balance all,
the seven rays upon our call.
Master Nada, rise and shine,
your radiant beauty most divine.

Master Nada, peace you give,
forevermore in peace we live,
our planet has a peaceful morn,
the Golden Age is hereby born.

9. Master Nada, radiate into the collective consciousness the awareness that when a nation makes the collective decision to raise the standard of living, to raise wages, so that no one is truly poor because all should share in the abundance and have a decent life, then the resources will be there.

> Nada Dear, your Presence here,
> filling up the inner sphere.
> Life is now a sacred flow,
> God Peace we do on all bestow.

> **Master Nada, peace you give,**
> **forevermore in peace we live,**
> **our planet has a peaceful morn,**
> **the Golden Age is hereby born.**

Part 4

1. Master Nada, radiate into the collective consciousness the awareness that through a collective decision, the ascended masters release more energy to a nation, and that makes it possible to bring forth more abundance so the entire economy of a nation is raised to a higher level.

> O Jesus, blessed brother mine,
> I walk the path that you outline,
> a great example to us all,
> I follow now your inner call.

> **O Jesus, let the Fire of Joy,**
> **consume the devil's subtle ploy,**
> **transfigured is our planet earth,**
> **the Golden Age is given birth.**

2. Master Nada, radiate into the collective consciousness the awareness that it is *necessary* to raise all nations, and it is *possible* to raise all nations to a much higher level. This requires a collective decision, and it is a collective decision that cannot only be made by the Western nations.

> O Jesus, open inner sight,
> the ego wants to prove it's right,
> but this I will no longer do,
> I want to be all one with you.
>
> **O Jesus, let the Fire of Joy,**
> **consume the devil's subtle ploy,**
> **transfigured is our planet earth,**
> **the Golden Age is given birth.**

3. Master Nada, radiate into the collective consciousness the awareness that other nations need to decide that they want the same level of affluence that they see in the Western nations. Such a decision will open up for the resources to make it happen.

> O Jesus, I now clearly see,
> the Key of Knowledge given me,
> my Christ self I hereby embrace,
> as you fill up my inner space.
>
> **O Jesus, let the Fire of Joy,**
> **consume the devil's subtle ploy,**
> **transfigured is our planet earth,**
> **the Golden Age is given birth.**

4. Master Nada, radiate into the collective consciousness the awareness that nations need to recognize the value of making collective decisions. They have so far done this unconsciously, but there is no limit to how far they can take this if they do it more consciously.

> O Jesus, show me serpent's lie,
> expose the beam in my own eye,
> as Christ discernment you me give,
> in oneness I forever live.

**O Jesus, let the Fire of Joy,
consume the devil's subtle ploy,
transfigured is our planet earth,
the Golden Age is given birth.**

5. Master Nada, radiate into the collective consciousness the awareness that nations also need to take practical measures. However, once the decision is made, then the clearer it is, the shorter will be the time span before the condition is manifest.

> O Jesus, I am truly meek,
> and thus I turn the other cheek,
> when the accuser attacks me,
> I go within and merge with thee.

**O Jesus, let the Fire of Joy,
consume the devil's subtle ploy,
transfigured is our planet earth,
the Golden Age is given birth.**

6. Master Nada, radiate into the collective consciousness the awareness that the developed nations cannot grow further until they begin to selflessly serve others. There are nations in Eastern Europe and other parts of the world that could use that kind of cooperation and service from more developed nations.

> O Jesus, ego I let die,
> surrender ev'ry earthly tie,
> the dead can bury what is dead,
> I choose to walk with you instead.
>
> **O Jesus, let the Fire of Joy,**
> **consume the devil's subtle ploy,**
> **transfigured is our planet earth,**
> **the Golden Age is given birth.**

7. Master Nada, radiate into the collective consciousness the awareness that it is possible for nations to raise each other up, to raise their economies to an entirely different level. There is a model that can work. Therefore, Europe can be an example that can be adapted to other parts of the world.

> O Jesus, help me rise above,
> the devil's test through higher love,
> show me separate self unreal,
> my formless self you do reveal.
>
> **O Jesus, let the Fire of Joy,**
> **consume the devil's subtle ploy,**
> **transfigured is our planet earth,**
> **the Golden Age is given birth.**

8. Master Nada, radiate into the collective consciousness the awareness that we can never get beyond a certain level of abundance by human, physical, material power. We can only do so by the combined power of the minds of the citizens, which then opens up for a connection to the ascended masters.

> O Jesus, what is that to me,
> I just let go and follow thee,
> with this I do pass ev'ry test,
> to find with you eternal rest.
>
> **O Jesus, let the Fire of Joy,**
> **consume the devil's subtle ploy,**
> **transfigured is our planet earth,**
> **the Golden Age is given birth.**

9. Master Nada, radiate into the collective consciousness the awareness that when people can set aside their differences, their conflicts, and come together behind some goal, then there will be the multiplication from the Christ mind and from Source energy.

> O Jesus, fiery master mine,
> my heart now melting into thine,
> I love with heart and mind and soul,
> the God who is my highest goal.
>
> **O Jesus, let the Fire of Joy,**
> **consume the devil's subtle ploy,**
> **transfigured is our planet earth,**
> **the Golden Age is given birth.**

Part 5

1. Master Nada, radiate into the collective consciousness the awareness that when all people in a nation come together and stand behind a certain decision, then the Christ mind will provide the insights necessary and the multiplication of the energy that makes it possible.

> O Saint Germain, you do inspire,
> my vision raised forever higher,
> with you I form a figure-eight,
> your Golden Age I co-create.
>
> **O Saint Germain, what love you bring,
> it truly makes all matter sing,
> your violet flame does all restore,
> with you we are becoming more.**

2. Master Nada, radiate into the collective consciousness the awareness that it is not necessary that a nation has a particular religion or follows a specific spiritual teaching. It can be done by people having a vision of certain principles, a vision of certain conditions, having compassion for others, respect for other people, and desiring to manifest a better standard of living.

> O Saint Germain, what Freedom Flame,
> released when we recite your name,
> acceleration is your gift,
> our planet it will surely lift.

**O Saint Germain, what love you bring,
it truly makes all matter sing,
your violet flame does all restore,
with you we are becoming more.**

3. Master Nada, radiate into the collective consciousness the awareness that free energy cannot become a physical reality if it is monopolized by some multinational corporation that wants to use it to control the world and blackmail all nations.

O Saint Germain, in love we claim,
our right to bring your violet flame,
from you Above, to us below,
it is an all-transforming flow.

**O Saint Germain, what love you bring,
it truly makes all matter sing,
your violet flame does all restore,
with you we are becoming more.**

4. Master Nada, radiate into the collective consciousness the awareness that for people to receive the knowledge of how to use this unlimited energy, they have to step up to the attitude of wanting to serve life.

O Saint Germain, I love you so,
my aura filled with violet glow,
my chakras filled with violet fire,
I am your cosmic amplifier.

> **O Saint Germain, what love you bring,**
> **it truly makes all matter sing,**
> **your violet flame does all restore,**
> **with you we are becoming more.**

5. Master Nada, radiate into the collective consciousness the awareness that when scientists, inventors and visionaries have a motivation that is ego-based, they cannot receive new ideas and technology. It takes selfless service where we are not motivated by any earthly desires.

> O Saint Germain, I am now free,
> your violet flame is therapy,
> transform all hang-ups in my mind,
> as inner peace I surely find.

> **O Saint Germain, what love you bring,**
> **it truly makes all matter sing,**
> **your violet flame does all restore,**
> **with you we are becoming more.**

6. Master Nada, radiate into the collective consciousness the awareness that there is no doubt that the Golden Age is already being manifest increment by increment.

> O Saint Germain, my body pure,
> your violet flame for all is cure,
> consume the cause of all disease,
> and therefore I am all at ease.

> O Saint Germain, what love you bring,
> it truly makes all matter sing,
> your violet flame does all restore,
> with you we are becoming more.

7. Master Nada, radiate into the collective consciousness the awareness that many people chose to descend into embodiment at this time because we saw the opportunity, felt the joy, felt the excitement of wanting Saint Germain to have the victory of the manifestation of his Golden Age.

> O Saint Germain, I'm karma-free,
> the past no longer burdens me,
> a brand new opportunity,
> I am in Christic unity.

> O Saint Germain, what love you bring,
> it truly makes all matter sing,
> your violet flame does all restore,
> with you we are becoming more.

8. Master Nada, radiate into the collective consciousness the awareness that the Golden Age will be manifest when we accept that it is manifest *now*. We need to move on from all negativity and focus on the positive.

> O Saint Germain, we are now one,
> I am for you a violet sun,
> as we transform this planet earth,
> your Golden Age is given birth.

**O Saint Germain, what love you bring,
it truly makes all matter sing,
your violet flame does all restore,
with you we are becoming more.**

9. Master Nada, radiate into the collective consciousness the awareness that we cannot let what is present on earth prevent us from accepting what is not only possible but is already being lowered into physical manifestation.

O Saint Germain, the earth is free,
from burden of duality,
in oneness we bring what is best,
your Golden Age is manifest.

**O Saint Germain, what love you bring,
it truly makes all matter sing,
your violet flame does all restore,
with you we are becoming more.**

Sealing

In the name of the Divine Mother, I call to all ascended masters for the sealing of myself and all people in my circle of influence in the creative flow of the Divine Mother, the River of Life. I call for the multiplication of my calls by all ascended masters, so that we form the perfect figure-eight flow of "As Above, so below." Thus, I accept that this is fully manifest, because the mouth of the Lord, the Divine Mother that I AM, has spoken it. Amen.

15 | A NEW AWARENESS OF MENTAL FREEDOM

I AM the Ascended Master Saint Germain. I am the Chohan of the Seventh Ray. I am the leader of the Aquarian Age, the Hierarch of the Aquarian Age.

My beloved, you have heard a magnificent discourse from each of my six fellow Chohans who are all here with me, as we all stand before you in humility and awe over the fact that so many people on earth, yourselves included but far beyond yourselves, are able and willing to tune in to some of the new ideas that we are bringing forth.

We have called it the "Golden Age of Saint Germain," which is, of course, because I hold the position as the main director for the Aquarian Age. As you can clearly see from this conference, it is truly the Golden Age of all of the Chohans, all of the Archangels, all of the Elohim, all of the masters who are working with earth, including, of course, that wonderful Being that we all love, Mother Mary.

A universalist mindset

It is a cooperative effort up here and it will, of course, be a cooperative effort on earth. That is why we are looking to you – who are our direct students, who are open to our messages – to get yourselves out of any remnants of the sectarian mindset and adopt this universalist mindset that we have talked about. You are focused on raising up the All and not focused on getting any credit or recognition or converting people to a particular sectarian idea or philosophy.

We, my beloved, are not looking to bring in the Golden Age through one particular source but through many, many sources, for that is the only way that we can avoid the fallen beings taking control over it. Just look at how one particular church in Europe, the Catholic Church, became instantly the tool for the fallen beings and was so for so many years. This, of course, can be repeated over and over again until the people have had enough of it, but *we* have already long ago had enough of it. That is why we are bringing forth the Golden Age of Aquarius through many different sources, which fortunately is possible today.

It is possible for the major reason that Jesus himself set a foundation that many people have been able to use at inner levels to manifest a degree of personal Christhood so that they can be the open door for the influence from Spirit. Even if a person is the open door for one idea during a lifetime, that is a major contribution to bringing forth the Golden Age.

Freedom from and freedom to

I want to talk about what you have just done in this rosary where you have invoked an alchemical shift of perception. If

15 | A new awareness of mental freedom

you look at the history of humankind, you can interpret it, of course, in various ways but you can look at it as a continuing process of seeking greater and greater freedom for the people. Freedom has two aspects: freedom from and freedom to.

When you are oppressed, when you are limited by some external force, you naturally seek *freedom from* that force. There can come a higher recognition of freedom as a *freedom to* flow with the Spirit. If you look at the history of humankind so far, you can see that people have mainly been concerned about attaining freedom from. You might, with your knowledge, say that the population has been seeking freedom from the power elite.

This is a perfectly valid way to interpret history. It is clear that in the Aquarian Age the influence of the power elite will diminish. Many of the fallen beings in embodiment will be judged and then will be taken out of embodiment. Many of the fallen beings in the emotional, mental and identity realms will also receive their judgment and will be removed from this earth, possibly going to the second death (some of them). There will be an aspect of bringing the Aquarian Age that is a freedom from these external forces, but this in itself will not bring the Golden Age into manifestation.

In fact, you cannot attain freedom from the power elite through physical, material means. This is what the other Chohans have attempted to explain to you. There is no way to bring the Golden Age through physical means. You cannot, even if people were awakened to the existence of the power elite tomorrow, create some kind of institution that is meant to identify the power elite and dethrone them from power. It could not be done. It could not work at the present level of the collective consciousness.

What is it that is needed? What is needed is an alchemical shift in consciousness. What do I mean with alchemical? Well, even though alchemy has been somewhat the laughingstock of the scientific community and, of course, was persecuted by the religious community of the Catholics, there is a validity here. The validity is that there is a recognition that the substances that are in existence on earth right now can be transformed into a higher state. This is the essence of alchemy.

It is possible to take what is manifest on earth right now and transform it into a higher state. There is also implicit in the alchemical mindset that you need to find some ingredient that is not physical in order to accomplish this. This is implicit in true alchemy. There is, of course, a false alchemy, which thinks that there is some magical formula, some philosopher's stone, some chemical element that can bring about this transformation in a mechanical way. The true reality of alchemy is that the philosopher's stone that can transform one element into another is consciousness, the Christ consciousness or a "higher state of consciousness," if we are completely neutral.

Mental freedom is the norm

If there is one thing, from the perspective of the Seventh Ray, that I would like to see happen in society, it would be that the awakening that has already begun to happen would be accelerated so that people would realize that there is no condition in human psychology, in the human psyche, that cannot be transformed into a higher condition. When I, as the Chohan of the Seventh Ray of Freedom, look at humankind, I naturally want people to be free.

Of course, I want people to be free from the power elite and from any external oppression and limitation, but I also see that the only way, the *absolutely* only way, to accomplish this is to first free them from the limitations in their own psyches

15 | A new awareness of mental freedom

that are burdening them and weighing them down. Why is the power elite still in power? Because people have so many psychological burdens that they cannot raise themselves to the awareness of the power elite and the awareness that will simply flush out the power elite without much physical action having to be taken.

The most important single step, from my perspective, that could possibly happen on earth was a groundswell of an awareness that we have reached a point where the intensity and the frequency of mental illnesses and other psychological maladies has reached a level where we need to do something different, something we have not done before.

We cannot use the Christian paradigm to cure mental illness but neither can we use the materialistic paradigm to cure mental illness. Therefore, we need to find a new paradigm. We need to find not just one new paradigm but many different paradigms and modalities, many different approaches to mental illness, mental freedom. The concept I want to put into the collective consciousness of this planet is the concept of "mental freedom."

You have so much talk about mental illness and people think that mental illness is something you can ignore until it becomes a crisis that you can label as a depression or schizophrenia or this or that. Then you need to do something about it, but I want to put out the concept that ideally all human beings should enjoy and manifest mental freedom. Mental freedom is the normal state for a human being.

Right now, you have in every country a certain sense of normality based on how most people function, or rather how most people dysfunction. In all countries you still have a situation where virtually all people have unresolved psychology to the extent that they are not functioning at their optimum capacity. They do not have mental freedom, and therefore mental freedom should be the norm for a human being. It should be seen that until you have that mental freedom, you are not manifesting your highest potential. It is desirable – it is, in fact, *normal* – that all human beings, first of all, are striving for mental freedom and are engaging in a lifelong process to attain this mental freedom. Therefore, society should help in this process right from the kindergarten stage and even before. When the child is in the womb, there are things the parents can do to help facilitate the process of children engaging in this lifelong process of achieving and expanding mental freedom.

The next step is psychological welfare

Society, of course, also needs to help those who are already born, those who are already adults, those who are already elderly, attain mental freedom. My beloved, this does not have to be a particularly religious or even spiritual concept. Who can, in a free democratic society, object to the concept of mental freedom? Only the power elite. The question is: Do they dare to object to this if enough people grab on to the idea and demand that society does something to facilitate the process of people developing mental freedom? Who can really object to this if enough people grab on to the idea and begin expressing their desire to see this happen?

This, of course, has many different levels, and there are many different ways this will be done. It will be implemented in different ways in different countries. It will start like you have already started, with you pursuing it individually. What I am proposing is that we have reached a point where a next logical step for the more affluent societies is that we stop focusing on material welfare but begin focusing on psychological welfare and the goal is to help people develop mental freedom.

You see, my beloved, why is the power elite in power? Because they are using people's psychological hang-ups and wounds to keep them under their control. What happens if a critical mass of people work on their psychology to the point where they achieve a higher degree of mental freedom? Well, they simply will not respond to the control games of the power elite.

Do you understand? Many of you actually do not understand this point so let me make this very clear. You can look at certain societies, such as the Soviet Union, and you can see that there was a physical apparatus designed to control people. It was brutal, it was willing to kill anybody who did not submit to control and even randomly kill people to keep them in a constant state of fear. It is clear that such an apparatus has a certain power over the people, but could this apparatus prevent the Soviet Union from collapsing? You know the historical fact that it did not.

How society changes

Ask yourself this: How could a society that was so heavily controlled actually transition into a different phase? We can always discuss whether there has been improvement or not but there *has* been a shift, there *has* been a change. The control is not there that was there during the Stalinist era. How does this happen? Because there was a shift in the collective consciousness of the citizens of the Soviet Union so that they simply did not mentally submit to the control games of the elite.

The same has happened in the West. Why are you no longer living in feudal societies? Why are you no longer as controlled by certain industrialists as you were a hundred years ago? Why has the affluence been raised among the general population when, in fact, the power elite would do everything they could to avoid this happening?

There are physical means of control. If you focus on these, as they do in the conspiracy theories, you will be discouraged. You will think there is nothing that can be done. This is exactly what the power elite wants, exactly what the fallen beings want because this delays the inevitable, namely that people raise themselves above the control game. It especially delays it because it pulls those who are the most aware people into this negative attitude that nothing can be done, that conditions are so severe, that a big crash or collapse is coming and therefore there is no point in doing anything.

This is not mental freedom. What I am telling you is this, and we have said this over and over again: "Consciousness always precedes physical manifestation." When the consciousness of the people shifts, those physical control instruments, will no longer work the same way. In most cases what will happen is that the established power elite will not be able to adapt quickly enough because they are always behind. In most cases the established elite will collapse.

In many cases this has caused an aspiring elite to then come in and take power, but they never had quite the same amount of power as the old elite [If the consciousness had shifted.]. Even this has led to some progress, but what I am telling you is that if the shift can really happen towards mental freedom, there will be no new power elite. You will have a state where a power elite simply cannot exist, it cannot maintain a hold on the people. Why is this so? Because again, the hold that the power elite has may be expressed in the physical through physical instruments of control but the real hold that they have is on the minds of the people. When that slips, then the physical instruments will be of no avail.

A peaceful revolution in consciousness

You see why we have said it is possible to create a peaceful revolution that does not require a physical uprising and bloodshed and the overthrow of the power elite. It is a revolution in consciousness. This is true alchemy. The true alchemists of the Middle Ages (and there were few that were true alchemists but there were some), they knew that finding the philosopher's stone could only be done by raising their consciousness to such a level that they could be the open door for the influx of energy and consciousness from the ascended realm.

It was this influx from our level that would bring the increase that could transform a base substance into not only gold but a higher substance. This is what the other Chohans have been saying. It is our multiplication of the efforts of those in embodiment that will bring the increase that will bring about the Golden Age.

There are, of course, many modalities for how psychology can be transformed. There are already many modalities that are brought into the physical. We are not saying that we are looking for the ascended master teachings or that we are looking to bring forth a new modality that will replace all the others. They can all be used for different people at different stages of development. There are, of course, others that we will bring in through those who are sensitive to them.

The point of this is that when the awareness is raised, when the awareness shifts and people begin to demand mental freedom, then the tools will be there to bring this about. You, as the spiritual people, can hold the vision for this. You can make the calls for this. You can demand that this happen, and therefore you will see that the shift has actually already begun to happen.

It is just that there is hardly anybody who has grasped the vision I am giving you, namely that the next logical stage for the more developed societies is that they go beyond focusing on the material but they focus on psychological welfare and mental freedom. This is the new goal. This is the goal for the most advanced countries in the world, namely to give their citizens more than physical freedom, to give them mental freedom also or at least allow them to pursue mental freedom.

Citizen's income

This could be done in various ways. There has been talk in some countries about giving all citizens a certain basic income so that they do not have to work. This is a valid idea for consideration and experimentation. It would allow some people the freedom from making a living that could make them free to focus on developing their own psychology.

Surely, many would take advantage of it and do nothing but there are those who are spiritual people who could say: "I am going to focus, at least for some years, on developing my own psychology, healing my psychology, achieving mental freedom. Then I will see, when I have achieved some degree of freedom, what I might do for society."

You would actually find that there would be many young people who would have no clear conscious idea of why they are doing what they are doing, as you have seen many spiritual people who started the spiritual path without really knowing what they were doing. After some years, they reach a greater clarity and now they become free to actually begin to serve society rather than just pursuing their individual growth. As we have said, there comes a point where you cannot grow further unless you serve the All.

15 | A new awareness of mental freedom

An unfolding economy

This is just one possibility. What I also want to talk about in this discourse is, of course, the economy. It is clear that changes need to happen in the economy, not only with the money system. Again, I am not looking to bring forth one particular solution to this. There is a tendency, and it is a Piscean tendency, amongst spiritual students to think that when you become aware of a problem, it is necessary, first of all, to define the problem very clearly, in a very succinct way, in a very black-and-white way: "This is right, this is wrong about the problem." Then, you need to define a cause of the problem, a scapegoat, and then you have a simple solution. You do something with the scapegoat and you have solved the problem.

As we have tried to point out, this form of thinking (this epic mindset, this black-and-white thinking) is the creation of the fallen beings. In reality, my beloved, life is far more complex. The economy is an extremely complex topic. I know I have said before (and we have said before) that it need not be complex. It need not be complex, but it is still a topic that cannot be defined in very succinct black-and-white terms. There is not a single solution that can be pointed out that will suddenly solve all of your problems.

What I have said before is that the Golden Age is not a fixed creation. It is not that I, up here, have a fixed matrix for the Golden Age and I am looking to bring the earth closer and closer to that matrix, when suddenly: "Wham," the earth has reached the matrix, then the Golden Age will remain the same for a thousand years. That is not how I think. I see the Golden Age as a continually unfolding process and, of course, the economy during the Golden Age will also be continually unfolding.

The elite that pays no taxes

There is no point in telling you today how the economy will be two or five hundred years from now because you cannot bridge the gap from here to there and you are not meant to. You are meant to start where you are now and then gradually transform the economy through a series of steps and stages. The real concern is on the next step that humankind can take. What you have seen here in this year (which is, of course, the year of purity that flushes out impurity) is that the most significant event that has happened is the publication of the *Panama Papers*.

This was, of course, instrumented by me and sponsored by me but subject to the free will of those who had the powers to attain this information and publish it at great risk to themselves. What all people in all nations have the opportunity to become aware of here is that in every nation there is a group of people who have managed to attain great fortunes, greater fortunes than the majority of the population. Despite the fact that they have more wealth than they can possibly use for personal consumption, they are not willing to pay taxes. They are not willing to pay to the whole.

Now my beloved, what does that say to the people? It says that there is a power elite, which is taking advantage of the freedom that their society has given them, but they are not willing to give anything back. This can be built upon to make people realize that there is a power elite for whom the economy (the financial world, the stock market, the commodities markets, the currency markets) is just a tool to enrich themselves by stealing the value of people's labor, by stealing the value of what the population has brought forth by doing the actual physical work.

Extracting money from people's labor

What is it that brings greater wealth to a nation? It is that there are people who are doing something. They are producing goods, they are providing a service but they are doing actual physical work. It is this work that produces value, but what the fallen beings have done is that they have created a situation where the value produced by actual labor is immediately measured by and transferred into money. Therefore, when a person performs physical labor, that labor is measured as a certain sum of money and this allows those who are in control of the system to extract some of the money for themselves before it is given back to the people.

How is money given back to the people? Well, first of all through your salary, through your pensions but also through paying taxes to society so that it goes to the benefit of the all and to upholding the infrastructure and the institutions of society that benefit all people.

What the power elite has done is to create a situation where not all of the value of people's labor goes back to the people or to society but they can extract a percentage. They have actually created a situation where they are extracting a greater and greater percentage by manipulating every aspect of the economy, not only the money system but also the entire banking system, the currency markets, the stock markets.

The gambling economy

I have talked before about the fact that the stock markets and other markets have created a gambling economy where you are gambling that things will go up or down but you don't know if they will go up or down. What needs to be seen is that there is a power elite that has taken this gambling economy beyond the gambling stage. They are not gambling; they are *driving* the market.

If you go to Las Vegas and play the slot machines, you might get lucky and win a lot of money. If you step back from your own situation and look at all of the people who go to Las Vegas and play the slot machines (or other forms of gambling), you can see very clearly that how would these great hotels be built unless people leave more money in Las Vegas than they take out of Las Vegas? You know they say: "What happens in Vegas, stays in Vegas," and that applies to your money too. You can see that the gambling system could not exist unless those who are in control of the system take more money out than is being sent back to those who play. The same goes for the stock market, the currency markets and all other aspects of the economy. The same goes for the banking sector.

Are banks needed?

My beloved, may I raise a question for you: "Do you need banks in the modern age?" You see, would it not be possible to say that when we were dependent on physical money, it was reasonable that we had an institution that created a safe storage place where we could store our money so it could not easily be stolen? Would it not be possible for some institution, whether government or private, to provide this Internet security so that you had an account that was not associated with a bank? Would it not be possible to create a non-profit organization that could store your money electronically and give you much

15 | A new awareness of mental freedom

the same services as banks do today, but without allowing the banks the possibilities of manipulating or taking your money by doing what they have been doing: increasing the fees, by making the interest off the money that they lend. Is there not a different way in the electronic age so that banks could either be completely transformed or that new institutions could be created for managing money?

Why, why my beloved, is the entire dealing with money done through the banks that are making a profit off of doing this? I have said before that the greatest problem in the economy is that you are allowing some people to make money off of money but it is not just money. It is also stocks, bonds, currencies, commodities.

Why are you allowing people to speculate when it can be proven that this lowers the economy for the whole? It gives advantages to the few who know how to manipulate the system, but the cost is that it takes money out of the economy that benefits the general population and the nation. You are allowing the few to take money from the many. Why are you allowing this? Why should this be allowed? Certainly, it will not be allowed in the Golden Age.

The immediate step towards an improvement of the economy, that I want to put before you in this release, is that you make the calls, you hold the vision, you talk to people, you raise the question of why nations (modern developed nations that are based on democratic principles of the greatest good for the greatest number of people) are continuing to allow a small elite to steal money from the population? Why? This makes no sense and it should be possible to have an awakening where people like a wildfire would wake up and say: "This must stop. It is time to stop this madness."

Why Saint Germain is an optimist

I am, of course, the eternal optimist. Why else would I have accepted the job of being the overseer of the Aquarian Age? Why would I have stayed with earth when I certainly could have moved on to other planets with a higher level of development? I am the eternal optimist. Why am I an *optimist?* Because I am a *realist.* You know so many people say: "I'm not a pessimist, I'm a realist." I am an optimist because I am a realist. I know, as my beloved brother MORE said, we were winning from the beginning.

The fallen ones cannot win because they cannot use true alchemy. In his wonderful book [*The Mystical Initiations of Intention*] Serapis Bey explained to you that the fallen beings have managed to create what he called the secondary laws of nature. This is what allows a certain manipulation of matter. There are even those who were the false alchemists who could achieve some results through mechanical, physical means. Do you not understand that if you are using only the energy that has already been brought into the physical vibrational spectrum, then your energy will always be limited?

You can do something. That is why the fallen beings can attain a certain degree of control. It is the same as the energy sources you have today, namely that in order to get energy out, you have to put something in so you have to have something to put into the process. As humankind is beginning to realize, the material universe in its current condition has limited resources. The fallen beings cannot win in the long run for they *will* run out of energy.

The power elite limits itself

The reason for this is what we have already explained, namely that when you go into the dualistic mindset, anything you do creates an impulse. You can do something on earth, you can take power and you can manipulate the people. You can do what seems to be a very impressive feat, such as create the Roman Empire that had great power in the ancient world. It actually had greater power in the ancient world than any power has had ever since. When you consider the technology that was available at the time, then the Roman Empire had greater power than the United States has today or that the Soviet Union or China ever had. But everything the Romans did sent out an energy impulse into the universe. When it came back to them, it was an opposition to their expansion. At the same time, the Roman Empire was built on the fact that the empire itself was not producing enough energy to sustain itself.

That is why the Roman Empire had to expand, not only to take physical resources from the new provinces but to take energy from the people that were conquered. They had to expand in order to maintain their power. They could not stay still because they had not created a society that was able to produce enough energy internally to maintain itself so they had to expand.

Yet their previous expansion had created an impulse that came back to them from the universe and opposed their expansion and therefore there came a point where the Roman Empire simply stagnated. It could not expand anymore and since it did not produce enough energy from within, it started to collapse. This is also what happened to the Soviet Union. This is also what today is to some degree happening to the United States, which instead of allowing the state to take control has allowed corporations to take control.

There is a limit to how much you can expand, so the only way to get beyond this is to get energy from a source beyond the material. That is why a completely realistic evaluation of the situation will show you that the fallen ones are losing and they were losing from the beginning. The moment they started taking aggressive actions, they actually started creating the opposition that will inevitably defeat them.

The Golden Age can be now

The question is of course: "How long is it going to take before their self-created opposition defeats them?" As you saw with the Roman Empire, it took quite some time. Well, I don't know about you, my beloved, but I don't have time to wait for that.

Therefore, I am encouraging people (and giving people the teachings and the tools that will empower you) to accelerate the cycle, as it has already been accelerated by ascended master students, by other people who have grasped on to a higher vision. It is, of course, this acceleration that I look forward to. I am an *accelerating* master, I am not one who stands still. You may say I am impatient but I am not even impatient. I am simply saying: "Why should we wait two hundred years to have a Golden Age when we can have it now?"

Therefore, I am encouraging you to make that shift in consciousness. I am encouraging you to actually make the shift: "I am now living in the golden age consciousness and therefore I am living in the Golden Age. The Golden Age is where I have control, which is my own mind and energy field. I am not concerned necessarily about the rest of the planet, but where I am, there is the Golden Age." That is what you can all say, what you can all determine, and you can all live it.

There have been questions about what it means to hold the balance for the planet. How do you do this? What does it mean to hold the vision of what is going to happen and how the people are going to awaken? What it means is simply this: In your energy field, in your mind, you are deciding that you are living in a Golden Age. This does not mean that you are blind to what is going on in the world, but it *does* mean, very simply, that you have raised yourself above the level of fear and the level of doubt.

Look at so many well-meaning people in the world. They have a vision of a better age, they have a desire for a better age, but then something happens in the world and suddenly they go into a vibration of fear and think that now it is all going downhill, now we are no longer moving forward. Or they come across some conspiracy website or other website and all of a sudden they become so focused on a problem that they go into a vibration of doubt. Can this ever be overcome?

Holding a spiritual balance

When you are holding a spiritual balance for the planet, your aura, your force-field, can never be affected by this fear and doubt vibration. You *know* we are moving towards the Golden Age. You absolutely accept this and it is not that you are blind to what is happening in the world, but you are seeing that this is not a hindrance to the Golden Age. This is a step towards the Golden Age because it is, as we have said, sometimes necessary that a certain state of consciousness is outplayed to an extreme degree in order to make it so visible that people finally see it.

What did we say last year [*Help People Overcome the Past*]? Why did Nazism have to happen? Why did the Holocaust have to happen? Because someone had to outplay that state of consciousness to such an extreme degree that what people had denied for thousands of years, they could no longer deny. I am not saying this makes it excusable, but I am just saying that even though we would have preferred to avoid this event, it can be used as a step forward. It has been, to some degree, a step forward in the sense that if it had not been outplayed to that extreme extent that awoke people, it would just have continued to happen over and over again to a lesser degree.

You understand that there are some times when people are so good at adapting to certain conditions that they don't see a problem. They don't see it—they don't see it as a problem. They have become so tolerant of war, for example, that they say: "Oh, it's okay that we have a few minor wars here and there, it's inevitable. It's always been that way." How are people ever going to identify this as a problem and say: "We don't want it anymore," unless there is such an extreme outplaying of this consciousness that they are finally awakened because now they cannot ignore it anymore?

You come to the point where you realize that even these kind of things are simply necessary to awaken people because they would not be awakened in any other way. You are making a contribution to awakening people in a better way by you holding firm in your aura that the Golden Age is a manifest reality. You are staying in the golden age consciousness. You see, for example, when a certain event happens, there is a wave of panic that goes through the collective consciousness. You may even have read that scientists have created these machines that generate a completely random series of numbers, but when certain major events happen, such as 9/11, even these random generating machines are affected and this shows that there is a collective consciousness that affects everything.

Holding a spiritual balance

Do you understand that even when the collective consciousness is thrown into a panic, you are still firm? That is how you hold the balance so that the collective consciousness can come back much quicker and so that fewer people are pulled into the negative and many more people can come back from it more quickly. You also hold the vision by realizing that, no matter what happens out there, it will not deter the manifestation of the Golden Age. It will not destroy it; it will not delay it.

You hold the vision by holding firm that the Golden Age is in the process of manifesting and that it is happening at an ever-accelerated rate. Maybe that is what flushes out some of the darkness, but nevertheless it is a sign that the Golden Age is moving forward. When more and more people can hold this vision, then more people out there (who are not aware of the ascended masters) can also believe in the vision, can lock in to the ideas. They can come to accept the Omega aspect of manifestation where you not only see a vision but you actually accept that it is realistic to manifest it.

How, my beloved, shall the general population ever accept that it is possible to manifest a Golden Age if you, who are the ascended master students, do not firmly believe and accept this? If you have doubt in your beings, how is the general population going to overcome their doubt? I am asking you to seriously consider this. It is just a matter of going through what I have talked about: an alchemical shift in your consciousness. Sometimes, my beloved, you who are our best students are still trapped in looking beyond yourself and thinking the change has to happen "out there." As I am holding up a mirror, I am saying: "You and you and you, look at your consciousness and see the need to go through an alchemical shift in your mind. Raise your vibration. Raise your energy field beyond fear, beyond doubt. Accept that I am Saint Germain and I am manifesting my Golden Age on earth. You are part of it and therefore you and I together are in a figure-eight flow and we together *are* the manifestation of the Golden Age on earth. And thus, I thank you.

16 | INVOKING MENTAL FREEDOM

In the name I AM THAT I AM, Jesus Christ, I call to all ascended masters working on manifesting the Golden Age, especially Archangel Zadkiel, Elohim Arcturus, Saint Germain, Divine Director and Alpha, to radiate into the collective consciousness a new awareness of the concept of mental freedom. Help people see that we can build a new future by working with the ascended masters and letting go of the old way of looking at life, including…

[Make personal calls.]

Part 1

1. Saint Germain, radiate into the collective consciousness the awareness that there is a need for all progressive people to leave behind any remnants of the sectarian mindset and adopt a universalist mindset that is focused on raising up the All and not focused on getting any credit or converting people to a particular sectarian idea or philosophy.

> Zadkiel Archangel, your flow is so swift,
> in your violet light, we instantly shift,
> into a vibration in which we are free,
> from all limitations of the lesser me.
>
> **Zadkiel Archangel, encircle the earth,**
> **Zadkiel Archangel, with your violet girth,**
> **Zadkiel Archangel, unstoppable mirth,**
> **Zadkiel Archangel, our planet's rebirth.**

2. Saint Germain, radiate into the collective consciousness the awareness that the ascended masters are not looking to bring in the Golden Age through one particular source but through many sources, for that is the only way to avoid the fallen beings taking control over it.

> Zadkiel Archangel, we truly aspire,
> to being the master of your violet fire,
> wielding the power, of your alchemy,
> we use Sacred Word, to set all life free.

16 | Invoking mental freedom

> **Zadkiel Archangel, encircle the earth,**
> **Zadkiel Archangel, with your violet girth,**
> **Zadkiel Archangel, unstoppable mirth,**
> **Zadkiel Archangel, our planet's rebirth.**

3. Saint Germain, radiate into the collective consciousness the awareness that the history of humankind has been a continuing process of seeking greater and greater freedom for the people.

> Zadkiel Archangel, your violet light,
> transforming the earth, with unstoppable might,
> so swiftly our planet, beginning to spin,
> with legions of angels, our victory we win.

> **Zadkiel Archangel, encircle the earth,**
> **Zadkiel Archangel, with your violet girth,**
> **Zadkiel Archangel, unstoppable mirth,**
> **Zadkiel Archangel, our planet's rebirth.**

4. Saint Germain, radiate into the collective consciousness the awareness that there is freedom *from* and freedom *to*. So far, the population has been seeking freedom from the power elite.

> Zadkiel Archangel, the earth is now free,
> from burdens put on her by humanity,
> all people are free from their inner strife,
> embracing the freedom to start a new life.

> **Zadkiel Archangel, encircle the earth,**
> **Zadkiel Archangel, with your violet girth,**
> **Zadkiel Archangel, unstoppable mirth,**
> **Zadkiel Archangel, our planet's rebirth.**

5. Saint Germain, radiate into the collective consciousness the awareness that we cannot attain freedom from the power elite through physical, material means. There is no way to bring the Golden Age through physical means.

> Zadkiel Archangel, the earth will now spin,
> much faster as we Christ victory win,
> for in Christ the captives are truly set free,
> bathed in Christ Light the earth now will be.
>
> **Zadkiel Archangel, encircle the earth,**
> **Zadkiel Archangel, with your violet girth,**
> **Zadkiel Archangel, unstoppable mirth,**
> **Zadkiel Archangel, our planet's rebirth.**

6. Saint Germain, radiate into the collective consciousness the awareness that what is needed is an alchemical shift in consciousness, based on the recognition that the substances that are in existence on earth right now can be transformed into a higher state.

> Zadkiel Archangel, the forces of night,
> are bound by your penetrating Freedom Light,
> the earth is now cleared by forces so dark,
> as your Violet Light provides a new spark.
>
> **Zadkiel Archangel, encircle the earth,**
> **Zadkiel Archangel, with your violet girth,**
> **Zadkiel Archangel, unstoppable mirth,**
> **Zadkiel Archangel, our planet's rebirth.**

7. Saint Germain, radiate into the collective consciousness the awareness that the true reality of alchemy is that the philosopher's stone that can transform one element into another is a higher state of consciousness.

> Zadkiel Archangel, we truly love you,
> and to Saint Germain we will always be true,
> help us now see our plans so Divine,
> so we on this planet our full light can shine.

Zadkiel Archangel, encircle the earth,
Zadkiel Archangel, with your violet girth,
Zadkiel Archangel, unstoppable mirth,
Zadkiel Archangel, our planet's rebirth.

8. Saint Germain, radiate into the collective consciousness the awareness that there is no condition in human psychology that cannot be transformed into a higher condition.

> Zadkiel Archangel, there is no more night,
> a new day is born from your great Violet Light,
> transforming all manifestations of fear,
> we know that the Golden Age is now here.

Zadkiel Archangel, encircle the earth,
Zadkiel Archangel, with your violet girth,
Zadkiel Archangel, unstoppable mirth,
Zadkiel Archangel, our planet's rebirth.

9. Saint Germain, radiate into the collective consciousness the awareness that the only way to free people from the power elite is to first free them from the limitations in their own psyches that are burdening them and weighing them down.

Zadkiel Archangel, your violet flame,
the earth and humanity, never the same,
Saint Germain's Golden Age, is a reality,
what glorious wonder, we joyously see.

Zadkiel Archangel, encircle the earth,
Zadkiel Archangel, with your violet girth,
Zadkiel Archangel, unstoppable mirth,
Zadkiel Archangel, our planet's rebirth.

Part 2

1. Saint Germain, radiate into the collective consciousness the awareness that the power elite is still in power because people have so many psychological burdens that they cannot raise themselves to the awareness of the power elite and the awareness that will flush out the power elite without much physical action having to be taken.

Beloved Arcturus, release now the flow,
of Violet Flame to help all life grow,
in ever-expanding circles of light,
it pulses within every atom so bright.

Beloved Arcturus, your Violet Flame pure,
is for every ailment the ultimate cure,
against it no darkness could ever endure,
earth's freedom it will forever ensure.

2. Saint Germain, radiate into the collective consciousness the awareness that there is a need for a groundswell of an awareness that we have reached a point where the intensity and frequency of mental illnesses proves we need to do something different, something we have not done before.

> Beloved Arcturus, thou Elohim Free,
> we open our hearts to your reality,
> we have no attachments to life here on earth,
> we claim a new life in your Flame of Rebirth.
>
> **Beloved Arcturus, your Violet Flame pure,**
> **is for every ailment the ultimate cure,**
> **against it no darkness could ever endure,**
> **earth's freedom it will forever ensure.**

3. Saint Germain, radiate into the collective consciousness the awareness that we cannot use the Christian paradigm to cure mental illness but neither can we use the materialistic paradigm.

> Beloved Arcturus, be with us alway,
> reborn, we are ready to face a new day,
> expanding our hearts into Infinity,
> your flame is the key to our God-victory.
>
> **Beloved Arcturus, your Violet Flame pure,**
> **is for every ailment the ultimate cure,**
> **against it no darkness could ever endure,**
> **earth's freedom it will forever ensure.**

4. Saint Germain, radiate into the collective consciousness the awareness that we need to find many different paradigms and modalities, many different approaches, to mental illness, mental freedom. The real goal of a free society is mental freedom for all people.

> Beloved Arcturus, your bright violet fire,
> now fills every atom, raising them higher,
> the space in each atom all filled with your light,
> as matter itself is shining so bright.

> **Beloved Arcturus, your Violet Flame pure,**
> **is for every ailment the ultimate cure,**
> **against it no darkness could ever endure,**
> **earth's freedom it will forever ensure.**

5. Saint Germain, radiate into the collective consciousness the awareness that ideally all human beings should enjoy and manifest mental freedom. Mental freedom is the normal state for a human being.

> Beloved Arcturus, your transforming Grace,
> empowers us now every challenge to face,
> with your Freedom's Song filling the ear,
> we know that to God we're ever so dear.

> **Beloved Arcturus, your Violet Flame pure,**
> **is for every ailment the ultimate cure,**
> **against it no darkness could ever endure,**
> **earth's freedom it will forever ensure.**

16 | Invoking mental freedom

6. Saint Germain, radiate into the collective consciousness the awareness that virtually all people have unresolved psychology to the extent that they are not functioning at their optimum capacity. They do not have mental freedom, and therefore mental freedom should be the norm for a human being.

> Beloved Arcturus, we surrender all fear,
> we're feeling your Presence so tangibly near,
> as your violet light floods our inner space,
> towards the ascension we willingly race.
>
> **Beloved Arcturus, your Violet Flame pure,**
> **is for every ailment the ultimate cure,**
> **against it no darkness could ever endure,**
> **earth's freedom it will forever ensure.**

7. Saint Germain, radiate into the collective consciousness the awareness that until we have mental freedom, we are not manifesting our highest potential. It is normal that all human beings are striving for mental freedom and are engaging in a lifelong process to attain this freedom.

> Beloved Arcturus, bring in a new age,
> help earth and humanity turn a new page,
> your transforming light gives us certainty,
> Saint Germain's Golden Age is a reality.
>
> **Beloved Arcturus, your Violet Flame pure,**
> **is for every ailment the ultimate cure,**
> **against it no darkness could ever endure,**
> **earth's freedom it will forever ensure.**

8. Saint Germain, radiate into the collective consciousness the awareness that society needs to facilitate that people engage in this lifelong process of achieving and expanding mental freedom.

> Beloved Arcturus, illusions you pierce,
> no serpent can stand against angels so fierce,
> no forces of darkness can stop Violet Flame,
> all discord on earth it will instantly tame.

> **Beloved Arcturus, your Violet Flame pure,**
> **is for every ailment the ultimate cure,**
> **against it no darkness could ever endure,**
> **earth's freedom it will forever ensure.**

9. Saint Germain, radiate into the collective consciousness the awareness that this does not have to be a religious or spiritual concept. In a free democratic society, who can object to the concept of mental freedom except the power elite. But they will lose if enough people demand mental freedom.

> Beloved Arcturus, we love Saint Germain,
> and therefore we call forth again and again,
> your Violet Flame to flood all the earth,
> so Saint Germain's eyes are filling with mirth.

> **Beloved Arcturus, your Violet Flame pure,**
> **is for every ailment the ultimate cure,**
> **against it no darkness could ever endure,**
> **earth's freedom it will forever ensure.**

Part 3

1. Saint Germain, radiate into the collective consciousness the awareness that the next logical step for the more affluent societies is that we stop focusing on *material* welfare but begin focusing on *psychological* welfare, and the goal is to help people develop mental freedom.

> Saint Germain, your alchemy,
> with violet fire now sets us free.
> Saint Germain, we ever grow,
> in freedom's overpowering flow.
>
> **O Saint Germain, your Golden Age,**
> **sets people free from psychic cage,**
> **the earth is raised to starry height,**
> **as we project with Freedom's Sight.**

2. Saint Germain, radiate into the collective consciousness the awareness that if a critical mass of people work on their psychology to the point where they achieve a higher degree of mental freedom, they will not respond to the control games of the power elite.

> Saint Germain, your mastery,
> of violet flame geometry.
> Saint Germain, in you we see,
> the formulas that set us free.

**O Saint Germain, your Golden Age,
sets people free from psychic cage,
the earth is raised to starry height,
as we project with Freedom's Sight.**

3. Saint Germain, radiate into the collective consciousness the awareness that any progress in society comes about because the collective consciousness has shifted upwards. No physical means of control can stop this.

Saint Germain, in Liberty,
you give the love that sets all free.
Saint Germain, we do adore,
the violet flame that makes all more.

**O Saint Germain, your Golden Age,
sets people free from psychic cage,
the earth is raised to starry height,
as we project with Freedom's Sight.**

4. Saint Germain, radiate into the collective consciousness the awareness that consciousness always precedes physical manifestation. When the consciousness of the people shifts, the physical control apparatus will no longer work the same way.

Saint Germain, in unity,
we will transcend duality.
Saint Germain, the self so pure,
your violet chemistry so sure.

> **O Saint Germain, your Golden Age,**
> **sets people free from psychic cage,**
> **the earth is raised to starry height,**
> **as we project with Freedom's Sight.**

5. Saint Germain, radiate into the collective consciousness the awareness that in most cases the established power elite will not be able to adapt quickly enough and it will collapse.

> Saint Germain, reality,
> in violet light we are carefree.
> Saint Germain, our auras seal,
> your violet flame our chakras heal.

> **O Saint Germain, your Golden Age,**
> **sets people free from psychic cage,**
> **the earth is raised to starry height,**
> **as we project with Freedom's Sight.**

6. Saint Germain, radiate into the collective consciousness the awareness that if the shift can happen towards mental freedom, there will be no new power elite. We will have a state where a power elite simply cannot exist, it cannot maintain a hold on the people.

> Saint Germain, your chemistry,
> with violet fire set atoms free.
> Saint Germain, from lead to gold,
> transforming vision we behold.

**O Saint Germain, your Golden Age,
sets people free from psychic cage,
the earth is raised to starry height,
as we project with Freedom's Sight.**

7. Saint Germain, radiate into the collective consciousness the awareness that the hold that the power elite has may be expressed in the physical through physical instruments of control, but the real hold that they have is on the minds of the people. When that slips, then the physical instruments will be of no avail.

Saint Germain, transcendency,
as we are always one with thee.
Saint Germain, from soul we're free,
we so delight in knowing thee.

**O Saint Germain, your Golden Age,
sets people free from psychic cage,
the earth is raised to starry height,
as we project with Freedom's Sight.**

8. Saint Germain, radiate into the collective consciousness the awareness that it is possible to create a peaceful revolution that does not require a physical uprising, bloodshed or the overthrow of the power elite. It is a revolution in consciousness.

Saint Germain, nobility,
the key to sacred alchemy.
Saint Germain, you balance all,
the seven rays upon our call.

**O Saint Germain, your Golden Age,
sets people free from psychic cage,
the earth is raised to starry height,
as we project with Freedom's Sight.**

9. Saint Germain, radiate into the collective consciousness the awareness that when the collective consciousness is raised, it opens for an influx of energy from the ascended realm, and this is what shifts society.

Saint Germain, your Presence here,
filling up the inner sphere.
Life is now a sacred flow,
God Freedom we on all bestow.

**O Saint Germain, your Golden Age,
sets people free from psychic cage,
the earth is raised to starry height,
as we project with Freedom's Sight.**

Part 4

1. Saint Germain, radiate into the collective consciousness the awareness that when the awareness shifts and people begin to demand mental freedom, then the tools will be there to bring about the healing of psychology.

Divine Director, I now see,
the world is unreality,
in my heart I now truly feel,
the Spirit is all that is real.

> **Divine Director, send the light,**
> **from blindness clear my inner sight,**
> **my vision free, my vision clear,**
> **your guidance is forever here.**

2. Saint Germain, radiate into the collective consciousness the awareness that the next logical goal for the most advanced countries in the world is to give their citizens more than physical freedom, to give them mental freedom also or at least allow them to pursue mental freedom.

> Divine Director, vision give,
> in clarity I want to live,
> I now behold my plan Divine,
> the plan that is uniquely mine.

> **Divine Director, send the light,**
> **from blindness clear my inner sight,**
> **my vision free, my vision clear,**
> **your guidance is forever here.**

3. Saint Germain, radiate into the collective consciousness the awareness that one way to do this is to give citizens a basic income so that they do not have to work and are free to focus on developing their own psychology.

> Divine Director, show in me,
> the ego games, and set me free,
> help me escape the ego's cage,
> to help bring in the Golden Age.

**Divine Director, send the light,
from blindness clear my inner sight,
my vision free, my vision clear,
your guidance is forever here.**

4. Saint Germain, radiate into the collective consciousness the awareness that the economy is an extremely complex topic that cannot be reduced to the black-and-white thinking that is the creation of the fallen beings.

Divine Director, I'm with you,
my vision one, no longer two,
as karma's veil you do disperse,
I see a whole new universe.

**Divine Director, send the light,
from blindness clear my inner sight,
my vision free, my vision clear,
your guidance is forever here.**

5. Saint Germain, radiate into the collective consciousness the awareness that instead of looking for a final economic model, we are meant to start where we are now and gradually transform the economy through a series of steps and stages.

Divine Director, I go up,
electric light now fills my cup,
consume in me all shadows old,
bestow on me a vision bold.

> **Divine Director, send the light,**
> **from blindness clear my inner sight,**
> **my vision free, my vision clear,**
> **your guidance is forever here.**

6. Saint Germain, radiate into the collective consciousness the awareness that in every nation there is a group of people who have managed to attain great fortunes, but they are not willing to pay taxes. They are not willing to pay to the whole.

> Divine Director, heart of gold,
> my sacred labor I unfold,
> o blessed Guru, I now see,
> where my own plan is taking me.

> **Divine Director, send the light,**
> **from blindness clear my inner sight,**
> **my vision free, my vision clear,**
> **your guidance is forever here.**

7. Saint Germain, radiate into the collective consciousness the awareness that there is a power elite, which is taking advantage of the freedom that their society has given them, but they are not willing to give anything back.

> Divine Director, by your grace,
> in grander scheme I find my place,
> my individual flame I see,
> uniqueness God has given me.

> Divine Director, send the light,
> from blindness clear my inner sight,
> my vision free, my vision clear,
> your guidance is forever here.

8. Saint Germain, radiate into the collective consciousness the awareness that there is a power elite for whom the economy is just a tool to enrich themselves by stealing the value of people's labor, by stealing the value of what the population has brought forth by doing the physical work.

> Divine Director, vision one,
> I see that I AM God's own Sun,
> with your direction so Divine,
> I am now letting my light shine.

> Divine Director, send the light,
> from blindness clear my inner sight,
> my vision free, my vision clear,
> your guidance is forever here.

9. Saint Germain, radiate into the collective consciousness the awareness that the fallen beings have created a situation where the value produced by actual labor is immediately measured by and transferred into money, allowing those who are in control of the system to extract some of the money for themselves before it is given back to the people.

> Divine Director, what a gift,
> to be a part of Spirit's lift,
> to raise mankind out of the night,
> to bask in Spirit's loving sight.

> Divine Director, send the light,
> from blindness clear my inner sight,
> my vision free, my vision clear,
> your guidance is forever here.

Part 5

1. Saint Germain, radiate into the collective consciousness the awareness that the power elite has created a situation where not all of the value of people's labor goes back to the people or to society. They are extracting a greater and greater percentage by manipulating the money system, the banking system, the currency markets and the stock markets.

> Beloved Alpha, God's great plan,
> in Central Sun it all began,
> what wondrous vision of a world,
> the cosmic spheres were then unfurled.
>
> **Beloved Alpha, in your light,**
> **I now see God with inner sight,**
> **as man I will no longer live,**
> **my life to God I fully give.**

2. Saint Germain, radiate into the collective consciousness the awareness that the markets have created a gambling economy, but the power elite has taken this gambling economy beyond the gambling stage. They are not gambling; they are driving the market.

> Beloved Alpha, serve the All,
> this is Creator's timeless call,
> from out Creator's perfect whole,
> sprang lifestreams with a sacred goal.
>
> **Beloved Alpha, in your light,**
> **I now see God with inner sight,**
> **as man I will no longer live,**
> **my life to God I fully give.**

3. Saint Germain, radiate into the collective consciousness the awareness that banks are not needed in the Golden Age. It is possible to create a non-profit organization that can store money electronically and give the same services as banks do today, but without allowing the banks the possibilities of manipulating the economy.

> Beloved Alpha, all was one,
> as we were sent from Central Sun,
> to you we shall in time return,
> for cosmic union we do yearn.
>
> **Beloved Alpha, in your light,**
> **I now see God with inner sight,**
> **as man I will no longer live,**
> **my life to God I fully give.**

4. Saint Germain, radiate into the collective consciousness the awareness that the greatest problem in the economy is that we are allowing some people to make money off of money, including stocks, bonds, currencies and commodities.

Beloved Alpha, I now see,
you with Omega form the key,
it was from your polarity,
that I received identity.

Beloved Alpha, in your light,
I now see God with inner sight,
as man I will no longer live,
my life to God I fully give.

5. Saint Germain, radiate into the collective consciousness the awareness that allowing people to speculate lowers the economy for the whole. It gives advantages to the few who know how to manipulate the system, but the cost is that it takes money out of the economy that would benefit the general population and the nation.

Beloved Alpha, cosmic gate,
the nexus of your figure-eight,
I sprang from Cosmic Cube so bright,
I am at heart a spark of light.

Beloved Alpha, in your light,
I now see God with inner sight,
as man I will no longer live,
my life to God I fully give.

6. Saint Germain, radiate into the collective consciousness the awareness that modern developed nations, that are based on democratic principles of the greatest good for the greatest number of people, are allowing a small elite to steal money from the population. This must stop.

16 | Invoking mental freedom

Beloved Alpha, from your womb,
I did descend to matter's tomb,
but buried I will be no more,
my inner vision you restore.

**Beloved Alpha, in your light,
I now see God with inner sight,
as man I will no longer live,
my life to God I fully give.**

7. Saint Germain, radiate into the collective consciousness the awareness that the fallen ones are losing and they were losing from the beginning. The moment they started taking aggressive actions, they started creating the opposition that will inevitably defeat them.

Beloved Alpha, I now know,
the love you did on me bestow,
a co-creator, I will bring,
the light to make all matter sing.

**Beloved Alpha, in your light,
I now see God with inner sight,
as man I will no longer live,
my life to God I fully give.**

8. Saint Germain, radiate into the collective consciousness the awareness that the more progressive people need to make the shift in consciousness: "I am now living in the golden age consciousness and therefore I am living in the Golden Age. The Golden Age is where I have control, which is my own mind and energy field. I am not concerned about the rest of the planet, but where I am, there is the Golden Age."

Beloved Alpha, on this earth,
a new age we are giving birth,
for we are here to bring the love,
that you are sending from Above.

**Beloved Alpha, in your light,
I now see God with inner sight,
as man I will no longer live,
my life to God I fully give.**

9. Saint Germain, radiate into the collective consciousness the awareness that all spiritual people need to hold a spiritual balance for the planet so that no matter what happens, we hold firm that the Golden Age is in the process of manifesting and that it is happening at an ever-accelerated rate. We are in a figure-eight flow with Saint Germain, and together we are making the Golden Age a manifest reality, NOW!

Beloved Alpha, you and me,
we form a true polarity,
as up Above, so here below,
with life's own river I do flow.

**Beloved Alpha, in your light,
I now see God with inner sight,
as man I will no longer live,
my life to God I fully give.**

Sealing

In the name of the Divine Mother, I call to all ascended masters for the sealing of myself and all people in my circle of influence in the creative flow of the Divine Mother, the River of Life. I call for the multiplication of my calls by all ascended masters, so that we form the perfect figure-eight flow of "As Above, so below." Thus, I accept that this is fully manifest, because the mouth of the Lord, the Divine Mother that I AM, has spoken it. Amen.

17 | SPIRITUAL COMMUNITIES IN THE GOLDEN AGE

I AM the Ascended Master Gautama Buddha. It has been my privilege to seal many of these gatherings of ascended master students where you have been willing to come together in order to experience what you desire to experience, but also in order to give us a better platform for releasing the light and the teachings we desire to release.

The effect of people coming together

Do you truly understand the effect of coming together in a spirit of harmony, unity, oneness of purpose? When we release a dictation, there is an outer teaching that your outer mind can study. You may even go into analyzing the teaching in whatever level of detail you desire. Some, of course, analyze it to death, but others know how to use a teaching to stimulate getting their intuitive insights that go beyond the outer words.

This is, of course, very valuable, but when we release a dictation, we also release the teaching with a certain momentum of energy—light. This gives it greater penetrating power to go into the mass consciousness and therefore awaken more and more people so that they suddenly are able to grasp the ideas we are bringing forth, or even accelerate themselves on their own path, whatever that path may be.

It is clear that if the messenger sits alone and releases a dictation, there is a certain momentum. When more people come together in a group, then your chakras combine and they form a greater amplifier. You have, for example, seen musical concerts where they have a big number of speakers that are working together because they are synchronized. This is a crude illustration of what happens to your chakras when you come together, when you know each other, when you have a spirit of harmony, when you have given invocations together. Over the course of these few days, you actually build a great amplifier of the combination of your chakras, and this greatly increases and multiplies the momentum of a dictation so it penetrates much further into the collective consciousness.

What I want to impress upon you is, as we have said before, that the multiplication of this is exponential. You know that two plus two plus two is six whereas two times two times two is more. The greater the number of people who come together, and the greater the level of harmony and oneness they can attain, the greater the multiplication factor will be. I want to congratulate you for once again, this year, creating an event that has had a very powerful effect on the collective consciousness of Europe.

We are grateful for this multiplication factor. As happened last year, you have exceeded the potential for this conference, and therefore you have earned the release of Mother Mary's visualization and transformative process last night. It was not necessarily a given that this would be released at this conference. Because you had already done the work that we wanted to see done, by supporting the release of the eight dictations from the Chohans and Mother Mary, then it was determined that we would release that also at this conference so that you who were here could have that firsthand experience of being taken by the hand by Mother Mary back to see your birth trauma.

The Aquarian community

What you have done here is that you have, in this short amount of time, built a community. You will know that when I was in embodiment as the Buddha, I emphasized three elements: the Buddha, the Sangha, the Dharma. The Sangha, of course, is another word for community. The reason for this is that we live on a planet that is quite difficult, quite challenging—in many ways quite dark. As we have seen in the past, there have been a few individuals who were able to walk the path alone, but in the Aquarian Age, we are looking at an entirely different model. We are looking for an age of community where people support each other.

When I was in embodiment as the Buddha, I elected – for a set of complex reasons that really are not so interesting today – to withdraw from society and create a community that was set apart. I was sitting there in the community, and I had the students come to this protected sphere. This has value. It is not that this model has become outdated by the end of the Piscean Age. It is not that this model will not be seen in the Age of Aquarius. There will be communities in Aquarius that are set apart from the mass consciousness.

However, what you have seen in the Age of Pisces is that there has been a creation of communities that saw it as their role to isolate and insulate themselves from the world and its problems, however they defined them. You have seen some communities where people would make a lifetime commitment to become a monk, a nun or a member of that community, whatever the name was for those members. This is a model that will not be as useful in the Aquarian Age.

In fact, even in the Piscean Age there were many examples of how such communities did not actually help either its members nor the collective consciousness grow. The people simply became trapped in a very comfortable state where nothing challenged them, and therefore they did not grow. There are many examples of Christian monks and nuns, but also many Buddhist monks and nuns, who have entered a community and simply did not grow beyond a certain point for the rest of that lifetime. Instead, they would actually have grown more by remaining in society where they would have been challenged more. What we look for in the Aquarian Age is a different approach to community where you realize that community is not an end in itself. Community only has meaning when it exists as part of the trinity of the Buddha, the Sangha, the Dharma.

Buddha, Sangha, Dharma

What is the Buddha? Well, the Buddha is a representation of what you experience as the flow of the Spirit from the ascended masters, the impulse from Spirit. What is it the impulse from Spirit ultimately wants? It wants to be expressed in the world. As you know, for the impulse of Spirit to be expressed, the Law of Free Will mandates that there must be people in embodiment who become the open doors for expressing the impulse from Spirit. This is where the Sangha has its most important role. It is a place where people can go, or where they can help each other where they are—support each other so that they become able to be the open doors for the expression of Spirit. Then, when they have attained that certain level of consciousness (mastery, openness), then they go out in society and express it in society.

There is little point in attaining mastery in an ideal situation and then keeping your mastery confined to that ideal situation. First of all, for your own growth you need to actually test if you can maintain the mastery in a less than ideal situation. You also need to – in order to grow further – use your mastery to raise the All, to help others. This, of course, requires you to go out where people are and help them there. It is not that I want to put any limitations on the exact form of spiritual communities in the Golden Age. I do not want to give you a certain matrix and say: "This is the ideal matrix for how they should function." There are many ways to implement this, but what I would like to give you is the thought that the Sangha is not a physical place.

There are many, many examples – and you can find them today all over India and also in the West – where a certain guru has set himself or herself up with an ashram. Then they have gotten followers to come in and receive whatever teachings, darshans and blessings they receive. The guru sits there, much like the queen bee in a beehive or the queen in an ant hill, and all of the students are running around, making sure that the guru can function in his or her capacity. This is not the Sangha. This is not the community. A true community, a true "coming-into-unity," can only be done among those who are somewhat equal in their level of consciousness but, more importantly, who have overcome the ego's need for being special, for being superior. You cannot come into unity unless you have transcended the entire need to feel that you are better, more important or more special than others.

Coming into unity, not conformity

When you have a group of people who have transcended that need, they can come into unity even if they are not at the same level of spiritual maturity and attainment. There may still be some who are further along on the path. There may still be some who serve in certain capacities, be it as a messenger, be it as a minister, be it as a healer—in various ways. If all have overcome that egoic need for validation, for feeling special, then you can come into unity. There are many examples of the creation of a physical ashram where people come together and it seems that they are coming into unity because they are all working for a certain goal. They are all working in cooperation, and they are all working in a seeming harmony because there is no conflict among them. However, coming into unity is not the same as coming into conformity.

There are many examples of how a guru has managed to create what from the outer looks like a state of unity because he has gotten all of the followers to submit to whatever matrix he has created for the ashram. This is not coming into unity because it is actually setting aside, getting the students to set aside, their individuality.

You understand that we of the ascended masters do not want you to set aside anything. We want you to see and transcend the egoic patterns so that you actually free yourself from them. Therefore, you can be who you really are and express your Divine, your spiritual, individuality that is anchored in your I AM Presence. We are not looking to create a community in the Golden Age where there is one person who has reached some state, whatever you may choose to call it, and all the others have suppressed the expression of their individuality. This is not the kind of community that we are looking for in the Aquarian Age.

That is also why we are not primarily looking to create a community that has a certain physical location where everybody comes together physically. How can you, in creating a certain community, avoid setting a certain matrix for how the community functions? A community by definition cannot be all things to all people. A community that is isolated and set aside must make a choice and say: "These are the activities we elect to express in our community in the circle of the Sangha. And these are the activities that we select out, that we select not to express in the Sangha." This is not necessarily wrong, as I said, for the purpose of helping people come together and, for example, overcome the ego, heal their psychology, attain Christhood. What we are looking for is the broader community. It is a community where you are not having to set aside your individuality in order to fit into the community. That is why we look for the building of a community that uses the technology of the Internet and other communications technology to still build a sense of community, but you do not need to be all in the same physical location.

Non-physical communities

Now, I know that I started out saying that there is value in coming together for a conference, but coming together for a conference is one thing. Living together permanently is another. You will see that as you grow on your individual path, as you overcome the ego, as you overcome your birth traumas and other psychological wounds, what naturally happens is that you become free to express your Divine individuality and your Divine plan. Well, my beloved, if your Divine individuality wants to be expressed in a certain way by working with other people, helping them where they are, giving them certain gifts, teachings or whatever, this is not necessarily expressed in the best way in a closed community. It is expressed better in a society.

We may say that a community cannot be all things to all people, but a society can be many more things to many more people. That is why we ask you not to fixate your minds on the old model of a community where it has to be a physical location that is set aside, it has to be a community that has a strict definition of rules and regulations. Instead, look for a more open community where you can still support each other around certain common goals, but you also have your individual lives where there is plenty of room for individual expression.

What I suggest is that it would be valuable to do what you have already started to do and have a way to communicate where you can support each other around two primary goals. One is to invoke light together so that you multiply your efforts of invoking light for particular issues. Certainly, there is a great acceleration in being physically together in one location, but coming all together at the same time, giving decrees over the Internet, also has a very significant multiplication. This is one goal that we would like to see as a start.

The other goal is a little more diffuse because it relates to supporting each other on your path towards Christhood, on your spiritual path in general. This can involve many different things, from sharing your experiences to decreeing for each other, to talking with each other, to helping each other in various ways, to even having certain therapists in the community who can help people in a more direct personal way, and so forth and so on. I do not want to give you a matrix because what we have seen in the past, my beloved, is that when we give our students a certain goal, then all hell breaks loose, so to speak. Not only is there an opposition from the dark forces, but there is also an opposition from people's egos. Many times it actually causes our students to go into an almost frantic state where they feel they now absolutely have to manifest this goal, and so they seek to force it, rather than flowing with it.

Downward spirals in history

When you look at our teachings with the linear mind, it is possible to find certain things that from the perspective of the linear mind seem like contradictions. For example, in this conference you have heard the Chohans bring out the concept that we were winning from the beginning because the fallen beings cannot stop the River of Life. At the same time, we have talked about the possibility that people can create downward spirals that hinder their growth, that keep them trapped in such a spiral.

I want to give you an image, and you might benefit from actually physically going to a river if there is one within a reasonable distance from where you live. It does not need to be a big river. It can be a stream, but it needs to have two qualities. It needs to have some stretches that are calm and some that are more turbulent. You can even imagine this in your mind's eye, for you have probably all seen rivers and know what I am talking about.

When you look at a river, you can see that there are some places where, for example, the current of the water passes around a rock. This means that the stream of water is now compressed and it is given a direction that is not exactly the same as the direction of the river. It is going to the side, it is being compressed, the speed is being increased and suddenly a whirlpool, a maelstrom, appears in the river. You now have this small vortex where the water is swirling around in a circle that becomes narrower and narrower. Everything that is close enough gets sucked into it, and once you are inside that vortex, you are spinning around, seemingly out of control, and your mind feels like it is out of control. This is the illustration of what we call a downward spiral.

You have seen in history many of these downward spirals. You see them today as well where suddenly a group of people can be pulled into this maelstrom of emotional energy, mental energy, where they are swirling around and they have no control. It is like their minds have become a mass mind, as you saw in the rallies of Adolph Hitler and as you see today at a rock concert, for example, where people's minds have lost their individuality. They have surrendered to the mob consciousness, and they are being pulled into this.

You can go to a river that has a stretch where there are lots of rocks and twists and turns and you can see that there is no calm stretch of the river. It is all swirling energy, fast-flowing energy, seemingly chaos. Then you can go a little further downstream, and now there is a stretch where there are no rocks and where the river is straight and all of a sudden the water is flowing calmly. Then you can ask yourself: "Is that the same river as what I just saw up there in the turbulence?" And you realize that it *is* the same river.

This makes you realize that when you look at earth, if you go into one of these downward spirals, one of these vortexes, you can easily feel as if the world is going backwards, that things are bad, that some calamity must happen. If you step back from this, you realize that this particular whirlpool, as powerful as it may be on the inside, the whirlpool itself is actually being carried along by the greater current of the river. This is what we mean by the River of Life. This is what we mean when we say that an event on earth is just an event. It does not stop the river of the raising of the collective consciousness and of the entire universe where the earth is being pulled along by the billions of planets that are in an upward spiral.

The reality beneath surface appearances

What we desire for you who are our students is, of course, to have you lock in to the river. Do not focus your attention on all the whirlpools, and certainly do not go into them if you can possibly avoid it. When you find yourself in them, then do what you need to do to get out of them. Focus on the river and see that whatever happens in these whirlpools that come up, it is necessary to outplay a certain state of consciousness physically so that people can see it. You don't need to focus on this because you have overcome that consciousness. Or if you have not, then you look at yourself and overcome it. Then you focus on the river, the ongoing flow of the river, and you allow yourself to experience and feel that you are in the river, that you are being carried along with the river.

You know very well that if you are in a train, you can walk back and forth in the train, and you can walk as easily in the opposite direction of the direction in which the train is moving as you can walk with the movement of the train. In fact, if the train is one of these modern trains that is quiet and you are not looking out the window, you might get the impression that you are standing still. This is why it is easy, when you are in embodiment, to get the impression that you are either standing still or you are going backwards because you are trapped in this whirlpool of energy. Part of discernment, part of developing the Christ consciousness and certainly the Buddhic consciousness, is to become aware of that flow of the river that underlies everything that is happening on earth.

You might even see that whatever is happening on earth, my beloved, the earth is moving through space. As we have said before, the earth is not moving in a stationary orbit around the sun, for the sun is moving in a greater orbit, and that means the earth is moving in a spiral around the sun. Therefore, the earth never comes back to the same place twice and this is part of the movement where the earth and the sun (and the entire solar system and the entire galaxy) are actually being pulled along by this directional movement of the material universe.

Scientists have not yet realized, cosmologists have not yet realized, how directional the material universe actually is. It is not just directional in a spatial way but also in a vibrational way. This is the way to understand that there are multiple dimensions and that the universe can move from one dimension to another, and that it will gradually move through various levels of frequencies until it is ready to ascend. The universe is directional, not just in a physical sense but also in an energetic, vibratory sense. You can, even though you are in embodiment on a heavy planet like earth, learn to sense this.

Spontaneous Golden Age communities

Why am I telling you this in a discourse on community? Because it should be obvious that you cannot come into unity as long as you are individually trapped in these little whirlpools and vortexes. You cannot truly come into unity if your aura is an individual vortex of swirling energy because you have unresolved psychological issues or you have too much unresolved, untransmuted, energy in your four lower bodies. You

17 | Spiritual communities in the Golden Age

do, of course, need to do the work that needs to be done to transform the energy, to resolve your psychology, to see your illusions.

When you have done that to a sufficient level, you can benefit greatly from making an effort to focus on the river. This is how you create the kind of communities we look for in Aquarius. What have I said earlier? A guru decides to create a Sangha or an ashram, he sets certain rules, he gives certain teachings, and he says: "Those who are willing to come into conformity with the matrix I have set, they are welcome here and others are not welcome."

What we are looking for in the Aquarian Age is the spontaneous emergence of communities because a group of individuals have, on an individual level, tuned in, first of all, to their individual Divine plans and then to the River of Life. When you know who you are, what you desire to express, and when you are attuned to the river, then all of those who have a similar Divine plan, a similar expression and who are attuned to the river, they will be brought together by the river—not by outer means, my beloved. When you tune in to the river, the river brings you together with other people who are also attuned and who resonate with you and your mission and your expression. Therefore, you can find a higher form of community that is based on supporting each other. You always have the awareness, as I said, of the Buddha, which is the driving force behind the river, and the Dharma, which is how the river wants to be expressed in the world, how it wants to flow into physical events on earth.

This is how you can form a kind of community that has been seen on earth before, but has *rarely* been seen on earth before. It is not based on these outer characteristics that require you to come into conformity because you do not have a set outer framework, such as living together at a certain place and having a certain type of community. You are living individually, but you still have a community where you support each other. You help each other not only overcome hindrances on the path, but you help each other tune in to the river. You help each other express what it is you individually desire to express. There is no competition here. There is no requirement that somebody has to set aside their outer expression of their Divine plan or set aside their psychology in order to fit into the community. Having set this as the ideal model, it should be clear also that such communities, such spontaneous communities, can only form when people are serious about walking the spiritual path, raising their consciousness, healing their psychology and tuning in to the River of Life.

Ego-based organizations

I want to bring to your attention what Saint Germain already mentioned about the fact that we of the ascended masters have defined a level and have said: "We will not sponsor any community that is still outplaying the ego games that have been seen so often in the Piscean Age." You have all heard the story of the devil saying that he is not worried about people finding the truth; he is just going to ask them to organize it. Many spiritual people have taken that statement to mean that there is an inherent problem with organizing anything.

This, of course, is not correct. There is no inherent problem with anything on earth. There is an inherent problem with anything that is done from the fallen or the egoic consciousness. What has happened up to this point on this planet is that the devil had an easy time because whenever he asked people to organize something, it was a given that they would be coming from the level of the ego. Therefore, their egos would begin to clash, and the usual games that you have seen over and over again would outplay themselves. It would not take long before the organization itself had actually created its own whirlpool of energy.

The conflict between the people kept everybody transfixed in this whirling downward spiral where they often thought that they were being good spiritual students working for some higher cause. In reality, they were slowly or quickly moving in a downward spiral, often without noticing it. This is why you have seen many spiritual movements that actually had a certain momentum for a while but eventually started to diminish or even collapse or be split apart by internal conflicts. The devil knew that because people had no real awareness of the ego, because they had no willingness to face and confront the ego, all he needed to do was to get them to organize it. Then, the rest, as they say, is history.

Transparent communities and societies

In the Aquarian Age we are, of course, looking at you all to come to a higher level, to come to that level of having resolved enough of these ego patterns that you can begin to come into unity without having that unity, that outer unity, be taken over by the ego patterns. This, of course, requires us to create what Saint Germain said: a community where you have resolved enough ego that you can be free to talk about anything and to tell each other anything without somebody being insulted and walking out in a huff.

The kind of communities that we desire to see in Aquarius, the kind of organizations we desire to see in Aquarius, are those where there is this kind of transparency. I am not only talking about spiritual communities but about organizations of all kinds—even organizations in society, even, for that matter, the organization that a society is, that a nation is.

Do you begin to see what is happening in this age where the Internet makes it possible to spread information instantly and makes it very difficult to suppress certain types of information that the people who are targeted by the information would rather see hidden? Do you see what is happening with something like the *Panama Papers* or even what is happening on Facebook where a certain idea can be spread very quickly? It is very simply that there is an outer technology that now allows you to spread information, making it more and more difficult to suppress information.

What is it that this is moving society towards? It is moving society towards a place where, as we have said, nothing can really be hidden. It does not mean that in the Aquarian Age you cannot have a private life. You will, of course, still be able to live in a personal relationship or a family, and it is not like anybody can monitor what you are doing in your home. What I am talking about is that in the public space, when it comes to any kind of organization that involves many people – and it potentially affects many more people, such as society – nothing can be hidden. There must be and there will be transparency.

The mindset of having nothing to hide

I know very well that even as spiritual people there is still, for many of you, a certain element of ego that resists this and says: "Oh, but I certainly don't want people to know everything about me." It is not that people need to know everything about you, but you need to come to a point – as the spiritual people who are the forerunners for the Age of Aquarius – where you have nothing in your consciousness or your life that you want to hide.

I am not here talking about only a situation where you know you have done something and you want to hide it, or you know you have a certain element of your psychology and you want to hide it. I am talking about you coming to a point where you have acquired the attitude that there is nothing you want to hide, that there is nothing that could possibly come up in the future that you are not willing to look at, that there is no situation you could imagine on earth that you would not be willing to confront and move through if that was part of your path.

What I am saying is this: In order to fully lock in to the flow of the river, you must surrender yourself into the flow of the river. You must be aware: "I am in the river. I am not standing on the bank looking at the stream flowing by me. I have immersed myself in the river. I am flowing with it, and wherever the river takes me downstream, whatever experiences the river brings up, I am not going to stand aside and just watch. I am not going to hold on to some branch on the bank of the river. I am not going to resist the flow. I am not going to cling to a rock. I am going to flow with the river through that experience. Even while I am flowing through it, I am going to be aware that I am flowing with the river. Even if it might be unpleasant right now, I know that the river will carry me through this experience, and there will again be a calm phase of the river afterwards."

You see, you cannot fully tune in to the River of Life if you are resisting its flow, if you are saying: "Yes, I want to flow with the River of Life, but only if it flows nicely and gives me good experiences." That is not flowing with the river.

No more secret organizations

This, again, applies to society at large. In the Aquarian Age it will become more and more impossible for any organization to function in secret. It will become more and more impossible to stay hidden. My beloved, what is it in you that wants to hide something? It is the ego. Who are the people who want to hide something in society? Who are the people who want to exercise power and hide this from the population? Well, of course, the people who are completely trapped in the ego, and they are the ones we have called the fallen beings or those who are completely trapped in the fallen consciousness.

Do you see that when you tune in to the River of Life, you can see that behind all the turbulence there is an ongoing movement? You can see that there may be all of these organizations, there may be some secret organizations, there may be some conspiracies, there may be all of these things going on right now, but beyond making the calls and holding the vision, you do not need to be worried about this. You need to tune in to the river and flow with the river whereby you reinforce the flow in the collective consciousness. You bring society more quickly to the point where all of these secrets, all of these barriers, will fall away and people will not be able to hide anything anymore.

Therefore, those who want to hide because they have something to hide, will begin to realize that they had better not seek any kind of public office or position because they will not be able to hide. You have already seen – not publicly but if you go to the hidden levels – a certain selection process where there are those who have elected not to run for office because they knew they had done something that would not remain hidden if they had to go through the much more public process that it is today to be elected in many countries. There are also people who have certain psychological issues where they know that they will react with anger when they are challenged and who have elected not to run for office. This means that those who were the dictators of the past have in some cases given up trying to run for a democratic office, and this has then saved a certain society from going into a blind alley of being taken over by someone who has a more dualistic state of consciousness. I am asking you who are our spiritual students to hold that vision and to also in your own minds work on getting to the point where there is nothing you want to hide.

Making an effort and flowing with the river

I will give you a little bit of an insight here that might help you. When you begin to lock in to the river, you can see what the river means for you. The river means growth. The River of Life is not a downward stream—it is an upward accelerating stream. How do you personally have maximum growth? By flowing with the River of Life. It is actually so that there are many of you who are in an in-between state where you have come to see spiritual growth as a process that requires effort on your part. Some of you think that the more effort you exert individually, the more you must be growing.

We have said before that the path has stages. There is a stage on the path where the primary goal for you is to pull yourself away from the mass consciousness, to pull yourself out of whatever downward spirals you may have been in with other people or with groups of people. It is true that you need to pull yourself up and away, and this requires an effort. It requires you to invoke light, it requires you to study, it requires you to work on your psychology. There is a stage where this is perfectly in order, but what I am pointing out is that many of you have come to a point where it is not the amount of effort that is going to pull you further. It is actually that in order to go further, you need to lock in to the ongoing flow that we have called the River of Life or the Holy Spirit.

You need to recognize that the upward path of the Buddha, the Buddhic consciousness, the upward path of all of the beings in the material universe who are growing, is not a path where billions of separate individuals are walking their own path. The goal of the path is to come into unity, and that means that the higher you go on the path, the more you come into unity with the whole, and that means you are flowing with the whole. There comes a point where you realize that it is no longer a matter of the individual effort you are making, it is actually more a matter of surrendering into the flow.

This does not mean that you don't do anything, that you become passive. It means that you shift your attitude to how you are walking the path. It is not so much a matter of effort, of pulling yourself away from something. It is a matter of becoming more aware that there are certain situations where you sense something in yourself. You sense a certain resistance, you sense a certain attachment, you sense a certain pattern, a reaction, a strong reaction. Then, you realize that at the bottom of this is what I have called an attachment, and it is necessary sometimes to invoke energy, to consume the energy that keeps you attached to something. It is necessary to see the attachment, to see the belief, but in the end letting go of the attachment is an act of surrender. An attachment is created by force. You cannot force yourself out of an attachment. You have to stop using force. You have to surrender.

There are some of you who know that there is a phenomenon called quicksand. If you walk into an area with quicksand, you will start sinking, and some of you have even died this way in past lifetimes. What you see is that when people fall into this and start sinking, they start struggling. The more they struggle, the more they sink because it is the disturbance of the quicksand that actually creates the opening whereby your body sinks deeper and deeper. If you could lie perfectly still and relaxed, you would not sink into the quicksand. The problem with quicksand is that even if you were relaxed, you would not get out of it either so while you would not drown, you would eventually starve to death. That is why I am pointing out to you that when you lock in to the River of Life, you are not in quicksand.

Now shift your perception to one of these whirlpools in a river. When you go into such a whirlpool, you are feeling that there is a force sucking you down and you are resisting. You are struggling, you are resisting the force because you think that if you allow yourself to be pulled down, something really bad will happen. Think about what happens in one of these whirlpools, maybe even observe it. You will see that there is a swirling movement that goes down into the water, but it becomes thinner and thinner. The reason is that momentum is dissipated, and at the bottom of one of these swirls in the water there are just bubbles. Below that is calm water that is flowing.

What I submit to you is this: There is a point where you need to exercise a certain activity in order to pull yourself away from these downward momentums you are in. When you are able to lock in to the river, you see that if you are flowing with the river and you suddenly see a whirlpool ahead, you do not need to react with fear. You allow yourself to flow into it, and then, instead of struggling against it, you surrender into it and you actually allow yourself to go into the experience. You know that there will come a point where you have reconnected to the river, and the river will carry you on, away from the experience. I am not saying that all can do this. There is a certain level of the path where you cannot do this. I am not saying that you should go into a negative experience and surrender yourself into it and let yourself be pulled down. There are, of course, many situations on earth that are designed by the fallen beings to pull you down to a point where you get trapped and cannot get out. What I am saying is that there comes a point on the spiritual path where it is not effort, it is not resistance that is going to help you grow—it is surrender into the ongoing flow of the River of Life and the absolute knowledge and the absolute conviction that this will carry you through.

Having the Buddha as part of your path

As long as you maintain your attunement to the river, you can be calm even in the most violent whirlpools of situations you may encounter on earth. Even though you are in the situation and you see everybody else around you panicking and running around like chickens with their heads cut off, you can remain attuned to the Buddha because the Buddha is there. This is what it means, actually, to have the Buddha as part of your path.

You recognize that behind everything that happens on earth, there is the Buddha, the Buddha nature. Everything *is* the Buddha nature. In every situation, the Buddha is there and therefore it is always possible to tune in to the Buddha. The Buddha is not the static Buddha that some of you have come to see based on the statues of me. The Buddha is the flow, the ongoing flow that is behind everything that happens in the material world. When you lock in to that, there is nothing that could possibly happen on earth that can define you. If you know that no experience can define you, why would you resist going into it? Why would you be afraid or hesitant to let the River of Life take you where it takes you? You know that either it takes you to a point where you need to see something for your own learning, or it takes you to a situation where you can be of service to the whole.

Therefore, you do not resist. You are not trying to look ahead and decide where you want the river to go or to take you. You are flowing, you are being in the moment, and you are not worried about what is going to happen tomorrow or ten years down the road. You are flowing with the River of Life now, and you are enjoying it. You are joyful, you are at peace in being in that flow. Whenever something comes up, you do what needs to be done in the outer situation, but you do it with non-attachment because you are still attuned to the flow. You know that whatever the situation is, the flow will take you beyond it. You do not resist the situation, for in doing that you sometimes resist the flow and actually attach yourself to the situation. You allow yourself to surrender, and in that surrender the river can carry you through it much quicker.

My beloved hearts, I have had my say, as we have had our say at this conference. I simply want to again express the gratitude of all of us. Mother Mary especially wants me to convey to you her gratitude for being here and for allowing her to bring forth this visualization that can truly help many people make tremendous progress on the path by getting in tune with the trauma that they received when they first embodied on earth, the trauma that has set the matrix, the pattern, for all of the embodiments that followed.

Once you resolve that central trauma, it is much easier for you to resolve the lesser traumas that were often a result of you trying to avoid ever experiencing that first trauma again. When you stop compensating for that first trauma, many of the others and many of the patterns in your psychology become so much easier to resolve by coming to see it and just surrendering into the flow of the River of Life.

Thus, I seal this conference. I seal you each one in the true Sangha of the Buddha that I AM, wherever you are.

18 | ENVISIONING THE MONEY SYSTEM OF THE GOLDEN AGE

Saint Germain I AM. My greater vision for America and the world is the vision of people from many different backgrounds coming together, transcending those divisions created by their backgrounds, and locking in to the I AM spirit, the spirit of the I AM people, that transcends all outer divisions and therefore forms a bulwark of freedom, a bastion of freedom, against the forces of anti-freedom that would seek to enslave the people.

In so doing, these forces must divide the people, and therefore use the divide-and-conquer tactic, the divide-and-conquer consciousness, to divide the people into all these factions based on outer characteristics. Then, it must make the people believe that they have to be enemies of those who are different from themselves, and that the only way to resolve the conflicts that they see is to go to war and destroy those who are different.

The true vision of Saint Germain and the true vision of the ascended masters is to create unity among the people of this planet. The perversion of that vision by the fallen beings is, of course, to create a forced unity. They try to get people to kill all of those who are different from themselves until there is uniformity by eliminating all differences. This, by the way, would only be possible if in the end there was only one person left on this planet. Truly, even two people trapped in the duality consciousness would soon find a way to create animosity and conflict between them so that one would have to kill the other.

World peace begins with the individual

There is no way to create peace this way, to create unity among people through violence, through division. There is no way, as we have said before, to solve a problem with the same state of consciousness that created the problem. You cannot possibly overcome division while you are still trapped in the very consciousness, that created the division in the first place. The only practical – the only *possible* – solution is to transcend that state of consciousness entirely, to rise to a higher level.

How can people do this, as long as they are identified with the outer divisions on earth? There is only one solution and it is that people realize that they are more than these outer human identities that have been created for them. They are more than these molds that have been created and which they are supposed to fit into from cradle to grave. They are truly the I AM people, and when you recognize this, you can transcend these outer divisions.

This can only happen on an individual basis. There is no way to overcome the divisions except through individuality. It cannot be done collectively, my beloved, and that is why the Lord Christ himself came to this planet 2,000 years ago to inaugurate an age in which humankind was meant to grow in individuality and attain a greater individualism that pulled them out of the tribal consciousness—that is truly the cause of many divisions on this planet.

Real and perverted individualism

It was, of course, foreseeable and inevitable that some among humankind – especially those who had already become trapped in the consciousness of duality before they came to this planet – would pervert this concept of the Christ. They would turn the concept of the individual Christ into the perverted concept of individualism, based on the ego that does not consider anyone but itself. This is simply the "cost of doing business," as they say these days. It was foreseeable that this would happen and that it would create atrocities.

Nevertheless, I ask you to raise your vision and see that even all of the warfare and strife you have seen over these last 2,000 years was a necessary element of raising humankind, not only out of the tribal consciousness but also out of the perverted consciousness of individuality. People need to realize that individuality does not mean that you are an island. As has been said, no man, no woman, is an island. It means that you find your divine individuality as an extension of, as an individualization of, your Creator. When you recognize your oneness with God and say with Christ: "I and my father are one," well then you will quickly take the next step and realize that all of your brothers and sisters also have an I AM Presence, also came out of the God Presence, and therefore they too are part of the Body of God on earth.

While it may seem illogical to some, the reality is that humankind started out in more of a collective consciousness where very few individuals on this planet had a strong enough individuality to raise themselves above that collective consciousness. Humankind had to go through becoming stronger individually before they could engage in the path of individual Christhood. This would lead them to the greater oneness in Spirit that will then form the basis for a greater oneness in the material realm. One that is not based on sameness but is based on the reality that differences, divine differences, sprang from the same source and therefore differences are not the source of conflict.

They are, indeed, individual facets of the diamond mind of God where each of you is a facet on that diamond. When you come together, you can create a much more beautiful shine than when you stand apart, or even when you try to oppose each other and thereby hide your light under a bushel. You cannot engage in conflict with other people unless you first hide your own light unless you deny that light and therefore accept a lower sense of identity, whether you created it yourself or whether you stepped into a role created for you by society or even by the false leaders of humankind. They have used the divide-and-conquer consciousness to create all of these false identities that can only be in opposition to each other.

They have set up a culture of vain competition where those who have attained a stronger individuality, instead of moving on to the path of individual Christhood, are trapped on the outer path, the broad way that leads to destruction. The false path goes through the false individuality, and it must – according to the Law of Free Will – allow people to pursue the building of this false individuality until they finally tire of it. Or they run out of time and thus are no more because they are not willing to see the folly of that false identity. They are not willing to let it die. They are not willing to give up that ghost, even though their false identity has paralyzed them and nailed them to the cross of their own making, as they have misused the four levels of the mind – the etheric, mental, emotional and physical – to create that false identity.

Christ came not only to show the path but to show the only way out of that path, my beloved, which is to let the false identity die. You need to contemplate how you can not only let your personal ego and false identity die, but you can also do it for the collective consciousness, in whatever aspect of the collective consciousness that you have taken on, including the aspects you have worked on so far.

You need to let that false identity die on the cross, to give up that ghost with Jesus and therefore let it go. You can then be free of the false identity, free to be resurrected in Christ, to be resurrected *with* Christ when the cycle is completed and you individually are ready to pass through that initiation of accepting your oneness with your divine identity.

Raising up the Mother in the economy

I will now shift gears and give you a discourse on raising up the Mother, the Mother Light. You realize, I am sure, that anything that takes place in this material realm is part of the Mother. For there to be a Golden Age, we must raise up the expressions of the Mother in all aspects of society. Based on the recent turmoil in the economy, I wish to make a few remarks about the golden age economy and how there must be change compared to the economy you see today.

I will begin my going to the very core of the issue of the economy, which of course is money itself. Money is an expression of the Mother. Money, in its pure form, is a pure expression of the Mother. I know that as spiritual people, you may often have had a somewhat ambivalent, or even negative, attitude towards money, being based on Jesus' statement that you cannot serve God and mammon, or the commonly circulated statement that money is the root of all evil. In its pure form, money is not the root of all evil nor is money actually the mammon that Jesus talked about when he made the remark that you cannot serve two masters. The two masters that you cannot serve are the true master of the Christ and the false master of anti-christ—the false identity of the ego.

Money is – in its pure form – two things: It is a medium of exchange, and it is a way to store value for different times when that value is needed and cannot be produced on a short-term basis. If the money system in the world was still in its pure form as a medium of exchange and a short-term storage of value, well then you would not have the problems that you have in the economy today.

After money was created, a different possibility came into being, namely that money could be more than a medium of exchange and a storage of value. Instead of being a means to an end, some people turned money into an end in itself. They saw that by perverting the money system beyond its original intent and design, they could use money not only to gather privileges for themselves (that they could buy with money that they hoard for themselves), but they could go beyond that and use money to further their never-ending quest for power and control over the people.

Understanding the divine economy

As we have explained, there is indeed a power elite on this planet who want to enslave the people and have the people work for them as worker bees to create privileges. What you are dealing with in the economy is two different states of

18 | Envisioning the money system of the Golden Age

consciousness that are opposing one another. In Jesus' parable about the servants who received different numbers of talents, you see the principle for how the divine economy works. You are given certain talents through your ingenuity and your labor and your willingness to take initiative. You multiply those talents, and then you receive more in return because you have been willing to fulfill your role as a co-creator with God on this planet.

As Jesus also said: "Fear not little flock, for it is your Father's good pleasure to give you the kingdom." It is your Father's good pleasure to give you the abundant life. When all people take what they have been given – whatever talents that may be individually – and they make the best of it, they multiply what they have. Then, they bring forth more abundance than what they were given.

This opens up the doorway to heaven where we can multiply what you have multiplied and bring forth even more abundance whereby the total amount of abundance available on this planet is increased. This opens the possibility that the entire economy can grow whereby all people receive more abundance. This does not happen in the way of the communist dream where supposedly all are given an equal share. It happens because the money system and the economy become another tool for the path of individual Christhood where people are rewarded according to their willingness to multiply their talents. There are three ways you multiply the talents:

- Through your ingenuity of bringing forth new ideas, new inventions, better ways of doing the same old tasks.

- Through your willingness to take risks by taking an initiative by doing something that no one has done before—and therefore you cannot know what the outcome will be.

- By your willingness to put forth the labor that is needed in order to get the economy to run.

These are three legitimate ways to multiply your talents. When you look at history, you will see that the majority of the people on this planet have been willing to multiply their talents in at least one of these ways. The majority, of course, choosing the role of doing the actual labor but yet many other people also being inventors or taking the initiative.

The perverted economy

This is the consciousness of multiplying the talents and thereby increasing the amount of abundance. This is, of course, the Christ consciousness, or aspects of the Christ consciousness. In contrast to this consciousness is the consciousness that springs from the mind of anti-christ, and it is the consciousness of wanting something for nothing. Or as a variant of that, the perversion of wanting to reap the reward of other peoples' labor.

This is the perversion of the father-mother element. Wanting something for nothing is the perversion of the Mother where you seek to reap without sowing. Wanting to reap the reward of other peoples' labor is the perversion of the Father element where you seek to control and suppress others and set yourself up above them because you have created the division of separating man from God. Therefore, all cannot be equal in God, for as I said, only through the connection to the spiritual realm can you have true equality.

When that connection is lost in a civilization, you inevitably open up for the creation of an elite who will then suppress the people and reap the rewards of the labor of the people. This is what you saw in the feudal societies of Europe, with a noble class who had the physical power to suppress the people and make them work for them.

When people are physically suppressed, it is very difficult for them, of course, to fail to notice that they are suppressed. When the feudal societies collapsed, there were those among the elite who realized that this was not the ultimate way to suppress the people. There was a much better way to suppress and control the people, namely in hidden ways so that the people did not realize they were suppressed.

What is real money?

Some among these fallen beings realized that with the growing economy that actually resulted from the collapse of the feudal societies – giving rise to better trade and the Industrial Revolution – the creation of this new medium of money gave them an opportunity to control the people by controlling the money system. They realized that the money system, if they could manage to pervert it, would give them incredible opportunities for suppressing the people and stealing the value of their labor—without the people understanding what was happening. This has now been going on for a long time, and the people still are not realizing how the value of their labor is being stolen through a manipulation of the money system. Without going into a long and overly complex discourse, I will give you the few highlights you need to understand.

What you need to understand is that when money is used correctly as a medium of exchange, then you have only the amount of money that is needed to exchange the total amount of goods and services that are produced by a society. There is, so to speak, a one-on-one relationship between the amount of money and the amount of something that has real, actual value, be it goods or services. Or even, in the case of gold money, that the gold itself has a certain value. You see a direct relationship between money and something that has real value.

When people actually multiply their talents, they can, as a result of that multiplication, accumulate a certain amount of money, which they can then choose, if they will, to store for times when they may not be able to make the money. Even this is legitimate, as long as the money was created as a result of providing a real service to life, be it an invention, taking the initiative, or performing physical labor. There is nothing wrong with then storing that money, although, of course, when it is put to use in investing, then it will help the economy grow. Thus, savings should really only be a temporary thing and should not mean that the money is permanently taken out of circulation. Money is indeed meant to flow and thereby help the entire economy grow.

When there is a direct correspondence between money and something of real value, well, then it is not possible to create money out of nothing, money that has no real value associated with it. This means that even though the money supply can grow, the value of money is not degraded, for you still only have the money needed to buy goods and services. Therefore, you can have a society that has a steadily growing economy and a steady increase in the money supply without having an increase in the prices of goods and services. What is the need of such an increase when you do not have excess money that has no correspondence to real value? You still only have the amount of money needed to exchange goods and services, which means that the value of the money – what you can buy for that money – will remain constant.

When money is disassociated from real value

Perhaps it is even possible that as productivity increases – as new methods for producing goods and services cheaper and with less labor are invented – well, then prices can actually decrease. Or you could say that the value of your labor goes up so that you can buy more for the same amount of labor put in. Thus, everyone experiences an increase in abundance.

This, my beloved, is the divine economy, which we might also call the spiritual economy or even the natural economy. You see in nature that if you take even the theory of evolution, as flawed as it is, it does point out the very fact that nature itself has a built-in force that produces greater and greater abundance of life forms, more complex life forms and greater numbers in different species so that every niche in nature is filled and there is nothing wasted. Nature has a built-in force that leads towards greater abundance for all life.

How do you then get away from this divine economy? Well, you do so very simply by perverting the money system so that you disassociate money from something that has real value. This has been done in various societies – starting in Europe – over time. Why did this happen? Well, if you look at the history of this, you will see that it started with some of the kings in Europe who needed money to wage war with each other. They needed excess money, more money than could be raised through the production of goods and services.

War cannot *produce* something of value. It can only *destroy* something of value. Even though there are those who will say that war leads to economic growth, this is actually a fallacy. War can only lead to a loss through the destruction of something that has real value, including the killing of soldiers who could have otherwise been put to productive work and therefore produce something of value instead of killing each other. What you see is that the very kings that I attempted to work with during my sojourn on the European continent as the Wonderman of Europe – the very kings that rejected me and rejected the idea of the United States of Europe – well, those very kings were the ones who in their greed for money (more money than they could tax from their subjects) set the stage for the emergence of a money system that was perverted.

Even though the kings of the Middle Ages and later had great power, even they had a fear of their own people. Thus, they knew that if they raised taxes in order to finance their wars, well, then the people might actually revolt against them and they might lose their power and privilege. They saw that they needed to find some other way to finance their wars, and they entered into an unholy alliance with the emerging bankers of Europe. They started out as the goldsmiths who stored the excess money that people had legitimately earned. They stored the gold in their vaults, and they started realizing that they could make money out of lending that gold and charging interest. Since it was very rare that all of the people would demand all of their gold at the same time, they started lending out the money that people had deposited in their vaults, even though it was not theirs to lend, and you see the beginning of the banking system.

The kings of Europe were open to the suggestions of the bankers who suggested that instead of having money that was based on gold or silver – thus the money had an inherent, indigenous value – you created a new type of money, called fiat money. This was money by decree where the king issued a law that this newly created money was now the legal tender, the legally approved form of money in society, and all people had to accept it as payment for goods and services. Thereby, the bankers could create this money, lend it to the king who could then use it to buy the goods and services needed to finance his war.

The deception of fractional reserve banking

You see now the beginning of a money system where there is no longer a direct correspondence between the amount of money and the amount of goods and services. There is now a disconnect between the money and something of real value, which means you can now create excess money. You can create money that is not the result of someone multiplying their talents. It is literally created out of nothing by the bankers lending money, charging interest for it, but actually lending more money than they have reserves for in their vaults. This is the emergence of the system called fractional reserve banking, which is what your banking system in the United States and most of the civilized world is based on even today.

You see now the emergence of a money supply that is disconnected from real value, which means that the kings and the bankers can now increase the money supply beyond what is needed to trade goods and services that have real value. What happens when you increase the amount of money? Well, suddenly there is more money in circulation, and what does that mean? It means that the first people who get a hold of the newly issued money, those people who did not have to work for it, they can now spend it.

In so doing, they will inevitably bid up prices of goods and services, including real estate. They increase prices, which gradually filters through the economy until the prices of all goods and services have gone up.

To simplify this process for you, if you have a certain amount of goods and services and you have a certain amount of money needed to trade those goods and services, well, if you doubled the amount of money by creating money that is not backed by precious metals or other things of value, then eventually – in fact in a short period of time – this will result in the prices of most goods and services also doubling. Or at least, they will go up to some degree to adjust to the fact that there is now more money in circulation.

Inflation steals the value of your labor

What has happened in this process? Well, what has happened is that the value of the labor of the majority of the population has now been reduced because you still only work x amount of hours, and you are still paid x amount of whatever the monetary unit is. But you need more money to pay for the goods and services you need in order to survive.

This then leads to a spiral where in the beginning of the Industrial Revolution – when this new money system started becoming the norm – the people who did the actual work, the value of their labor was degraded to the point where they could hardly maintain a living. This necessitated that the workers started organizing into labor unions who then demanded higher wages, which then the employers were forced to pay. In so doing, they created a spiral where, again, those in the power elite simply created more money out of nothing to pay the higher wages. For a time the workers were happy, but as the filter-down effect on prices took place, then again the value of their labor was degraded. This has continued to the present day.

How the people uphold the system of the elite

You might look back at history and see that if you compare what an ordinary laborer is paid today to what a laborer was paid a hundred years ago, you will say the laborer today can buy more goods and services and has a higher standard of living than they had a hundred years ago. This is true, but why is this true?

It is true because part of the money that was created out of nothing has been, so to speak, absorbed into the system through the fact that people have continued to multiply their talents. They have taken initiative, they have brought forth new inventions, better methods for fabrication, and they have become more productive in their work. The average worker today can produce much more than the average worker could a hundred years ago. Those people who are still functioning in the state of consciousness of not wanting something for nothing – but being willing to work to earn a living – well they have, so to speak, underwritten the system of the elite by adding real value to the economy.

This has prevented the inflation created by an increase in the money supply from reaching such proportions that the economy literally would collapse because the money had no value. You have indeed seen this happen in certain circumstances, such as Argentina and Germany, where you needed a wheelbarrow full of paper bills in order to buy a loaf of bread because the money was worth next to nothing. In fact, there have been periods where the money itself literally was not worth the paper it was printed on. It was cheaper for people to light the fire with money than to use the money to buy firewood.

Inflation is a hidden form of taxation

The money system – the fiat money system based on fractional reserve banking, based on creating money out of debt – has a built-in inflationary factor that inevitably will cause the system to collapse. Those who are in charge of such a money system cannot contain their greed. The king will want more money, the bankers will want to make a greater profit, and why not when all they need to do is roll the printing presses and print more money? They inevitably become blinded by that greed, and they set the economy into an inflationary spiral that will destroy the economy—if it is not balanced by the real people performing real labor, creating real goods and services. Therefore, they increase the amount of services so quickly that the money supply, the money system, does not collapse, does not go into the tailspin of an inflationary cycle that cannot be stopped.

Even though you can say that the average worker, the average citizen, is better off today, this is true—but this is only true because they have been willing to multiply their talents. What I want you to understand here is that through the money system, the people have not reaped the natural God-given reward of the multiplication of their talents. Through the increase of the money supply and inflation, they have, in fact been taxed. Inflation is indeed a hidden form of tax where the people do not realize they are taxed. They do not see on their tax bill or their paycheck that x amount of dollars have been taken out of their paycheck. What they do not see is that the value of the money, and thereby the value of their labor, has been reduced.

Concentrating wealth in the hands of the elite

If there had been a divine economy over this last century and more, then the standard of living that you see today would have been even higher. If that economy had been truly divine, then you would see a state where there would not be any poverty left for any people in the Western civilized nations. Indeed, you would also have seen a worldwide economy where the standard of living would have gone up tremendously in what you today consider the poor nations—where, indeed, so many people must exist on less than two dollars a day. This would not have taken place in a divine economy because the value of the abundance would have increased so greatly that there would have been enough to pull everybody up to a decent standard of living.

What you see here is that the power elite – through the perversion of the money system, and through eroding the value of the fiat money that they have created – have managed to actually delay the God-ordained growth in the economy and the manifestation of the abundant life that should have come about by now—if it had not been for this intervention of the power elite. What has happened instead is, as I explained, that the first people who can spend the newly created money – the money that has no correspondence to real value – they can, of course, buy goods and services with that money at (close to) the old prices. Only as the new money circulates through the economy, will prices go up.

Over the past century and more, you have seen a greater and greater concentration of wealth under the control of a smaller and smaller elite. You now, literally, have five to ten percent of the population in the United States who control the majority of the wealth in this nation. Even the top two percent control the majority of that wealth. This, of course, is not the divine economy where there is abundance for all.

How today's "kings" finance their wars

You need, as the spiritual people, to educate yourself to how this works, and we will indeed provide more instruction on this. I encourage you to come to understand this by studying at least the basics of how the money system currently works. You will see that this is an absolute perversion of the abundant life of God. This is nothing more than the power elite – those who are trapped in the duality consciousness – seeking to control the people through the money supply. You will know that one of the original bankers that created this system said that if you allowed him to control a nation's money, he did not care who made the nation's laws, for he knew that the nation could be controlled through the money system.

You need to see that – even in today's world – this is still going on. In the United States, for example, you have the unholy alliance between the federal government – which is at least a federal agency – and the Federal Reserve, which (as most of *you* know but which most Americans do not know) is not a federal agency. Therefore, it is not answerable to the people in a direct manner by the people being able to vote. What is happening here is that the government of today also faces the situation that they want to spend more money than they know the people are willing to pay in taxes. Where to do they get the money? They create it, or they let the bankers create it out of nothing, thereby eroding the entire value of the money

18 | Envisioning the money system of the Golden Age

supply—and thus taxing the people without the people being aware of this.

Take a modern example of this, and imagine that President Bush in 2003 had said to the American people in his State of the Union Address: "I have decided to go to war against Saddam Hussein, and my people tell me that this will cost each American family 2,000 dollars over the next year, so expect to see an increase in your tax bill." Well, my beloved, do you think the American people would have been very positive towards such an announcement? Many of them, surely, would have revolted against this—a war that they from the beginning were not really sure was necessary and would rather have avoided. What did the president do? Well, he simply set the money machine in motion and the Federal Reserve created the money out of nothing, lending it to the federal government so that they could spend it to buy the goods and services that were needed to start the military invasion in Iraq.

The magical money machine

This is not only done for war. It is done for many other aspects of the economy where the government wants to spend more than they think the people are willing to pay in taxes. They simply camouflage it as inflation so that the people pay it anyway but now they do not notice and thus they do not object.

Of course, the bankers and those in the top financial elite, they make the money off of it. You, the people, not only have the degradation of the value of the money but you also pay the interest of the federal debt. Or perhaps you do not pay it, but your children or grandchildren might end up paying it—unless, of course, they continue the scheme indefinitely. The bankers are not necessarily concerned about having you pay back the debt—as long as you keep paying the interest and allowing them to create more money out of nothing so that they can keep their money machine rolling.

You do need to educate yourself to the connection between war and money. Even though I said that the kings were open to creating fiat money to finance their wars, you should not be so blind that you do not see that the bankers quickly realized that there was no better way to earn a profit than to set nations against each other in Europe so that they went to war. Once two nations are committed to war, well, is it not so that suddenly they feel a need to spend whatever money is needed to defeat their enemy? They spend more money than they ever would have done in peacetime.

Who makes the money off of it? Well, certainly the bankers, who in many cases in Europe financed both sides of the conflict and also opened the weapons plants that produced the weapons used in the conflict. They made a profit all around, while the people paid not only with their blood in the war but also with their sweat and blood as they worked to produce the real value that was needed to keep the system going.

The modern form of slavery through money

This is a form of slavery that is far beyond the physical slavery that you have seen with the native peoples of this continent being sold into slavery, or people from Africa being imported into slavery. Again, this was a physical slavery that the people were surely aware of. The slavery that you are under is a slavery that most people do not understand. They cannot object to it because they do not even know. They just notice that they have to work harder and harder, and they do not understand why this is so. They do not muster the will to be more and to educate themselves as to why they have to work harder, as to why it seems their dollar is not stretching as far as it used to.

You have the situation that everything that happens in the material realm is an outpicturing in matter of the consciousness of the people. The people themselves – by not being willing to take responsibility for their society, for their money system – well, they draw unto them those who are willing to pervert the system and take advantage of the people. This becomes a vicious circle that only has two potential outcomes. Either the people wake up, educate themselves, and demand the return to a divine economy with a sound money system. Or the power elite will inevitably keep increasing the money supply in their greed and their blindness and even their spiritual pride where they think they will never have to suffer the consequences of their actions. They are so used to the people bearing the karma and the consequences of their actions that they think they can get away with anything.

You cannot expect the power elite to stop this downward spiral. If the people do not put on the brakes, then it is just a matter of time before the money machine will run amok. You see this with a train that runs faster and faster and faster until the wheels start coming off and everything flies apart and the whole system collapses. Then, you will be faced with the necessity to return to a sound money system.

A golden age economy

This will create immense suffering and pain, and thus it would be far preferable to me that you would see an awakening among the people. They would realize that when you have a sound money system – where money is tied to real value – you have the foundation for a golden age economy. In the Golden Age, you will see a steady growth in the amount of abundance available, a steady growth in opportunity. People can see that when they put forth the effort, when they are willing to work harder, they get a return, a multiplication of their return. Instead of simply going into the consciousness that we will go to work for eight hours and be happy with the money we get – or at least get by with the money we get – people see that if they are willing to work harder, they can reap a much greater return.

They are willing to put in the effort, which then creates even more abundance. You see now a positive spiral where the people are reaping the rewards of their own labor, and therefore they are willing to work even more. Not necessarily that they work harder but that they work smarter and therefore produce even more value. Everything then becomes an upward spiral.

Surely, you do not envision, do you, that in the Golden Age – the Golden Age of Saint Germain – you would still have billions of people living at the starvation level or living at the poverty level? Surely, the vision that I hold for the Golden Age is a vision where no one is poor, no one is lacking for food, no one is lacking for a decent standard of living. No one is lacking for the free time to pursue the spiritual aspects of life according to their own choosing.

Those who do not want to accumulate greater material wealth can still make a living with a relatively small investment in time, and therefore can focus most of their attention, energy, and time, on spiritual pursuits that will raise the consciousness. As you raise the consciousness, you open the door for the bringing forth of new inventions, new methods of fabrication, new forms of energy, that will allow you again to increase the amount of abundance so that the economy can grow even further. There literally is no end to the growth in the economy in a golden age society. Again, the concept of limits to growth is put upon you by the fallen beings who want you – the people – to accept limits for *your* growth, while they, of course, have no intention whatsoever of limiting their own accumulation of wealth, power, and privilege. They have to find a way to get the people to be satisfied with less so that they can have more.

In the Golden Age, the people are not satisfied with less, for they realize that it is the Father's good pleasure to give them more. It is thereby their divine birthright to reap the reward of their initiative, their labor. They want that "more" because why not? It is part of bringing forth the Kingdom of God on earth.

Poverty is a perversion of Father and Mother

I desire you to tune in (in your hearts) to the reality that money is not evil, but that money in its pure form is simply an expression of the Mother. If you did not have money, the economy could not grow beyond a certain level, for it is impossible with a barter economy where you have to exchange one item for another or for a particular service without having the convenience of the medium of exchange that money provides. Money is an expression of the Mother and the Mother flame. Again, if the Mother is disconnected from the Father, then the Mother becomes an end in itself. Money becomes an end in itself—rather than a means to the end of keeping the divine economy going, bringing forth greater abundance.

When you have the perversion of the Mother, you see that instead of an upward spiral of increasing the amount of abundance, you have a situation where you limit the growth so that there is either little growth or no growth. You now have a concentration of wealth in the hands of a small group of people who actually do not want to increase the amount of abundance. They want to concentrate it in their own hands.

They do not care that the total amount of abundance is not increased for they do not care that the people live in poverty. In fact, they almost prefer it because then they seem richer in comparison—when the people are poorer.

Surely, you can see today that the feudal lords of medieval Europe – living in their cold stone castles, their drafty castles – were not living with a very high standard of living compared to what even the average person has today. Nevertheless, their standard of living seemed very high in comparison to the majority of the people who lived in very poor conditions.

The members of the power elite are trapped in the duality consciousness, which is relative and therefore compares everything based on a relative value judgment, based on a judgment of appearances. They are raising themselves in comparison to others, not by actually increasing, not by multiplying, their talents and increasing the amount of wealth. They do it by keeping others down, by limiting the value of their labor, thereby limiting the total amount of wealth. This is the total perversion of both the Divine Father and the Divine Mother where the Divine Father provides the increase in the total amount of abundance. The justice of the Divine Mother distributes that among all people so that all can have a decent standard of living and pursue their Divine plans as they see fit individually.

Money and the displacement of native peoples

Keep this in mind, for you will see (if you connect it to what you have talked about with the forced displacement of the native peoples) that what was really behind this was the greed for money, the greed for value by removing the native peoples from their lands. The white people could start farming that land in more efficient ways so that they would then increase

18 | Envisioning the money system of the Golden Age

the amount of abundance produced on the same acreage of land.

Even then, the people would not reap the full reward of their labor, for it was to some degree concentrated in the hands of an elite—those who controlled the trade, those who controlled the government. Do you see that it was not the little people, so to speak, who wanted the Indians forcefully moved off their land? It was the elite of the time who wanted to make more money off of the land, and therefore wanted white farmers to farm the land and produce more than the native peoples were willing or able to produce on the same amount of land. They could then reap the rewards of the farmers' labor and concentrate the money in their own hands.

Behind this mentality of: "Well, let us just take these indigenous people and move them out West where they are out of the way," was the power elite and their insensitivity to life and the consciousness of wanting to reap the fruit of other people's labor. This all ties together with the perversion of the Mother, the unbalanced use of the Mother, where the money becomes the means to control the people. It therefore allows those who are the controllers in the elite (allows their greed) to run amok and become a never-ending quest for more and more in the material realm. Rather than using the abundance in the material realm as a platform for spiritual pursuits that then raises the consciousness of the people and brings forth the Kingdom of God.

The elite does not want the Kingdom of God—for in the Kingdom of God they cannot be the elite. In fact, they cannot even remain on this planet so they want to stop the Kingdom of God. They do this by perverting every aspect of society where the people are not awake, are not aware, are not taking responsibility for educating themselves and making their own decisions. Instead, people want the elite to make decisions for them. It is the absolute requirement for a Golden Age to manifest that the people wake up realize how every aspect of society has been perverted by the consciousness of anti-christ, the dualistic consciousness, and decide that they will no longer be pawns in this game. They will no longer be the slaves, they will no longer be the worker bees for the elite.

They will take back their birthright to be the people of God—those who do not identify themselves based on the divisions created by the elite, but those who identify themselves based on the I AM consciousness. Thus, they become the I AM people who are the foundation for the true America, which is not limited to this particular nation but is a universal principle, a universal idea, that can spread to every nation on earth. When it does, you will see the Golden Age of Saint Germain manifest.

Decide that you want the Golden Age to be manifest

Surely, my beloved, you do not for a moment believe – do you – that I, Saint Germain, sponsored America so that America could be the only country that had the Golden Age? I sponsored America as a platform, as a springboard, for bringing forth the universal ideas of the Golden Age that could then spread to all other nations. In this way all nations and all people could have the benefits of the Golden Age that I sponsored—not just for this continent and this nation, but for the entire planet. I do not limit myself to one nation. I am the sponsor of all people for the Golden Age in the Age of Aquarius.

Thus, I say to all people everywhere: "Wake up and claim your birthright!" I, Saint Germain, am indeed ready to give you the Golden Age. As the father of the Golden Age, it is my good pleasure to give you my kingdom. Claim it, accept it, bring it into manifestation! Prove me herewith, sayeth the Lord, and I shall pour you out a blessing that there shall not be room enough to receive it. Not only shall there not be physical room, but even your minds can scarcely conceive of the wonders that I am ready to release—when there are people who are ready to put them to use for the benefit of all, rather than the misuse of concentrating wealth in the hands of the elite.

Thus, I say to you, I, Saint Germain, am ready to manifest my Golden Age on this planet. Are you ready to accept it? Then be it so, and then envision that all other people also will wake up and be ready to accept it and realize that there is a better way, there is a Golden Age waiting to be brought into manifestation. They need only play their part and multiply the talents that I am ready to give you, many of which I have already given you by sponsoring technology, science and invention.

I thank you for providing me a platform, for doing the spiritual work, that allowed me to release a greater concentration of light than I could have done, had you not been willing to raise up a chalice so that I have something to multiply. You recognize, my beloved, that we of the ascended masters can multiply, but we must have something to multiply. You must provide it so that we can do our part and provide the increase. In gratitude, I seal you in the heart of Saint Germain. I seal you in the Freedom Flame that I AM.

19 | INVOKING THE MONEY SYSTEM OF THE GOLDEN AGE

In the name I AM THAT I AM, Jesus Christ, I call to all ascended masters working on manifesting the Golden Age, especially the seven archangels and Saint Germain to radiate into the collective consciousness the matrix for the golden age economy. Help people see that we can build a new future by working with the ascended masters and letting go of the old way of looking at life, including…

[Make personal calls.]

Part 1

1. Saint Germain, radiate into the collective consciousness the awareness that money, in its pure form, is a pure expression of the Mother. Money is not the root of all evil.

Michael Archangel, in your flame so blue,
there is no more night, there is only you.
In oneness with you, we're filled with your light,
what glorious wonder, revealed to our sight.

Michael Archangel, your Knowing so strong,
Michael Archangel, oh sweep us along.
Michael Archangel, we're singing your song,
Michael Archangel, with you we belong.

2. Saint Germain, radiate into the collective consciousness the awareness that in its pure form money is a medium of exchange and a short-term storage of value.

Michael Archangel, protection you give,
within your blue shield, we ever shall live.
Sealed from all creatures, roaming the night,
we remain in your sphere, of electric blue light.

Michael Archangel, your Knowing so strong,
Michael Archangel, oh sweep us along.
Michael Archangel, we're singing your song,
Michael Archangel, with you we belong.

3. Saint Germain, radiate into the collective consciousness the awareness that after money was created, the fallen beings turned money into an end in itself.

Michael Archangel, what power you bring,
as millions of angels, praises will sing.
Consuming the demons, of doubt and of fear,
we know that your Presence, will always be near.

**Michael Archangel, your Knowing so strong,
Michael Archangel, oh sweep us along.
Michael Archangel, we're singing your song,
Michael Archangel, with you we belong.**

4. Saint Germain, radiate into the collective consciousness the awareness that the fallen beings saw that by perverting the money system, they could use money to gather privileges for themselves and to gain control over the people.

Michael Archangel, God's will is your love,
you bring to us all, God's light from Above.
God's will is to see, all life taking flight,
transcendence of self, our most sacred right.

**Michael Archangel, your Knowing so strong,
Michael Archangel, oh sweep us along.
Michael Archangel, we're singing your song,
Michael Archangel, with you we belong.**

5. Saint Germain, radiate into the collective consciousness the awareness that when all people take what they have been given and make the best of it, the ascended masters can bring forth even more abundance whereby the total amount of abundance is increased.

Michael Archangel, you are the best friend,
from all worldly dangers you do us defend,
the devil no match for your power of light,
and therefore our souls can freely take flight.

> **Michael Archangel, your Knowing so strong,**
> **Michael Archangel, oh sweep us along.**
> **Michael Archangel, we're singing your song,**
> **Michael Archangel, with you we belong.**

6. Saint Germain, radiate into the collective consciousness the awareness that the consciousness that springs from the mind of anti-christ is the consciousness of wanting something for nothing or wanting to reap the reward of other peoples' labor.

> Michael Archangel, as children we play,
> we're bringing the earth into a new day,
> we raise it from all of the patterns so old,
> our planet's life story is by us retold.

> **Michael Archangel, your Knowing so strong,**
> **Michael Archangel, oh sweep us along.**
> **Michael Archangel, we're singing your song,**
> **Michael Archangel, with you we belong.**

7. Saint Germain, radiate into the collective consciousness the awareness that the fallen ones have set themselves up as being above the people because they have created the division of separating man from God.

> Michael Archangel, God's power you show,
> that you are invincible, this we do know,
> you are undivided and thus can withstand,
> anything coming from serpentine band.

**Michael Archangel, your Knowing so strong,
Michael Archangel, oh sweep us along.
Michael Archangel, we're singing your song,
Michael Archangel, with you we belong.**

8. Saint Germain, radiate into the collective consciousness the awareness that only through the connection to the spiritual realm can we have true equality. When this connection is lost, an elite will suppress the people and reap the rewards of their labor.

Michael Archangel, come raise now the earth,
giving her thus a complete rebirth,
collective the mind that we do now raise,
for this we do give our infinite praise.

**Michael Archangel, your Knowing so strong,
Michael Archangel, oh sweep us along.
Michael Archangel, we're singing your song,
Michael Archangel, with you we belong.**

9. Saint Germain, radiate into the collective consciousness the awareness that when people are suppressed physically, they know they are suppressed. The fallen beings know it is better to suppress people in hidden ways so that the people do not realize they are suppressed.

Michael Archangel, the earth is now new,
covered in Blue-flame as the morning dew,
our planet now sparkles throughout all of space,
as we are receiving your infinite Grace.

**Michael Archangel, your Knowing so strong,
Michael Archangel, oh sweep us along.
Michael Archangel, we're singing your song,
Michael Archangel, with you we belong.**

Part 2

1. Saint Germain, radiate into the collective consciousness the awareness that some fallen beings realized that the creation of this new medium of money gave them an opportunity to control the people by controlling the money system.

Jophiel Archangel, in wisdom's great light,
all serpentine lies exposed to our sight.
So subtle the lies that creep through the mind,
yet you are the greatest teacher we find.

**Jophiel Archangel, exposing all lies,
Jophiel Archangel, cutting all ties.
Jophiel Archangel, clearing the skies,
Jophiel Archangel, the mind truly flies.**

2. Saint Germain, radiate into the collective consciousness the awareness that the fallen beings realized that if they could pervert the money system, they could suppress the people and steal the value of their labor—without the people understanding what was happening.

Jophiel Archangel, your wisdom we hail,
your sword cutting through duality's veil.
As you show the way, we know what is real,
from serpentine doubt, we instantly heal.

Jophiel Archangel, exposing all lies,
Jophiel Archangel, cutting all ties.
Jophiel Archangel, clearing the skies,
Jophiel Archangel, the mind truly flies.

3. Saint Germain, radiate into the collective consciousness the awareness that when money is used correctly as a medium of exchange, then we only have the amount of money needed to exchange the goods and services produced by society.

Jophiel Archangel, your reality,
the best antidote to duality.
No lie can remain in your Presence so clear,
with you on our side, no serpent we fear.

Jophiel Archangel, exposing all lies,
Jophiel Archangel, cutting all ties.
Jophiel Archangel, clearing the skies,
Jophiel Archangel, the mind truly flies.

4. Saint Germain, radiate into the collective consciousness the awareness that when there is a direct correspondence between money and something of real value, then it is not possible to create money out of nothing, money that has no real value associated with it.

Jophiel Archangel, God's mind in in me,
and through your clear light, its wisdom we see.
Divisions all vanish, as we see the One,
and truly, the wholeness of mind we have won.

Jophiel Archangel, exposing all lies,
Jophiel Archangel, cutting all ties.
Jophiel Archangel, clearing the skies,
Jophiel Archangel, the mind truly flies.

5. Saint Germain, radiate into the collective consciousness the awareness that even though the money supply can grow, the value of money is not degraded, for we still only have the money needed to exchange goods and services.

Jophiel Archangel, now show us the way,
that leads us beyond duality's fray,
we long to discern the truth and the lie,
so we the serpentine knots can untie.

Jophiel Archangel, exposing all lies,
Jophiel Archangel, cutting all ties.
Jophiel Archangel, clearing the skies,
Jophiel Archangel, the mind truly flies.

6. Saint Germain, radiate into the collective consciousness the awareness that we can have a society that has a steadily growing economy and a steady increase in the money supply without having an increase in the prices of goods and services.

19 | Invoking the money system of the Golden Age

> Jophiel Archangel, your Presence is here,
> and therefore our minds are perfectly clear,
> in wisdom's great fount we do take a bath,
> and now we withstand the devil's own wrath.
>
> **Jophiel Archangel, exposing all lies,**
> **Jophiel Archangel, cutting all ties.**
> **Jophiel Archangel, clearing the skies,**
> **Jophiel Archangel, the mind truly flies.**

7. Saint Germain, radiate into the collective consciousness the awareness that as productivity increases, prices can decrease. The value of our labor goes up so that we can buy more for the same amount of labor put in. Everyone experiences an increase in abundance.

> Jophiel Archangel, it is your great task,
> to raise all mankind, if only we ask,
> so now on behalf of those who are blind,
> we ask for your help in wisdom to find.
>
> **Jophiel Archangel, exposing all lies,**
> **Jophiel Archangel, cutting all ties.**
> **Jophiel Archangel, clearing the skies,**
> **Jophiel Archangel, the mind truly flies.**

8. Saint Germain, radiate into the collective consciousness the awareness that this is the natural economy because nature has a built-in force that leads towards greater abundance for all life.

Jophiel Archangel, your Presence we hail,
your Light cutting through the serpentine veil,
the serpents can no longer people deceive,
for all now your Flame of Wisdom receive.

Jophiel Archangel, exposing all lies,
Jophiel Archangel, cutting all ties.
Jophiel Archangel, clearing the skies,
Jophiel Archangel, the mind truly flies.

9. Saint Germain, radiate into the collective consciousness the awareness that the fallen beings took us away from the natural economy by perverting the money system so that they disassociated money from something that has real value.

Jophiel Archangel, where else can we go,
when we long the highest wisdom to know?
You share with us gladly all that you are,
and now our vision goes ever so far.

Jophiel Archangel, exposing all lies,
Jophiel Archangel, cutting all ties.
Jophiel Archangel, clearing the skies,
Jophiel Archangel, the mind truly flies.

Part 3

1. Saint Germain, radiate into the collective consciousness the awareness that this started because the kings in Europe needed money to wage war with each other. They needed excess money, more money than could be raised through the production of goods and services.

> Chamuel Archangel, in ruby ray power,
> we know we are taking a life-giving shower.
> Love burning away all perversions of will,
> we suddenly feel our desires falling still.
>
> **Chamuel Archangel, descend from Above,**
> **Chamuel Archangel, with ruby-pink love,**
> **Chamuel Archangel, so often thought-of,**
> **Chamuel Archangel, o come Holy Dove.**

2. Saint Germain, radiate into the collective consciousness the awareness that war cannot produce something of value. It can only destroy something of value.

> Chamuel Archangel, a spiral of light,
> as ruby ray fire now pierces the night.
> All forces of darkness consumed by your fire,
> consuming all those who will not rise higher.
>
> **Chamuel Archangel, descend from Above,**
> **Chamuel Archangel, with ruby-pink love,**
> **Chamuel Archangel, so often thought-of,**
> **Chamuel Archangel, o come Holy Dove.**

3. Saint Germain, radiate into the collective consciousness the awareness that the kings of Europe were the ones who, in their greed for more money than they could tax from their subjects, set the stage for the emergence of a perverted money system.

> Chamuel Archangel, your love so immense,
> with clarified vision, our lives now make sense.
> The purpose of life you so clearly reveal,
> immersed in your love, God's oneness we feel.
>
> **Chamuel Archangel, descend from Above,**
> **Chamuel Archangel, with ruby-pink love,**
> **Chamuel Archangel, so often thought-of,**
> **Chamuel Archangel, o come Holy Dove.**

4. Saint Germain, radiate into the collective consciousness the awareness that the kings knew that if they raised taxes in order to finance their wars, the people might revolt against them. They needed to find some other way to finance their wars, and they entered into an unholy alliance with the emerging bankers of Europe.

> Chamuel Archangel, what calmness you bring,
> we see now that even death has no sting.
> For truly, in love there can be no decay,
> as love is transcendence into a new day.
>
> **Chamuel Archangel, descend from Above,**
> **Chamuel Archangel, with ruby-pink love,**
> **Chamuel Archangel, so often thought-of,**
> **Chamuel Archangel, o come Holy Dove.**

5. Saint Germain, radiate into the collective consciousness the awareness that these bankers had realized that they could make money out of lending gold and charging interest. Yet their profits were limited by the amount of gold available.

Chamuel Archangel, God't Love Flame bestow,
on all those longing God's true love to know,
conditions we know can never be real,
and this is the love you always reveal.

**Chamuel Archangel, descend from Above,
Chamuel Archangel, with ruby-pink love,
Chamuel Archangel, so often thought-of,
Chamuel Archangel, o come Holy Dove.**

6. Saint Germain, radiate into the collective consciousness the awareness that the kings of Europe were open to the suggestions of the bankers that instead of having money that was based on gold or silver, you create fiat money.

Chamuel Archangel, love's seed you have sown,
in hearts of all those who don't seek to own,
for love that possesses is nothing but fear,
that pierces the heart with duality's spear.

**Chamuel Archangel, descend from Above,
Chamuel Archangel, with ruby-pink love,
Chamuel Archangel, so often thought-of,
Chamuel Archangel, o come Holy Dove.**

7. Saint Germain, radiate into the collective consciousness the awareness that fiat money is created by decree where the king issued a law that this newly created money was now the legal tender and all people had to accept it as payment for goods and services.

> Chamuel Archangel, we don't want control,
> for this is the devil's hold on the soul,
> your love will now break the serpentine chain,
> so we are set free God's love to reclaim.

> **Chamuel Archangel, descend from Above,**
> **Chamuel Archangel, with ruby-pink love,**
> **Chamuel Archangel, so often thought-of,**
> **Chamuel Archangel, o come Holy Dove.**

8. Saint Germain, radiate into the collective consciousness the awareness that this allowed the bankers to create this money, lend it to the king who could then use it to buy the goods and services to finance his war.

> Chamuel Archangel, you are so adept,
> at helping us God's true love to accept,
> we know that the love for which we so yearn,
> is not something we on earth have to earn.

> **Chamuel Archangel, descend from Above,**
> **Chamuel Archangel, with ruby-pink love,**
> **Chamuel Archangel, so often thought-of,**
> **Chamuel Archangel, o come Holy Dove.**

9. Saint Germain, radiate into the collective consciousness the awareness that there is now a disconnect between the money and something of real value, which means you can now create excess money. You can create money that is not the result of someone multiplying their talents.

> Chamuel Archangel, for love to accept,
> we do not need to be so perfect,
> for love is not static but always a flow,
> demanding only we're willing to grow.
>
> **Chamuel Archangel, descend from Above,**
> **Chamuel Archangel, with ruby-pink love,**
> **Chamuel Archangel, so often thought-of,**
> **Chamuel Archangel, o come Holy Dove.**

Part 4

1. Saint Germain, radiate into the collective consciousness the awareness that money is now created out of nothing by the bankers lending money, charging interest for it, but actually lending more money than they have reserves for in their vaults.

> Gabriel Archangel, your light we revere,
> immersed in your Presence, nothing we fear.
> Disciples of Christ, we do leave behind,
> the ego's desire for responding in kind.

> **Gabriel Archangel, of this we are sure,**
> **Gabriel Archangel, Christ light is the cure.**
> **Gabriel Archangel, intentions so pure,**
> **Gabriel Archangel, in you we're secure.**

2. Saint Germain, radiate into the collective consciousness the awareness that the money system in most parts of the world is based on fractional reserve banking.

> Gabriel Archangel, we fear not the light,
> in purifications' fire, we delight.
> With your hand in ours, each challenge we face,
> we follow the spiral to infinite grace.

> **Gabriel Archangel, of this we are sure,**
> **Gabriel Archangel, Christ light is the cure.**
> **Gabriel Archangel, intentions so pure,**
> **Gabriel Archangel, in you we're secure.**

3. Saint Germain, radiate into the collective consciousness the awareness that when you increase the money supply beyond what is needed to trade goods and services, there is now more money in circulation. The first people who get a hold of the newly issued money, those people who did not have to work for it, they can now spend it.

> Gabriel Archangel, your fire burning white,
> ascending with you, out of the night.
> The ego has nowhere to run and to hide,
> in ascension's bright spiral, with you we abide.

19 | Invoking the money system of the Golden Age

**Gabriel Archangel, of this we are sure,
Gabriel Archangel, Christ light is the cure.
Gabriel Archangel, intentions so pure,
Gabriel Archangel, in you we're secure.**

4. Saint Germain, radiate into the collective consciousness the awareness that in spending money created out of nothing, people inevitably bid up prices of goods and services, including real estate. They increase prices, which gradually filters through the economy until the prices of all goods and services have gone up.

Gabriel Archangel, your trumpet we hear,
announcing the birth of Christ drawing near.
In lightness of being, we now are reborn,
rising with Christ on bright Easter morn.

**Gabriel Archangel, of this we are sure,
Gabriel Archangel, Christ light is the cure.
Gabriel Archangel, intentions so pure,
Gabriel Archangel, in you we're secure.**

5. Saint Germain, radiate into the collective consciousness the awareness that if we doubled the amount of money by creating money that is not backed by real value, then eventually the prices of most goods and services would also double.

Gabriel Archangel, the earth is now free,
embracing a nondual reality,
the judgment of Christ upon forces so dark,
who deny that all have a spiritual spark.

> **Gabriel Archangel, of this we are sure,**
> **Gabriel Archangel, Christ light is the cure.**
> **Gabriel Archangel, intentions so pure,**
> **Gabriel Archangel, in you we're secure.**

6. Saint Germain, radiate into the collective consciousness the awareness that in this process, the value of the labor of the majority of the population has been reduced because people still only work so many hours and are paid so much money, but they need more money to pay for goods and services.

> Gabriel Archangel, with angels so white,
> raising our planet out of the dark night,
> as we now intone the Word of the Lord,
> the beings who fell are bound by your sword.

> **Gabriel Archangel, of this we are sure,**
> **Gabriel Archangel, Christ light is the cure.**
> **Gabriel Archangel, intentions so pure,**
> **Gabriel Archangel, in you we're secure.**

7. Saint Germain, radiate into the collective consciousness the awareness that this led to a spiral where the people who did the actual work had the value of their labor degraded to the point where they could hardly make a living.

> Gabriel Archangel, we call now to you,
> the astral plane your light burning through,
> entities, demons, discarnates are bound,
> as you and we intone Sacred Sound.

> **Gabriel Archangel, of this we are sure,**
> **Gabriel Archangel, Christ light is the cure.**
> **Gabriel Archangel, intentions so pure,**
> **Gabriel Archangel, in you we're secure.**

8. Saint Germain, radiate into the collective consciousness the awareness that this caused workers to organize and demand higher wages, but those in the power elite simply created more money out of nothing to pay the higher wages. This spiral has continued to the present day.

> Gabriel Archangel, what glorious day,
> your radiant angels have come here to stay,
> your purifications fire burning white,
> intentions so pure, our hearts taking flight.

> **Gabriel Archangel, of this we are sure,**
> **Gabriel Archangel, Christ light is the cure.**
> **Gabriel Archangel, intentions so pure,**
> **Gabriel Archangel, in you we're secure.**

9. Saint Germain, radiate into the collective consciousness the awareness that people have a higher standard of living today because part of the money that was created out of nothing has been absorbed into the system by people continuing to increase productivity.

> Gabriel Archangel, our planet so pure,
> in our bright new future we do feel secure,
> with your band of light encircling the earth,
> Saint Germain's Golden Age is now given birth.

> Gabriel Archangel, of this we are sure,
> Gabriel Archangel, Christ light is the cure.
> Gabriel Archangel, intentions so pure,
> Gabriel Archangel, in you we're secure.

Part 5

1. Saint Germain, radiate into the collective consciousness the awareness that those people who are still willing to work to earn a living have underwritten the system of the elite by adding real value to the economy.

> Raphael Archangel, your light so intense,
> raise us beyond all human pretense.
> Mother Mary and you have a vision so bold,
> to see that our highest potential unfold.
>
> **Raphael Archangel, for vision we pray,**
> **Raphael Archangel, show us the way,**
> **Raphael Archangel, your emerald ray,**
> **Raphael Archangel, our lives a new day.**

2. Saint Germain, radiate into the collective consciousness the awareness that this has prevented the inflation created by an increase in the money supply from reaching such proportions that the economy would collapse because the money had no value.

> Raphael Archangel, in emerald sphere,
> to immaculate vision we always adhere.
> Mother Mary enfolds us in her Sacred Heart,
> from Mother's true love, we're never apart.
>
> **Raphael Archangel, for vision we pray,**
> **Raphael Archangel, show us the way,**
> **Raphael Archangel, your emerald ray,**
> **Raphael Archangel, our lives a new day.**

3. Saint Germain, radiate into the collective consciousness the awareness that the fiat money system based on fractional reserve banking, based on creating money out of debt, has a built-in inflationary factor that inevitably will cause the system to collapse.

> Raphael Archangel, all ailments you heal,
> each cell in our bodies in light now you seal.
> Mother Mary's immaculate concept we see,
> perfection of health our new reality.
>
> **Raphael Archangel, for vision we pray,**
> **Raphael Archangel, show us the way,**
> **Raphael Archangel, your emerald ray,**
> **Raphael Archangel, our lives a new day.**

4. Saint Germain, radiate into the collective consciousness the awareness that those who are in charge of such a money system cannot contain their greed. The king will want more money, the bankers will want to make a greater profit, and all they need to do is roll the printing presses and print more money.

Raphael Archangel, your light is so real,
the vision of Christ in us you reveal.
Mother Mary now helps us to truly transcend,
in emerald light with you we ascend.

**Raphael Archangel, for vision we pray,
Raphael Archangel, show us the way,
Raphael Archangel, your emerald ray,
Raphael Archangel, our lives a new day.**

5. Saint Germain, radiate into the collective consciousness the awareness that the members of the power elite inevitably become blinded by that greed, and they set the economy into an inflationary spiral that will destroy the economy.

Raphael Archangel, diseases are done,
as you help us see that all life is One,
we no longer do your true love reject,
immaculate vision on all we project.

**Raphael Archangel, for vision we pray,
Raphael Archangel, show us the way,
Raphael Archangel, your emerald ray,
Raphael Archangel, our lives a new day.**

6. Saint Germain, radiate into the collective consciousness the awareness that this can be balanced by real people performing real labor and increasing the amount of services so quickly that the money system does not collapse, does not go into an inflationary cycle that cannot be stopped.

Raphael Archangel, we're healing the earth,
in immaculate vision we give her rebirth,
a new era has on this day begun,
your emerald light now shines like a sun.

Raphael Archangel, for vision we pray,
Raphael Archangel, show us the way,
Raphael Archangel, your emerald ray,
Raphael Archangel, our lives a new day.

7. Saint Germain, radiate into the collective consciousness the awareness that even though the average worker is better off today, people have not reaped the natural God-given reward of the multiplication of their talents.

Raphael Archangel, the fall is behind,
as all of earth's people the Christ path do find,
we call now to you all people to heal,
as four lower bodies in love you do seal.

Raphael Archangel, for vision we pray,
Raphael Archangel, show us the way,
Raphael Archangel, your emerald ray,
Raphael Archangel, our lives a new day.

8. Saint Germain, radiate into the collective consciousness the awareness that through the increase of the money supply and inflation, people have been taxed. Inflation is a hidden form of tax where the people do not realize they are taxed.

Raphael Archangel, as you bring the light,
the forces of darkness swiftly take flight,
their day is now done as we claim the earth,
spreading to all an innocent mirth.

**Raphael Archangel, for vision we pray,
Raphael Archangel, show us the way,
Raphael Archangel, your emerald ray,
Raphael Archangel, our lives a new day.**

9. Saint Germain, radiate into the collective consciousness the awareness that if there had been a divine economy over the last century, the standard of living would have been even higher. There would not be any poverty left.

Raphael Archangel, our vision set free,
as we can now see God's reality,
as Saint Germain's vision is manifest here,
the earth is now sealed in immaculate sphere.

**Raphael Archangel, for vision we pray,
Raphael Archangel, show us the way,
Raphael Archangel, your emerald ray,
Raphael Archangel, our lives a new day.**

Part 6

1. Saint Germain, radiate into the collective consciousness the awareness that the power elite has managed to delay the God-ordained growth in the economy and the manifestation of the abundant life that should have come about by now.

19 | Invoking the money system of the Golden Age

> Uriel Archangel, immense is the power,
> of angels of peace, all war to devour.
> The demons of war, no match for your light,
> consuming them all, with radiance so bright.
>
> **Uriel Archangel, use your great sword,**
> **Uriel Archangel, consume all discord,**
> **Uriel Archangel, we're of one accord,**
> **Uriel Archangel, we walk with the Lord.**

2. Saint Germain, radiate into the collective consciousness the awareness that the first people who can spend the newly created money can often buy goods and services at the old prices. Only as the new money circulates through the economy, will prices go up.

> Uriel Archangel, intense is the sound,
> when millions of angels, their voices compound.
> They build a crescendo, piercing the night,
> life's glorious oneness revealed to our sight.
>
> **Uriel Archangel, use your great sword,**
> **Uriel Archangel, consume all discord,**
> **Uriel Archangel, we're of one accord,**
> **Uriel Archangel, we walk with the Lord.**

3. Saint Germain, radiate into the collective consciousness the awareness that over the last century there has been a greater and greater concentration of wealth under the control of a smaller and smaller elite. A few percent of the population control the majority of the wealth in most nations.

> Uriel Archangel, from out the Great Throne,
> your millions of trumpets, sound the One Tone.
> Consuming all discord with your harmony,
> the sound of all sounds will set all life free.

> **Uriel Archangel, use your great sword,**
> **Uriel Archangel, consume all discord,**
> **Uriel Archangel, we're of one accord,**
> **Uriel Archangel, we walk with the Lord.**

4. Saint Germain, radiate into the collective consciousness the awareness that this is an absolute perversion of the abundant life of God. This is nothing more than the power elite seeking to control the people through the money supply.

> Uriel Archangel, all war is now done,
> for you bring a message, from heart of the One.
> The hearts of all men, now singing in peace,
> the spirals of love, forever increase.

> **Uriel Archangel, use your great sword,**
> **Uriel Archangel, consume all discord,**
> **Uriel Archangel, we're of one accord,**
> **Uriel Archangel, we walk with the Lord.**

5. Saint Germain, radiate into the collective consciousness the awareness that one of the original bankers that created this system said that if you allowed him to control a nation's money, he did not care who made the nation's laws, for he knew that the nation could be controlled through the money system.

> Uriel Archangel, your infinite peace,
> from all warring beings our planet release,
> war is a prison from which we are free,
> embracing the peace of true unity.
>
> **Uriel Archangel, use your great sword,**
> **Uriel Archangel, consume all discord,**
> **Uriel Archangel, we're of one accord,**
> **Uriel Archangel, we walk with the Lord.**

6. Saint Germain, radiate into the collective consciousness the awareness that in the United States there is an unholy alliance between the federal government and the Federal Reserve, which is not a federal agency and thus not answerable to the people.

> Uriel Archangel, we send forth the call,
> reveal now the oneness that unifies all,
> help us the vision of peace now to see,
> so we from all conflicts and struggles are free.
>
> **Uriel Archangel, use your great sword,**
> **Uriel Archangel, consume all discord,**
> **Uriel Archangel, we're of one accord,**
> **Uriel Archangel, we walk with the Lord.**

7. Saint Germain, radiate into the collective consciousness the awareness that the governments of today also face the situation that they want to spend more money than they know the people are willing to pay in taxes.

Uriel Archangel, in service to life,
you give us release from struggle and strife,
forgetting the self is truly the key,
to living a life in true harmony.

**Uriel Archangel, use your great sword,
Uriel Archangel, consume all discord,
Uriel Archangel, we're of one accord,
Uriel Archangel, we walk with the Lord.**

8. Saint Germain, radiate into the collective consciousness the awareness that even modern governments let the bankers create money out of nothing, thereby eroding the value of the money—and thus taxing the people without the people being aware of this.

Uriel Archangel, the earth now you raise,
out of duality's death-bringing haze,
we call now upon your great Flame of Peace,
commanding that all petty squabbles do cease.

**Uriel Archangel, use your great sword,
Uriel Archangel, consume all discord,
Uriel Archangel, we're of one accord,
Uriel Archangel, we walk with the Lord.**

9. Saint Germain, radiate into the collective consciousness the awareness that whenever a government wants to spend more than they think the people are willing to pay in taxes, they simply camouflage it as inflation so that the people pay it anyway but now they do not notice and thus they do not object.

Uriel Archangel, as peace is the norm,
to your higher vision the earth does conform,
as people have found your peace from within,
a Golden Age is the prize that we win.

Uriel Archangel, use your great sword,
Uriel Archangel, consume all discord,
Uriel Archangel, we're of one accord,
Uriel Archangel, we walk with the Lord.

Part 7

1. Saint Germain, radiate into the collective consciousness the awareness that the bankers and the financial elite make money from this process. The people not only have the degradation of the value of the money but also have to pay the interest of the national debt.

Zadkiel Archangel, your flow is so swift,
in your violet light, we instantly shift,
into a vibration in which we are free,
from all limitations of the lesser me.

Zadkiel Archangel, encircle the earth,
Zadkiel Archangel, with your violet girth,
Zadkiel Archangel, unstoppable mirth,
Zadkiel Archangel, our planet's rebirth.

2. Saint Germain, radiate into the collective consciousness the awareness that there is a connection between war and money. The bankers quickly realized that there was no better way to earn a profit than to set nations against each other in war.

> Zadkiel Archangel, we truly aspire,
> to being the master of your violet fire,
> wielding the power, of your alchemy,
> we use Sacred Word, to set all life free.
>
> **Zadkiel Archangel, encircle the earth,**
> **Zadkiel Archangel, with your violet girth,**
> **Zadkiel Archangel, unstoppable mirth,**
> **Zadkiel Archangel, our planet's rebirth.**

3. Saint Germain, radiate into the collective consciousness the awareness that the bankers have often financed both sides of a conflict and also opened the weapons plants that produced the weapons used in the conflict.

> Zadkiel Archangel, your violet light,
> transforming the earth, with unstoppable might,
> so swiftly our planet, beginning to spin,
> with legions of angels, our victory we win.
>
> **Zadkiel Archangel, encircle the earth,**
> **Zadkiel Archangel, with your violet girth,**
> **Zadkiel Archangel, unstoppable mirth,**
> **Zadkiel Archangel, our planet's rebirth.**

4. Saint Germain, radiate into the collective consciousness the awareness that the bankers made a profit all around, while the people paid not only with their blood in the war but also with their sweat and blood as they worked to produce the real value that was needed to keep the system going.

> Zadkiel Archangel, the earth is now free,
> from burdens put on her by humanity,
> all people are free from their inner strife,
> embracing the freedom to start a new life.

> **Zadkiel Archangel, encircle the earth,**
> **Zadkiel Archangel, with your violet girth,**
> **Zadkiel Archangel, unstoppable mirth,**
> **Zadkiel Archangel, our planet's rebirth.**

5. Saint Germain, radiate into the collective consciousness the awareness that slavery through money is far beyond physical slavery. People cannot object to it because they do not even know. They just notice that they have to work harder and harder, and they do not understand why this is so.

> Zadkiel Archangel, the earth will now spin,
> much faster as we Christ victory win,
> for in Christ the captives are truly set free,
> bathed in Christ Light the earth now will be.

> **Zadkiel Archangel, encircle the earth,**
> **Zadkiel Archangel, with your violet girth,**
> **Zadkiel Archangel, unstoppable mirth,**
> **Zadkiel Archangel, our planet's rebirth.**

6. Saint Germain, radiate into the collective consciousness the awareness that we need to educate ourselves and have the will to demand a new money system. By not being willing to take responsibility for the money system, we attract those who are willing to pervert the system and take advantage of us.

> Zadkiel Archangel, the forces of night,
> are bound by your penetrating Freedom Light,
> the earth is now cleared by forces so dark,
> as your Violet Light provides a new spark.
>
> **Zadkiel Archangel, encircle the earth,**
> **Zadkiel Archangel, with your violet girth,**
> **Zadkiel Archangel, unstoppable mirth,**
> **Zadkiel Archangel, our planet's rebirth.**

7. Saint Germain, radiate into the collective consciousness the awareness that this becomes a vicious circle that only has two outcomes. Either we wake up and demand change or the power elite will keep increasing the money supply until the system collapses.

> Zadkiel Archangel, we truly love you,
> and to Saint Germain we will always be true,
> help us now see our plans so Divine,
> so we on this planet our full light can shine.
>
> **Zadkiel Archangel, encircle the earth,**
> **Zadkiel Archangel, with your violet girth,**
> **Zadkiel Archangel, unstoppable mirth,**
> **Zadkiel Archangel, our planet's rebirth.**

8. Saint Germain, radiate into the collective consciousness the awareness that the fallen beings, in their greed, blindness and spiritual pride, think they will never have to suffer the consequences of their actions because the people are bearing the karma and the elite can get away with anything.

> Zadkiel Archangel, there is no more night,
> a new day is born from your great Violet Light,
> transforming all manifestations of fear,
> we know that the Golden Age is now here.
>
> **Zadkiel Archangel, encircle the earth,**
> **Zadkiel Archangel, with your violet girth,**
> **Zadkiel Archangel, unstoppable mirth,**
> **Zadkiel Archangel, our planet's rebirth.**

9. Saint Germain, radiate into the collective consciousness the awareness that we cannot expect the power elite to stop this downward spiral. If the people do not put on the brakes, then it is just a matter of time before the money machine will run amok.

> Zadkiel Archangel, your violet flame,
> the earth and humanity, never the same,
> Saint Germain's Golden Age, is a reality,
> what glorious wonder, we joyously see.
>
> **Zadkiel Archangel, encircle the earth,**
> **Zadkiel Archangel, with your violet girth,**
> **Zadkiel Archangel, unstoppable mirth,**
> **Zadkiel Archangel, our planet's rebirth.**

Part 8

1. Saint Germain, radiate into the collective consciousness the awareness that in the Golden Age there will be a steady growth in the amount of abundance available, a steady growth in opportunity.

> O Saint Germain, you do inspire,
> my vision raised forever higher,
> with you I form a figure-eight,
> your Golden Age I co-create.
>
> **O Saint Germain, what love you bring,**
> **it truly makes all matter sing,**
> **your violet flame does all restore,**
> **with you we are becoming more.**

2. Saint Germain, radiate into the collective consciousness the awareness that in the Golden Age there is a positive spiral where the people are reaping the rewards of their own labor, and therefore they are willing to work more. Everything becomes an upward spiral.

> O Saint Germain, what Freedom Flame,
> released when we recite your name,
> acceleration is your gift,
> our planet it will surely lift.
>
> **O Saint Germain, what love you bring,**
> **it truly makes all matter sing,**
> **your violet flame does all restore,**
> **with you we are becoming more.**

3. Saint Germain, radiate into the collective consciousness the awareness that the vision you hold for the Golden Age is a vision where no one is poor, no one is lacking for a decent standard of living or the free time to pursue the spiritual aspects of life.

> O Saint Germain, in love we claim,
> our right to bring your violet flame,
> from you Above, to us below,
> it is an all-transforming flow.

> **O Saint Germain, what love you bring,**
> **it truly makes all matter sing,**
> **your violet flame does all restore,**
> **with you we are becoming more.**

4. Saint Germain, radiate into the collective consciousness the awareness that as we raise consciousness, we open the door for new inventions, new methods of fabrication, new forms of energy that will increase the amount of abundance so that the economy can grow even further.

> O Saint Germain, I love you so,
> my aura filled with violet glow,
> my chakras filled with violet fire,
> I am your cosmic amplifier.

> **O Saint Germain, what love you bring,**
> **it truly makes all matter sing,**
> **your violet flame does all restore,**
> **with you we are becoming more.**

5. Saint Germain, radiate into the collective consciousness the awareness that there is no end to the growth in the economy in a golden age society. The concept of limits to growth is put upon us by the fallen beings.

> O Saint Germain, I am now free,
> your violet flame is therapy,
> transform all hang-ups in my mind,
> as inner peace I surely find.

> **O Saint Germain, what love you bring,**
> **it truly makes all matter sing,**
> **your violet flame does all restore,**
> **with you we are becoming more.**

6. Saint Germain, radiate into the collective consciousness the awareness that the fallen beings only want to limit *our* growth, not their own wealth, power, and privilege. They have to find a way to get the people to be satisfied with less so that they can have more.

> O Saint Germain, my body pure,
> your violet flame for all is cure,
> consume the cause of all disease,
> and therefore I am all at ease.

> **O Saint Germain, what love you bring,**
> **it truly makes all matter sing,**
> **your violet flame does all restore,**
> **with you we are becoming more.**

7. Saint Germain, radiate into the collective consciousness the awareness that in the Golden Age, the people are not satisfied with less, for they realize that it is the Father's good pleasure to give them more. It is their divine birthright to reap the reward of their initiative and labor.

> O Saint Germain, I'm karma-free,
> the past no longer burdens me,
> a brand new opportunity,
> I am in Christic unity.

> **O Saint Germain, what love you bring,**
> **it truly makes all matter sing,**
> **your violet flame does all restore,**
> **with you we are becoming more.**

8. Saint Germain, radiate into the collective consciousness the awareness that money is not evil. In its pure form, it is an expression of the Mother. If we did not have money, the economy could not grow beyond a certain level.

> O Saint Germain, we are now one,
> I am for you a violet sun,
> as we transform this planet earth,
> your Golden Age is given birth.

> **O Saint Germain, what love you bring,**
> **it truly makes all matter sing,**
> **your violet flame does all restore,**
> **with you we are becoming more.**

9. Saint Germain, radiate into the collective consciousness the awareness that the Divine Father provides the increase in the total amount of abundance. The Divine Mother distributes that among all people so that all can have a decent standard of living and pursue their Divine plans.

> O Saint Germain, the earth is free,
> from burden of duality,
> in oneness we bring what is best,
> your Golden Age is manifest.

> **O Saint Germain, what love you bring,**
> **it truly makes all matter sing,**
> **your violet flame does all restore,**
> **with you we are becoming more.**

Part 9

1. Saint Germain, radiate into the collective consciousness the awareness that with the perversion of the Mother, money becomes the means to control the people. It allows the elite to run amok in a never-ending quest for more and more in the material realm.

> Divine Director, I now see,
> the world is unreality,
> in my heart I now truly feel,
> the Spirit is all that is real.

> **Divine Director, send the light,**
> **from blindness clear my inner sight,**
> **my vision free, my vision clear,**
> **your guidance is forever here.**

2. Saint Germain, radiate into the collective consciousness the awareness that the higher use of abundance in the material realm is to use it as a platform for spiritual pursuits that then raises the consciousness of the people and brings forth the Kingdom of God.

> Divine Director, vision give,
> in clarity I want to live,
> I now behold my plan Divine,
> the plan that is uniquely mine.

> **Divine Director, send the light,**
> **from blindness clear my inner sight,**
> **my vision free, my vision clear,**
> **your guidance is forever here.**

3. Saint Germain, radiate into the collective consciousness the awareness that members of the elite do not want the Kingdom of God—for in the Kingdom of God they cannot be the elite. They cannot even remain on this planet so they want to stop the Kingdom of God.

> Divine Director, show in me,
> the ego games, and set me free,
> help me escape the ego's cage,
> to help bring in the Golden Age.

**Divine Director, send the light,
from blindness clear my inner sight,
my vision free, my vision clear,
your guidance is forever here.**

4. Saint Germain, radiate into the collective consciousness the awareness that members of the elite do this by perverting every aspect of society where the people are not aware, are not taking responsibility for educating ourselves and making our own decisions.

Divine Director, I'm with you,
my vision one, no longer two,
as karma's veil you do disperse,
I see a whole new universe.

**Divine Director, send the light,
from blindness clear my inner sight,
my vision free, my vision clear,
your guidance is forever here.**

5. Saint Germain, radiate into the collective consciousness the awareness that it is the absolute requirement for a Golden Age to manifest that the people wake up realize how every aspect of society has been perverted by the dualistic consciousness and decide that we will no longer be pawns in this game.

Divine Director, I go up,
electric light now fills my cup,
consume in me all shadows old,
bestow on me a vision bold.

19 | Invoking the money system of the Golden Age

**Divine Director, send the light,
from blindness clear my inner sight,
my vision free, my vision clear,
your guidance is forever here.**

6. Saint Germain, radiate into the collective consciousness the awareness that we need to decide that we will no longer be the slaves, we will no longer be the worker bees, for the elite. We will take back our birthright to be the people of God.

Divine Director, heart of gold,
my sacred labor I unfold,
o blessed Guru, I now see,
where my own plan is taking me.

**Divine Director, send the light,
from blindness clear my inner sight,
my vision free, my vision clear,
your guidance is forever here.**

7. Saint Germain, in the name of the Christ, I say to all people everywhere: "Wake up and claim your birthright! Saint Germain is the father of the Golden Age and it is his good pleasure to give us his kingdom. Claim it, accept it, bring it into manifestation!"

Divine Director, by your grace,
in grander scheme I find my place,
my individual flame I see,
uniqueness God has given me.

> **Divine Director, send the light,**
> **from blindness clear my inner sight,**
> **my vision free, my vision clear,**
> **your guidance is forever here.**

8. Saint Germain, radiate into the collective consciousness the awareness that you are ready to manifest your Golden Age on this planet. I, for one, am ready to accept it.

> Divine Director, vision one,
> I see that I AM God's own Sun,
> with your direction so Divine,
> I am now letting my light shine.

> **Divine Director, send the light,**
> **from blindness clear my inner sight,**
> **my vision free, my vision clear,**
> **your guidance is forever here.**

9. Saint Germain, radiate into the collective consciousness the awareness that there is a Golden Age waiting to be brought into manifestation. We need only play our part and multiply the talents that you are ready to give us. Then, you will do your part and provide the increase.

> Divine Director, what a gift,
> to be a part of Spirit's lift,
> to raise mankind out of the night,
> to bask in Spirit's loving sight.

**Divine Director, send the light,
from blindness clear my inner sight,
my vision free, my vision clear,
your guidance is forever here.**

Sealing

In the name of the Divine Mother, I call to all ascended masters for the sealing of myself and all people in my circle of influence in the creative flow of the Divine Mother, the River of Life. I call for the multiplication of my calls by all ascended masters so that we form the perfect figure-eight flow of "As Above, so below." Thus, I accept that this is fully manifest, because the mouth of the Lord, the Divine Mother that I AM, has spoken it. Amen.

20 | AN ECONOMY FOR THE PEOPLE OR FOR THE ELITE?

I am indeed Saint Germain. I hold the Flame of Freedom for the earth, but what exactly does that mean? It means that I have become completely and utterly one with the God Flame of Freedom. I have vowed to radiate that Flame of Freedom to this planet for the next cycle of the Aquarian Age. Thus, my beloved, I have earned the title of the God of Freedom for the earth, as I have become one with that God flame. I prefer not to use this title, as it can easily be misunderstood and mistaken by human beings as an excuse for building idolatry. I would speak, in the beginning of this discourse, about idolatry. Indeed, idolatry is one of the main lessons that humankind was meant to overcome during the Piscean Age.

What people have done instead is that they have built an even greater idolatry of Jesus who came to set all people free from idolatry. Not only the idolatry of self but especially the idolatry of the fallen beings on this planet, those who are entirely trapped in the duality consciousness because they have become completely blinded by their own egos. They firmly believe the illusions of the ego, believe those illusions to be an absolute, undeniable and unquestionable truth. They have the ultimate idolatry of having elevated a lie to a truth, and thereby thinking that by adhering to the "absolute truth," they have elevated themselves to some ultimate status compared to other human beings.

Idolatry is the veil of ignorance, the veil of illusions, that keeps the majority of the population trapped in the illusion that they need an elite to stand between themselves and God. Was this not what Jesus challenged when he challenged the scribes, Pharisees, temple priests and money changers? They had set themselves up as an elite between the people and their God, perpetuating the illusion, the lie, that people were not free to go within their own hearts and find God directly. They could contact God only through the outer religion and its priesthood.

Idolatry in spiritual organizations

This is the ultimate lie that must be overcome before the Golden Age of Aquarius can begin to unfold. You will, if you take an honest look at many spiritual organizations, see this idolatry. There is even the idolatry that the messenger can stand between you and the ascended masters, between you and your I AM Presence, between you and God.

It is necessary for the students in the present age to overcome this idolatry, to be willing to look at it in yourselves. Some of you are called to enter spiritual organizations in order to demonstrate that one can be a student of the ascended masters without being trapped in idolatry. Although your examples may be ignored, nevertheless the example is given and thus the opportunity to make a choice is there, which it would not have been if there had been no one who had dared to go beyond the idolatry.

Those who are the most advanced students are those who are not concerned about dualistic appellations, such as advanced and non-advanced. They are simply looking for the beam in their own eye, realizing that it has no meaning to compare yourself to others. It is only a matter of comparing whether you have purified your own consciousness of the elements of the duality consciousness. If you have not, then you look at them and you use our teachings to go beyond them. Indeed, this is the flaw that you see in those who are trapped in idolatry. Inevitably, they believe that although they can clearly see the faults in others, they do not need to look for that beam in their own eye.

It is an inevitable law of God that if you see any fault in any other human being, you have that same fault in your own eye—or you would not be able to see it in others. Thus, if you keep focusing on the splinter in the eye of your brother, then you will only reinforce your own self-idolatry and therefore refuse to learn the lesson you were meant to learn by being in a particular organization.

You get the messenger you deserve, you get the guru you deserve. Or you get a guru who is willing to outpicture the particular flaws that you need to see in yourself. Thus, if you see them only in the guru, but refuse to see them in yourself, well, then you have failed the opportunity. Nevertheless, it will be an opportunity for the planet to rise higher, as those who refuse to look at their own consciousness will then go elsewhere. We can move on with raising this planet beyond the consciousness of the fallen beings and their self-idolatry of thinking they know better than God.

Idolatry and the economic crisis

Why do I choose to start talking about idolatry? Well, is it not because it is precisely idolatry that is the central problem in the current economic crisis? What have you seen perpetuated by the press and the media, by government officials, by leaders in various economic organizations, such as the Federal Reserve or big banks? Well, my beloved, is it not the consciousness that certain organizations, companies and institutions are "too big to fail," and thus the government must step in and prop up those colossuses so that they do not tumble?

What is this, if not idolatry? The underlying truth here is that it is the idolatry of the people, perpetuated throughout the Piscean Age and earlier, that they cannot exist without the power elite of fallen beings. This, my beloved, is precisely the problem that you see on earth. It is the illusion that prevents the people from standing up and taking back their God Power, the power of God within each and every one of them. It is the illusion that is being perpetuated by the elite itself—the elite in the media, the elite in the government, the elite in business, finance and banking.

They desperately cling to their positions of power and privilege. Underneath it all, some of them are beginning to realize that their days are numbered. The days of their power and privilege over the people, those days are numbered too. They see that this cannot go on forever. It is only a matter of a relatively short time before the people will rise up, as they have done before against the feudal system and other examples of the power elite having attained almost total control over the people.

Many among the power elite are, of course, still blind to this, but some of them are beginning to see it. What I desire you to be aware of, what I desire you to envision and what I desire you to make calls on is that the people are awakened from this idolatry of thinking that they need an elite. They do not need an elite of selfish and self-centered people in order to continue a society with stability. We of the ascended masters are not in any way, shape or form attached to stability. We want growth! Sometimes, growth means that you must throw off the old by letting it become shattered (if that is what is necessary) because the people cling to it to the point of almost insanity, of not being willing to let it go.

We certainly prefer a smooth transition from the current economic system to a golden age economy. We prefer to minimize the suffering and the loss. Nevertheless, we do not prefer this to the point where we are willing to prevent the people from learning their lesson. I trust you will see that it is not appropriate for you to make calls for the stabilizing of the economy. It is not appropriate for you to make calls for the propping up of the institutions created by the fallen beings. It is not appropriate for you to make calls that support the power elite.

You need to make the calls and hold the vision that the people learn their lesson. Those who will not learn, need to receive the judgment of Christ so that they can be removed. This is what will bring progress, and if it requires a few bumpy turns of the road, then so be it. I tell you, it is a necessity that the people learn what can be done to misuse the economy before they will be ready to accept the economy of the Golden Age.

If I had an instrument that could right now present the golden age economy to humankind, well, the vast majority of the people on this planet simply would not accept it. They would reject it as a hopeless, utopian pipe-dream that simply could never come to pass. They are so steeped in the consciousness of lack, again perpetrated by the fallen beings as a result of their idolatry. What is the essence of idolatry? It is the desire to raise yourself and your own group above other people. How can you raise yourself compared to others unless you are in an environment infused with the illusion of lack? In order for some to have more, others must have less. This state of an unequal distribution of wealth and privilege cannot exist in the abundant life of God. It can only exist when that abundant life has been rejected by a critical mass of human beings so that it cannot be physically manifest.

Spreading risk or masking risk?

When I talk about an equal distribution of wealth, I am not talking about the socialist dream where the state has usurped the position held by each person's I AM Presence. I am talking about the true realism of the Golden Age where the people realize that they have access to the power of God within themselves. Therefore, they can bring forth the abundant life without being dependent upon an elite here on earth, an elite who can make the decisions of how to run the complicated financial system that the elite has created precisely in order to hide their intentions and their manipulation from the people.

What you have seen lately is that the system has finally become so complicated that even the people who created it can no longer figure out how the system works. They can no longer assess the true risk of the dubious financial instruments they have created. Companies, who have been in business for over a century, can suddenly vanish in a week because their own leaders have become so deceived by the complexity of their financial instruments, and by the consciousness of greed, that they could not accurately assess the risk of those instruments. They could not even keep their own companies afloat.

This is the lesson that the people need to learn. When they are in the state of idolatry, blindly following the blind leaders, allowing the blind leaders to run the economy, well then, it is only a matter of time before those blind leaders back themselves and the entire nation (and in a sense the entire world) into a corner from which there is no easy way out. There is only a collapse of the system, my beloved. The lesson learned by those who desired to build the Tower of Babel (a tower that could reach into the heavens) is that when you build too high without having the foundation of the reality of the Christ consciousness (because you are building on the sand of the antichrist consciousness) there comes a point where your creation will tumble under its own weight. This is what you see in the financial system of the United States and beyond.

From blind greed to blind fear

What has driven this financial system now for decades is indeed unbridled, blind greed. This is a greed that has perverted the financial system to the point where it was so based on debt that it became impossible to accurately assess the risk of conducting business in that system. The risk had been spread out and thereby masked and camouflaged so that no one knew what was really going on. As long as the cycle of supposed growth and profit continued (because the people in the system blindly believed that it could continue forever) well, then the cycle did continue seemingly forever. It was built not only on the blindness and the greed of those on the top, but even the blindness and the greed of many among the people. There were people who thought that by investing their savings, their pension plans, in the stock market and other dubious hedge funds and mutual funds, they could get something for nothing, as I talked about when I last discoursed on the economy. Both the people at the top and the people who followed those blind leaders were blinded by that consciousness of something for nothing that is the essence of greed. You are no longer willing to work for a fair return, you are no longer willing to work to raise all life and thereby receive your just reward. No, you want to receive a reward without working, or you want to receive a reward that is greater than you could achieve by working. You want a shortcut, you want something for nothing.

This blinds you to greed. You suddenly think that anything goes—anything that seems to offer you a short-term profit should be pursued. After all, if *you* don't do it, all the other companies in the financial world will, and they will seem to be doing better than you. Everybody jumped into the fray and followed suit. The people who are investing see that those who are investing in these dubious instruments are making money, and they think they have to jump in as well. Everyone is caught up in the fray, in the frenzy, like the feeding frenzy of a school of fish that blindly snap at anything that moves in order to get a part before the party is over.

Most people did not realize that the party would be over. The profits that were claimed were not real profits, they were imaginary profits because the risk had been masked to the point where it seemed like there was no loss or the loss could be postponed to next year. We can make the money and get a good balance sheet this year (and make the bonuses for the people in the top) and then nobody bothered to think what would happen a year, two, five, ten years down the road. In the blindness of their greed, nobody bothered to ask their own accountants to project what would happen down the road if the present trend continued. Even the accountants had difficulty assessing the real risk of derivatives and other financial instruments so that the entire system was in this state of blindness. This is the blindness that is the inevitable companion of greed. Greed can only be based on an illusion and any illusion feeds further illusion, further blindness. What is the illusion behind greed? It is the illusion of the separate self where it seems possible that we can gain an advantage to ourselves and our company, and then never mind what happens down the road to these other people that we are taking money from or to the system itself.

Learn from the story of the golden goose

One of the great problems in today's world is that most children have been brought up without the knowledge of the old fairy tales, the old folk tales, that used to circulate among the population and thereby became a part of the awareness of most children as they grew up. Those tales were indeed inspired by the ascended masters to inject valuable life lessons in a playful format that children would take in. The problem is that most of the money managers in today's world never heard the tale of the golden goose—the goose that laid the golden eggs.

Let me retell it briefly. There was a man who had a goose, and one day he noticed that the goose had laid a golden egg. He was, of course, happy, but he was even more happy the next day when he realized that the goose would lay a golden egg every day! For a time, he was overjoyed and bought everything he desired for those golden eggs. Then, gradually he became greedy and started thinking: Why should I have to wait to get a golden egg every day, why should I not cut open the goose and get all the eggs at once. He cut open the goose and found only one egg in there, and he lost the goose and all the golden eggs of the future.

An economy based on the gambling consciousness

This is indeed what the money managers have done to the economy by creating an economy that is basically based on the same exact consciousness, the same exact principle, that you see driving Las Vegas and gambling in general. It is the desire of something for nothing where you make a small, seemingly insignificant, investment and then you hope that the outcome would be a tremendous return through some aspect of fate or luck. Basically, by masking the risk of derivatives and other financial instruments, the money managers entered into this state of gambling. They were thinking that because they were investing borrowed money, and because they had masked the risk, it was an insignificant investment that had the potential to give a very large return.

This is the exact principle of gambling. You think you can invest in gambling without losing. Therefore, you see millions of people who buy a lottery ticket every week, hoping that one day it will get the big return. Gambling is a business, is it not? A business can survive only if it makes a profit. This means that for all of the people who buy a lottery ticket, even though a prize is paid out every week, less money is paid out than is paid into the system, for otherwise the business could not continue. You now see the fallacy of gambling, for certainly some people seem to get something for nothing, but all people could not get something for nothing or the system would collapse.

This is the same you see on Wall Street. When Wall Street started investing not only money but borrowed money (money that was not only borrowed because they existed somewhere, but money that was created out of nothing), they gradually started creating the situation where sometimes there would be a big return on an investment. Then it became clear that the promise was that all of those who invested in these new financial instruments would make a return. *That* promise simply could not be fulfilled because it was an illusion to begin with, as it is an illusion that all who play the lottery can win the big prize.

For a time, the greed blinded the people so they went along with it. Inevitably, there comes a point of reckoning where the Tower of Babel has become so top-heavy that it starts to crumble and crack under its own weight. Then – suddenly – the people in the top start waking up and realizing that this cannot continue. Then they do what always happens—they switch from the illusion of greed to the illusion of fear. In their fear, they try to pull out what they have before others do the same. Thus, they create the downward spiral that threatens a complete meltdown of the entire system.

Is the government for the people or for the elite?

This suddenly wakes up the rest of the people and the government who up until now has been asleep at the helm, for they would not regulate these new financial instruments and thought the market would take care of it. Suddenly, the government wakes up and realizes that the market will indeed take care of it—by taking down the entire flawed financial system. Wait a minute, that would be too big of a shock to society, they think, and it will certainly overturn some of these venerable institutions that we think we cannot live without. Now, the government believes that it has to step in, in order to protect the people. I ask you to consider: Who is the government protecting? Is it the people—or the power elite?

Indeed, you will see that so far the American government is too trapped in the entire mindset of something for nothing – the mindset of greed, the mindset of elitism – that they are acting primarily to protect the elite rather than the people. I will therefore prophesy to you that if they do not thoroughly reform the entire financial system, then whatever they do will only prop up the system temporarily. It is a matter of months or a few years before the next crisis will roll along.

I will also tell you that there are intelligent and well-meaning people in the system – both in businesses and in the government – who have the potential to enact the kind of reforms that are necessary in order to not only stave off the current crisis, but actually to put the entire financial world back on a sustainable growth path where the system will not destroy itself out of blind greed. There is the potential that if these people are allowed to bring forth their ideas, and if those ideas are indeed carried out, the ship can be righted, so to speak. You can have a more smooth transition towards the golden age economy. I must tell you that the golden age economy is very far off from the current state of the economy world-wide, and especially in these United States. I am cautiously optimistic, but "cautious" being the operative word in that sentence.

I am indeed a realist, and I realize, that the power of God can truly correct all man-made problems. The reality of God is that the Ma-ter Light can as easily outpicture the abundant life as the state of lack and inequality projected by the elite and the people who have blindly followed them. I also see that there are many hurdles that need to be overcome—hurdles that most people, even the brightest in the financial world or the government, do not see, for they cannot look that far ahead.

They have not yet been willing to truly take a look at the system and say: "What is actually wrong with the system?" They are still trapped in the consciousness of saying: "What do we need to do to prevent a collapse of the system?" Instead of saying: "What do we need to do to create an economy that is sustainable, that promotes sustainable growth, growth not only for the elite, but for all people?"

A sustainable financial system

In this day and age – in the transition to the Aquarian Age – no economy can be sustainable unless it raises up all people towards the abundant life. It is not sustainable to have an economy on a world basis where two thirds of the world's population live near the starvation level or below the poverty level of a few dollars a day. This is not sustainable, and as long as the rich nations will not address that problem, well then their economies will always be in a state of going from one crisis to the next, always being threatened by collapsing under their own weight. They are fed by greed instead of the true desire to raise up all life.

What will it take to create a financial system that is sustainable? It will take that the government wakes up and acknowledges its rightful role. One of the primary reasons for the current financial crisis is indeed the lack of regulation. The government has been caught up in a false view of the free market economy that makes them think that the best they can do is stand back and let the market create whatever financial instruments they want to create. The market will eventually regulate itself, as the saying goes.

As I started out saying, I hold the Flame of Freedom for the earth, but what is freedom? Is it the freedom to exploit? Is it the freedom of a small power elite to dominate the population? Nay, my beloved. This is not freedom, for freedom cannot be found through the blindness of the human ego. Freedom cannot be found through the duality consciousness. Freedom can be found only in knowing the reality of the oneness of all life, knowing that only when you do something that seeks to raise the All, will you be doing something that will truly benefit yourself.

Misuse of economic freedom to create monopolies

What is the role of government, or the role of a free democratic government, the kind of government that the founding fathers envisioned, at least partly, and attempted to create through the United States Constitution? It is indeed to protect the people, to serve as the steward of the principles that will raise up all life towards greater freedom, even greater economic freedom and economic abundance.

It is a myth perpetrated by certain people among the elite that a free market economy can run itself without government intervention. It is a further myth that the United States has a free market economy and has always had such an economy. The reality – that even a superficial study of history will reveal – is that in the late 1800's there were certain financiers, certain industrialists, who had used the freedom of the free market to create businesses and financial institutions of such size that they began to realize that it was possible not only to adapt to market conditions, but to drive and control market conditions in order to create monopolies. They also realized that in a true free market economy – where competition is unrestricted and where the people are educated and informed – it is not possible to create a monopoly.

Freedom is the anti-thesis of monopolies, for a monopoly is not the inevitable result of free competition. Free competition will destroy, or rather prevent the creation of, monopolies by always making it possible for others to compete, no matter how big one business might become. A business will only remain big in a free economy as long as it serves its customers. When you create a monopoly and artificially raise prices, you are no longer serving your customers, and if there is free competition those customers will go elsewhere.

This was what was realized by some of the big industrialists and financiers, such as Morgan and Rockefeller and others in the late 1800's. They realized, that in a democratic nation, such as the United States, it was not possible to create a monopoly through competition. The only way to create a monopoly was to restrict competition by causing the government to be deceived by the illusion that the government had to enter the economy and use its power to regulate the economy for the purpose of creating stability. In the vision of these big financiers, this meant creating a stable situation where no smaller companies could come up and challenge the position of the big established companies.

This is what you have seen over this past century, namely that government regulations have been used to protect the big established companies from the free market, the free competition. Then, the master stroke of these financiers was the creation of the Federal Reserve, the Federal Reserve System, which served not only to prevent free competition in the banking industry. It also served to prevent the big companies from reaping the consequences of their own mistakes. In a free economy, those who make mistakes will reap the consequences and thus go down or be reduced in size. If a company got big and greedy and no longer served its customers, in a free economy the customers would go elsewhere, and thus the company would be either reduced in size or disappear completely.

In creating the Federal Reserve as the lender of last resort, the big banks could then make questionable investments, and if they turned out to be wrong, well, then the system would protect them from going down. This is to a large degree what you see today. Or do you not see, my beloved, that the investment banks that have so far been independent of the regular banks, are falling one by one? Who is taking them over? Well, is it not the big banks who are a part of the Federal Reserve System and therefore are backed by the taxpayers, for the taxpayers are liable for the money that the system creates out of nothing?

The role of government in the economy

As I said in my last discourse, when you create more money to prop up the failing system, well then you put more money in circulation. There is nothing of real value to support that money, and the inevitable result is that the value of the money is degraded, which means that the value of the labor of the majority of the population is degraded. Thus, people's standard of living inevitably goes down, for inflation eats up the value of people's labor.

This is what must be seen, what must be corrected. It must be seen by a large number – a critical mass – of the people who have so far not been willing to use their freedom in a relatively free society to go beyond the illusions and the lies fed by the mainstream press and educate themselves about the reality of how the economy works. They, themselves, must be the watchmen on the wall. Surely, the people in the media are not the watchmen, as they should be, nor are many people in the government the watchmen, as they should be.

The consequence here is that it is a myth that a free democratic government can stay out of the economy. It is indeed absolutely necessary that a modern government will keep a watchful eye on the economy and will regulate. The problem is that regulation should not be to give an advantage to the elite, to the establishment. It should be made to make sure that an elite cannot form, that an establishment cannot form, but that the people always have recourse to take their business elsewhere and to create smaller businesses that compete with the big ones.

Another concern that must be brought out and debated freely is: Is it necessarily the duty of a free democratic government to allow businesses to reach and go beyond a certain size? Is it truly a free economy if businesses are allowed to become so big that they cannot only out-compete smaller businesses but that they can actually drive the market? Thus, they can create a situation like what you have seen in the financial industry where the financial companies themselves created these new financial instruments that ended up destroying the entire system.

It is again the duty of a government to protect its citizens against the consequences of companies becoming so big that they can dominate the marketplace and therefore in some sense hold a monopoly. A monopoly that in many cases is protected by government regulations, but in other cases is protected by non-regulation so that once a company has become so big that it dominates the market, well it can effectively destroy any competition to itself.

Why laissez faire is not an option

Precisely because I am the God of Freedom, I realize that laissez faire is not an option on this planet, as long as so many people are blinded by the duality consciousness. Also, it is not an option as long as there is such a large number of people who are totally embodying the fallen consciousness, the self-centered, egotistical consciousness of wanting something for themselves regardless of the consequences for other people. A government cannot simply let the market take care of itself. The government should be elected by the people and should be *of* the people, *by* the people and *for* the people. The government must protect the people, not only from the elite but even from the people's own blindness when they are blinded by the duality consciousness. That is why such a government must be based on principles.

In this day and age it is clearly not enough to have a constitution based on principles, for that constitution will be undermined by people who do not see the truth behind those principles. Thus, in the Aquarian Age it is necessary to raise up people in all aspects of government, in the media, in business and in other branches of society who have the vision that beyond man-made ideas there is a greater reality. It is only when we reach for that greater reality that we can create a sustainable civilization. This means a civilization that does not collapse under its own weight—whether through financial crisis, through war or through other manifestations, such as natural disasters or even epidemic diseases that are an outpicturing of people's consciousness.

The real lesson that should be learned here is that if you allow any aspect of society to be dominated by the duality consciousness, then you will experience a crisis that will threaten the collapse of the entire society. The only way to avoid this cycle of ups and downs (what some people have mistakenly called the business cycle, as if it was an inevitable part of business) is to reach for something that is beyond the duality consciousness. As long as you have a business world based on the duality consciousness, well, then you will have a business cycle of ups and downs. This is inevitable. It is inevitable that sooner or later this system will collapse, although it is amazing to see the ingenuity used by those in the duality consciousness to prop up a financial system so that it has been able to sustain itself for as long as it has.

I would be far more glad to be amazed by the willingness of people to recognize the flaws in the current system and their willingness to reach for the ideas that we are surely ready to inspire upon people with the necessary knowledge of the economy. This way, we can indeed see the emergence of a sustainable system that avoids these ups and downs. As I said before, there are many people who have an in-depth knowledge of the economy and therefore have the chalice prepared so that they could receive the ideas from the ascended masters that are absolutely necessary to pull people – to pull society, to pull civilization – out of the current financial crisis.

The vision for people to hold

The vision I desire you, the spiritual people, to hold is that those people who have the knowledge and who have the potential to be open to higher ideas are indeed awakened and that they are recognized and are allowed to come to the forefront of the system. Hold the vision that they can play their intended role, the role that they elected to play before they came into embodiment, but that most of them have forgotten. They need someone to hold the vision for them so that they will awaken, realize why they are here and suddenly step forward. Envision that they will no longer maintain silence but step forward and demand influence in a balanced way that will indeed be recognized by the people as the voice of reason, the voice of higher principles.

The people are already there, they are already in position, we simply need that last step of pushing society over the brink so that those people come to the forefront and their ideas are recognized as what is necessary to take society forward. Hold that vision, my beloved, call it forth, demand that it be manifest. This is indeed the most valuable service that you who are the spiritual people can do for the economy. Do not seek to prop up the system of the fallen ones. Seek instead to bring forth the system of the ascended masters that can replace the old system and truly create and manifest a golden age economy.

I thank you for your attention. I thank you for your invocations, for your calls. I thank those of you who are participating in the Course of Christhood, for by being willing to look at the beam in your own eye, you are also looking at the beam in the collective consciousness. As you pull the beam from your own eye, you make it easier for thousands or millions of people to also see and pull that beam.

In the Aquarian Age we do not wish our students to have the idolatry that inevitably causes them to feel left out. We want people to feel involved, to feel they are part of what we are doing so that we are not up here doing something that you are on the receiving end of. You very much see the figure-eight flow that as you multiply what we give, we can give even more, and thus we all grow together in the River of Life.

Be sealed in that Flame of Freedom. Be sealed in that River of Life. Be at peace, my beloved. Do not for a second entertain any fear. Even if the whole world goes into a fear about the economy, hold the vision for the golden age economy. Hold the vision that the people learn their lessons, even if they are hard learned lessons. Envision that they learn their lessons and transcend the old consciousness that has created the present system. Hold that vision and be sealed in the peace that truly is an aspect of freedom, for how can you be at peace if you are not free?

21 | INVOKING AN ECONOMY FOR THE PEOPLE

In the name I AM THAT I AM, Jesus Christ, I call to all ascended masters working on manifesting the Golden Age, especially the seven Elohim and Saint Germain to radiate into the collective consciousness the matrix for an economy that is not dominated by an elite but gives abundance to all people. Help people see that we can build a new future by working with the ascended masters and letting go of the old way of looking at life, including…

[Make personal calls.]

Part 1

1. Saint Germain, radiate into the collective consciousness the awareness that Jesus came to set all people free from the idolatry of the fallen beings, those who are trapped in the duality consciousness because they are blinded by their egos.

> O Hercules Blue, we're one with your will,
> all space in our beings with Blue Flame you fill,
> a beacon that radiates light to the earth,
> bringing about our planet's rebirth.

> **O Hercules Blue, all life you defend,**
> **giving us power to always transcend,**
> **in you the expansion of self has no end,**
> **as we in God's infinite spirals ascend.**

2. Saint Germain, radiate into the collective consciousness the awareness that idolatry keeps the majority of the population trapped in the illusion that they need an elite to stand between themselves and God.

> O Hercules Blue, your wisdom so great,
> within us a sense of knowing create,
> a new frame of reference we suddenly gain,
> for going beyond duality's pain.

> **O Hercules Blue, all life you defend,**
> **giving us power to always transcend,**
> **in you the expansion of self has no end,**
> **as we in God's infinite spirals ascend.**

3. Saint Germain, radiate into the collective consciousness the awareness that the fallen beings are perpetuating the lie that people can contact God only through the outer religion and its priesthood.

> O Hercules Blue, we lovingly raise,
> our voices in giving God infinite praise,
> in feeling your flame, so clearly we see,
> transcending the self is the true alchemy.

> **O Hercules Blue, all life you defend,**
> **giving us power to always transcend,**
> **in you the expansion of self has no end,**
> **as we in God's infinite spirals ascend.**

4. Saint Germain, radiate into the collective consciousness the awareness that idolatry is the central problem in the economic crisis.

> O Hercules Blue, all life now you heal,
> enveloping all in your Blue-flame Seal,
> we're grateful for playing a personal part,
> In God's infinitely intricate work of art.

> **O Hercules Blue, all life you defend,**
> **giving us power to always transcend,**
> **in you the expansion of self has no end,**
> **as we in God's infinite spirals ascend.**

5. Saint Germain, radiate into the collective consciousness the awareness that the press, government officials and leaders in economic organizations or big banks all perpetuate the idolatry that certain companies are "too big to fail."

O Hercules Blue, your Temple of Light,
revealed to us all through our inner sight,
your power allows us to forge on until,
we pierce every veil and climb every hill.

**O Hercules Blue, all life you defend,
giving us power to always transcend,
in you the expansion of self has no end,
as we in God's infinite spirals ascend.**

6. Saint Germain, radiate into the collective consciousness the awareness that the lie that we cannot exist without the power elite of fallen beings prevents us from taking back the power of God within each of us.

O Hercules Blue, I pledge now my life,
in helping this planet transcend human strife,
duality's lies are pierced by your light,
restoring the fullness of our inner sight.

**O Hercules Blue, all life you defend,
giving us power to always transcend,
in you the expansion of self has no end,
as we in God's infinite spirals ascend.**

7. Saint Germain, radiate into the collective consciousness the awareness that some among the power elite see that their days are numbered. It is only a matter of a relatively short time before the people will rise up against the power elites.

> O Hercules Blue, we set all life free,
> from the subtlest lies of duality,
> the prince of this world no more has a bond,
> for with you we go completely beyond.
>
> **O Hercules Blue, all life you defend,**
> **giving us power to always transcend,**
> **in you the expansion of self has no end,**
> **as we in God's infinite spirals ascend.**

8. Saint Germain, radiate into the collective consciousness the awareness that will awaken people from the idolatry of thinking that they need an elite of selfish and self-centered people in order to continue a society with stability.

> O Hercules Blue, in oneness with thee,
> we open our hearts to your reality,
> your electric-blue fire within us reveal,
> our innermost longing for all that is real.
>
> **O Hercules Blue, all life you defend,**
> **giving us power to always transcend,**
> **in you the expansion of self has no end,**
> **as we in God's infinite spirals ascend.**

9. Saint Germain, radiate into the collective consciousness the awareness that will help people learn their lesson so that those who will not learn can receive the judgment of Christ and be removed.

> O Hercules Blue, you fill every space,
> with infinite Power and infinite Grace,
> you embody the key to creativity,
> the will to transcend into Infinity.
>
> **O Hercules Blue, all life you defend,**
> **giving us power to always transcend,**
> **in you the expansion of self has no end,**
> **as we in God's infinite spirals ascend.**

Part 2

1. Saint Germain, radiate into the collective consciousness the awareness that people must learn what can be done to misuse the economy before they will be ready to accept the economy of the Golden Age.

> Beloved Apollo, with your second ray,
> you open our eyes to see a new day,
> We see through duality's lies and deceit,
> transcending the mindset producing defeat.
>
> **Beloved Apollo, thou Elohim Gold,**
> **your radiant light our eyes now behold,**
> **as pages of wisdom you gently unfold,**
> **our planet is free from all that is old.**

2. Saint Germain, radiate into the collective consciousness the awareness that people are so steeped in the consciousness of lack that most of them would reject the design for the golden age economy.

21 | Invoking an economy for the people

> Beloved Apollo, in your flame we know,
> that your living wisdom is always a flow,
> in your light we see our own highest will,
> immersed in the stream that never stands still.
>
> **Beloved Apollo, thou Elohim Gold,**
> **your radiant light our eyes now behold,**
> **as pages of wisdom you gently unfold,**
> **our planet is free from all that is old.**

3. Saint Germain, radiate into the collective consciousness the awareness that the essence of idolatry is the desire to raise yourself above other people. To do this, you must be in an environment infused with the illusion of lack. In order for some to have more, others must have less.

> Beloved Apollo, your light makes it clear,
> why we have taken embodiment here,
> exposing all lies causing the fall,
> you help us reclaim the oneness of all.
>
> **Beloved Apollo, thou Elohim Gold,**
> **your radiant light our eyes now behold,**
> **as pages of wisdom you gently unfold,**
> **our planet is free from all that is old.**

4. Saint Germain, radiate into the collective consciousness the awareness that this state of an unequal distribution of wealth and privilege cannot exist in the abundant life of God. It can only exist when that abundant life has been rejected by a critical mass of human beings so that it cannot be physically manifest.

> Beloved Apollo, exposing all lies,
> we hereby surrender all ego-based ties,
> we know our perception is truly the key,
> to transcending the serpentine duality.
>
> **Beloved Apollo, thou Elohim Gold,
> your radiant light our eyes now behold,
> as pages of wisdom you gently unfold,
> our planet is free from all that is old.**

5. Saint Germain, radiate into the collective consciousness the awareness that the true realism of the Golden Age is where the people realize that they have access to the power of God within themselves. Therefore, we can bring forth the abundant life without being dependent upon an elite here on earth.

> Beloved Apollo, we heed now your call,
> drawing us into Wisdom's Great Hall,
> working to raise our own cosmic sphere,
> together we form the tip of the spear.
>
> **Beloved Apollo, thou Elohim Gold,
> your radiant light our eyes now behold,
> as pages of wisdom you gently unfold,
> our planet is free from all that is old.**

6. Saint Germain, radiate into the collective consciousness the awareness that we do not need an elite who can make the decisions of how to run the complicated financial system that the elite has created in order to hide their intentions and their manipulation from the people.

> Beloved Apollo, your wisdom so clear,
> in oneness with you, no serpent we fear,
> the beam in our eye we willingly see,
> we're free from the serpent's own duality.
>
> **Beloved Apollo, thou Elohim Gold,**
> **your radiant light our eyes now behold,**
> **as pages of wisdom you gently unfold,**
> **our planet is free from all that is old.**

7. Saint Germain, radiate into the collective consciousness the awareness that the system has finally become so complicated that even the people who created it can no longer figure out how the system works. They can no longer assess the true risk of the dubious financial instruments they have created.

> Beloved Apollo, you help us to see
> through your knowing eyes we truly are free,
> we willingly stand in your piercing gaze,
> empowered, we exit duality's maze.
>
> **Beloved Apollo, thou Elohim Gold,**
> **your radiant light our eyes now behold,**
> **as pages of wisdom you gently unfold,**
> **our planet is free from all that is old.**

8. Saint Germain, radiate into the collective consciousness the awareness that old companies can suddenly vanish because their leaders have become deceived by the complexity of their financial instruments and by the consciousness of greed.

Beloved Apollo, our vision we raise,
we see that the earth is in a new phase,
for nothing can stop the knowledge you bring,
exposing that there's no separate thing.

**Beloved Apollo, thou Elohim Gold,
your radiant light our eyes now behold,
as pages of wisdom you gently unfold,
our planet is free from all that is old.**

9. Saint Germain, radiate into the collective consciousness the awareness that when people are in a state of idolatry, blindly following the blind leaders, then it is only a matter of time before those blind leaders take the entire system to the brink of collapse.

Beloved Apollo, in wisdom's great mirth,
we all are together uplifting the earth,
as you now the true Flame of Wisdom reveal,
all of earth's people can see what is real.

**Beloved Apollo, thou Elohim Gold,
your radiant light our eyes now behold,
as pages of wisdom you gently unfold,
our planet is free from all that is old.**

Part 3

1. Saint Germain, radiate into the collective consciousness the awareness that what has driven the financial system is blind greed. This has perverted the system to the point where it is so based on debt that it is impossible to accurately assess the risk of conducting business in the system.

> O Heros-Amora, in your love so pink,
> we care not what others about us may think,
> in oneness with you, we claim a new day,
> as innocent children, we frolic and play.

> **O Heros-Amora, we reap what we sow,**
> **yet this is Plan B for helping us grow,**
> **for truly, Plan A is that we join the flow,**
> **immersed in the Infinite Love you bestow.**

2. Saint Germain, radiate into the collective consciousness the awareness that the cycle of growth and profit was built on the blindness and the greed of those at the top and many among the people.

> O Heros-Amora, a new life begun,
> we laugh at the devil, the serious one,
> the serpent is stuck in his duality,
> but we are set free by Love's reality.

> **O Heros-Amora, we reap what we sow,**
> **yet this is Plan B for helping us grow,**
> **for truly, Plan A is that we join the flow,**
> **immersed in the Infinite Love you bestow.**

3. Saint Germain, radiate into the collective consciousness the awareness that both the people at the top and those who followed the leaders were blinded by the consciousness of something for nothing that is the essence of greed.

> O Heros-Amora, awakened we see,
> in true love is no conditionality,
> we bathe in your glorious Ruby-Pink Sun,
> knowing our God allows life to be fun.

> **O Heros-Amora, we reap what we sow,**
> **yet this is Plan B for helping us grow,**
> **for truly, Plan A is that we join the flow,**
> **immersed in the Infinite Love you bestow.**

4. Saint Germain, radiate into the collective consciousness the awareness that when people want something for nothing, they think that anything goes. Anything that seems to offer a short-term profit should be pursued.

> O Heros-Amora, life is such a joy,
> we see that the world is like a great toy,
> whatever the mind into it projects,
> the mirror of life exactly reflects.

> **O Heros-Amora, we reap what we sow,**
> **yet this is Plan B for helping us grow,**
> **for truly, Plan A is that we join the flow,**
> **immersed in the Infinite Love you bestow.**

21 | Invoking an economy for the people

5. Saint Germain, radiate into the collective consciousness the awareness that the profits that were claimed were not real profits, they were imaginary profits because the risk had been masked to the point where it seemed like there was no loss or the loss could be postponed to next year.

> O Heros-Amora, conditions you burn,
> we know we are free to take a new turn,
> Immersed in the stream of infinite Love,
> we know that the Spirit came from Above.
>
> **O Heros-Amora, we reap what we sow,**
> **yet this is Plan B for helping us grow,**
> **for truly, Plan A is that we join the flow,**
> **immersed in the Infinite Love you bestow.**

6. Saint Germain, radiate into the collective consciousness the awareness that the entire system was in a state of blindness that is the inevitable companion of greed. Greed can only be based on an illusion and any illusion feeds further illusion, further blindness.

> O Heros-Amora, we feel that at last,
> we've risen above the trap of the past,
> in true love we claim our freedom to grow,
> forever we're one with Love's Infinite Flow.
>
> **O Heros-Amora, we reap what we sow,**
> **yet this is Plan B for helping us grow,**
> **for truly, Plan A is that we join the flow,**
> **immersed in the Infinite Love you bestow.**

7. Saint Germain, radiate into the collective consciousness the awareness that the illusion behind greed makes it seem possible that we can gain an advantage to ourselves and our company, and then never mind what happens to other people or to the system itself.

> O Heros-Amora, conditions are ties,
> forming a net of serpentine lies,
> but you have the antidote setting us free,
> you take us beyond conditionality.
>
> **O Heros-Amora, we reap what we sow,**
> **yet this is Plan B for helping us grow,**
> **for truly, Plan A is that we join the flow,**
> **immersed in the Infinite Love you bestow.**

8. Saint Germain, radiate into the collective consciousness the awareness that the money managers have created an economy that is based on the consciousness behind gambling.

> O Heros-Amora, your love is no bond,
> for love only wants to take us beyond,
> your love has no bounds, forever it flies,
> raising all life into Ruby-Pink skies.
>
> **O Heros-Amora, we reap what we sow,**
> **yet this is Plan B for helping us grow,**
> **for truly, Plan A is that we join the flow,**
> **immersed in the Infinite Love you bestow.**

9. Saint Germain, radiate into the collective consciousness the awareness that Wall Street created the promise that all who invested in these new financial instruments would make a return. That promise could not be fulfilled because it was based on the illusion that all who play the lottery can win the big prize.

> O Heros-Amora, love bathing the earth,
> filling all people with infinite mirth,
> for fear and despair there is no more room,
> as all are awakened by love's sonic boom.

> **O Heros-Amora, we reap what we sow,**
> **yet this is Plan B for helping us grow,**
> **for truly, Plan A is that we join the flow,**
> **immersed in the Infinite Love you bestow.**

Part 4

1. Saint Germain, radiate into the collective consciousness the awareness that when the Tower of Babel began to crack, the people at the top switched from the illusion of greed to the illusion of fear. In their fear, they created the downward spiral that threatened a meltdown of the system.

> Beloved Astrea, your heart is so true,
> your Circle and Sword of white and blue,
> cut all life free from dramas unwise,
> on wings of Purity our planet will rise.

> **Beloved Astrea, in oneness with you,**
> **your circle and sword of electric blue,**
> **with Purity's Light cutting right through,**
> **raising the earth into all that is true.**

2. Saint Germain, radiate into the collective consciousness the awareness that this woke up the government, who thought the market would take care of itself. Suddenly, the government realized that the market will take care of it by taking down the entire flawed system.

> Beloved Astrea, in God Purity,
> accelerate all of our life energy,
> we're rising beyond every impurity,
> as Purity's Light forever we see.

> **Beloved Astrea, in oneness with you,**
> **your circle and sword of electric blue,**
> **with Purity's Light cutting right through,**
> **raising the earth into all that is true.**

3. Saint Germain, radiate into the collective consciousness the awareness that the government suddenly decided that it had to protect the people. But is the government protecting the people or the power elite?

> Beloved Astrea, from Purity's Ray,
> send forth deliverance to all life today,
> acceleration to Purity, we are now free
> from all that is less than love's Purity.

> **Beloved Astrea, in oneness with you,**
> **your circle and sword of electric blue,**
> **with Purity's Light cutting right through,**
> **raising the earth into all that is true.**

4. Saint Germain, radiate into the collective consciousness the awareness that the American government is so trapped in the mindset of greed and elitism that they are acting primarily to protect the elite rather than the people.

> Beloved Astrea, accelerate us all,
> as for your deliverance we fervently call,
> set all life free from vision impure
> beyond fear and doubt, we're rising for sure.

> **Beloved Astrea, in oneness with you,**
> **your circle and sword of electric blue,**
> **with Purity's Light cutting right through,**
> **raising the earth into all that is true.**

5. Saint Germain, radiate into the collective consciousness the awareness that if the government does not thoroughly reform the entire financial system, another crisis will come along.

> Beloved Astrea, we're willing to see,
> all of the lies that keep us unfree,
> we surrender all lies causing the fall,
> forever affirming the oneness of All.

> **Beloved Astrea, in oneness with you,**
> **your circle and sword of electric blue,**
> **with Purity's Light cutting right through,**
> **raising the earth into all that is true.**

6. Saint Germain, radiate into the collective consciousness the awareness that will awaken the intelligent and well-meaning people in both businesses and government so they can enact the reforms that are necessary in order to put the financial world on a sustainable growth path where the system will not destroy itself out of blind greed.

> Beloved Astrea, accelerate life
> beyond all duality's struggle and strife,
> consume all division between God and man,
> accelerate fulfillment of God's perfect plan.
>
> **Beloved Astrea, in oneness with you,**
> **your circle and sword of electric blue,**
> **with Purity's Light cutting right through,**
> **raising the earth into all that is true.**

7. Saint Germain, radiate into the collective consciousness the awareness that we need to take a look at the system and say: "What is actually wrong with the system? What do we need to do to create an economy that promotes sustainable growth, not only for the elite but for all people?"

> Beloved Astrea, we lovingly call,
> break down separation's invisible wall,
> raising our minds into true unity
> with the Masters of love in Infinity.
>
> **Beloved Astrea, in oneness with you,**
> **your circle and sword of electric blue,**
> **with Purity's Light cutting right through,**
> **raising the earth into all that is true.**

8. Saint Germain, radiate into the collective consciousness the awareness that in the transition to the Aquarian Age no economy can be sustainable unless it raises up all people towards the abundant life.

> Beloved Astrea, help all of us find,
> the secret that we create with the mind,
> and thus what in ignorance we decreate,
> in knowledge we easily can recreate.

> **Beloved Astrea, in oneness with you,**
> **your circle and sword of electric blue,**
> **with Purity's Light cutting right through,**
> **raising the earth into all that is true.**

9. Saint Germain, radiate into the collective consciousness the awareness that it is not sustainable to have an economy on a world basis where two-thirds of the world's population live near the starvation level or below the poverty level of a few dollars a day.

> Beloved Astrea, we all do aspire,
> to learning to use your purity's fire,
> to raise every form in infamy sown,
> as Saint Germain makes this planet his own.

> **Beloved Astrea, in oneness with you,**
> **your circle and sword of electric blue,**
> **with Purity's Light cutting right through,**
> **raising the earth into all that is true.**

Part 5

1. Saint Germain, radiate into the collective consciousness the awareness that as long as the rich nations will not address that problem, their economies will always be in a state of going from one crisis to the next.

> Cyclopea so dear, the truth you reveal,
> the truth that duality's ailments will heal,
> your Emerald Light is like a great balm,
> our emotional bodies are perfectly calm.
>
> **Cyclopea so dear, in Emerald Sphere,**
> **in raising perception we shall persevere,**
> **as deep in our hearts your truth we revere,**
> **to immaculate vision the earth does adhere.**

2. Saint Germain, radiate into the collective consciousness the awareness that in order to create a financial system that is sustainable, the government must acknowledge its rightful role.

> Cyclopea so dear, with you we unwind,
> all negative spirals clouding the mind,
> we know pure awareness is truly our core,
> the key to becoming the wide-open door.
>
> **Cyclopea so dear, in Emerald Sphere,**
> **in raising perception we shall persevere,**
> **as deep in our hearts your truth we revere,**
> **to immaculate vision the earth does adhere.**

3. Saint Germain, radiate into the collective consciousness the awareness that one of the primary reasons for the current financial crisis is the lack of regulation.

> Cyclopea so dear, clear our inner sight,
> empowered, we pierce the soul's fearful night,
> we now see our life through your single eye,
> beyond all disease we're ready to fly.

> **Cyclopea so dear, in Emerald Sphere,**
> **in raising perception we shall persevere,**
> **as deep in our hearts your truth we revere,**
> **to immaculate vision the earth does adhere.**

4. Saint Germain, radiate into the collective consciousness the awareness that the government has been caught up in a false view of the free market economy that makes people think they need to let the market regulate itself.

> Cyclopea so dear, life can only reflect,
> the images that the mind does project,
> the key to our healing is clearing the mind,
> from the images the ego is hiding behind.

> **Cyclopea so dear, in Emerald Sphere,**
> **in raising perception we shall persevere,**
> **as deep in our hearts your truth we revere,**
> **to immaculate vision the earth does adhere.**

5. Saint Germain, radiate into the collective consciousness the awareness that a free society does not mean that a small power elite has freedom to exploit and dominate the population.

> Cyclopea so dear, we want to aim high,
> to your healing flame we ever draw nigh,
> through veils of duality we now take flight,
> bathed in your penetrating Emerald Light.
>
> **Cyclopea so dear, in Emerald Sphere,**
> **in raising perception we shall persevere,**
> **as deep in our hearts your truth we revere,**
> **to immaculate vision the earth does adhere.**

6. Saint Germain, radiate into the collective consciousness the awareness that freedom cannot be found through the duality consciousness. Freedom is when you know that only when you do something to raise the All, will you be doing something that will truly benefit yourself.

> Cyclopea so dear, your Emerald Flame,
> exposes every subtle, dualistic power game,
> including the game of wanting to say,
> that truth is defined in only one way.
>
> **Cyclopea so dear, in Emerald Sphere,**
> **in raising perception we shall persevere,**
> **as deep in our hearts your truth we revere,**
> **to immaculate vision the earth does adhere.**

7. Saint Germain, radiate into the collective consciousness the awareness that the role of a democratic government is to protect the people, to serve as the steward of the principles that will raise up all life towards greater economic freedom and abundance.

21 | Invoking an economy for the people

> Cyclopea so dear, we're feeling the flow,
> as your Living Truth upon us you bestow,
> from all dual vision we are now set free,
> planet earth in immaculate matrix will be.
>
> **Cyclopea so dear, in Emerald Sphere,**
> **in raising perception we shall persevere,**
> **as deep in our hearts your truth we revere,**
> **to immaculate vision the earth does adhere.**

8. Saint Germain, radiate into the collective consciousness the awareness that the power elite has perpetrated the myth that a free market economy can run itself without government intervention.

> Cyclopea so dear, the truth is now clear,
> we see higher purpose for which we are here
> we know truth transcends all systems below,
> immersed in your light, we continue to grow.
>
> **Cyclopea so dear, in Emerald Sphere,**
> **in raising perception we shall persevere,**
> **as deep in our hearts your truth we revere,**
> **to immaculate vision the earth does adhere.**

9. Saint Germain, radiate into the collective consciousness the awareness that it is a myth that the United States and other Western nations have a free market economy and have always had such an economy.

> Cyclopea so dear, we're feeling your joy,
> as creative vision we now do employ,
> in lifting earth out of serpentine cage,
> to manifest Saint Germain's Golden Age.
>
> **Cyclopea so dear, in Emerald Sphere,
> in raising perception we shall persevere,
> as deep in our hearts your truth we revere,
> to immaculate vision the earth does adhere.**

Part 6

1. Saint Germain, radiate into the collective consciousness the awareness that in the late 1800's certain fallen beings realized that the only way to create a huge profit was to drive and control market conditions in order to create monopolies.

> O Elohim Peace, in Unity's Flame,
> there is no more room for duality's game,
> we know that all form is from the same source,
> empowering us to plot a new course.
>
> **O Elohim Peace, through your tranquility,
> we are free from the chaos of duality,
> in oneness with God a new identity,
> we are raising the earth into Infinity.**

2. Saint Germain, radiate into the collective consciousness the awareness that in a true free market economy, where competition is unrestricted and people are educated and informed, it is not possible to create a monopoly.

21 | Invoking an economy for the people

> O Elohim Peace, the bell now you ring,
> causing all atoms to vibrate and sing,
> we give up the sense of a separate "me,"
> we're crossing Samsara's turbulent sea.
>
> **O Elohim Peace, through your tranquility,**
> **we are free from the chaos of duality,**
> **in oneness with God a new identity,**
> **we are raising the earth into Infinity.**

3. Saint Germain, radiate into the collective consciousness the awareness that freedom is the anti-thesis of monopolies. Free competition will destroy monopolies by always making it possible for others to compete, no matter how big one business might become.

> O Elohim Peace, you help us to know,
> that Jesus has come your Flame to bestow,
> upon all who are ready to give up the strife,
> by following Christ into infinite life.
>
> **O Elohim Peace, through your tranquility,**
> **we are free from the chaos of duality,**
> **in oneness with God a new identity,**
> **we are raising the earth into Infinity.**

4. Saint Germain, radiate into the collective consciousness the awareness that a business will only remain big in a free economy as long as it serves its customers. When you create a monopoly and artificially raise prices, the customers will go elsewhere.

> O Elohim Peace, through your eyes we see,
> that only in oneness will we ever be free,
> we now see that there is no separate thing,
> to the ego-based self we no longer cling.
>
> **O Elohim Peace, through your tranquility,**
> **we are free from the chaos of duality,**
> **in oneness with God a new identity,**
> **we are raising the earth into Infinity.**

5. Saint Germain, radiate into the collective consciousness the awareness that the big industrialists realized that in a democratic nation it is not possible to create a monopoly through competition. The only way to gain a monopoly is to use the government to limit the competition.

> O Elohim Peace, you show us the way,
> for clearing the mind from duality's fray,
> you pierce the illusions of both time and space,
> separation consumed by your Infinite Grace.
>
> **O Elohim Peace, through your tranquility,**
> **we are free from the chaos of duality,**
> **in oneness with God a new identity,**
> **we are raising the earth into Infinity.**

6. Saint Germain, radiate into the collective consciousness the awareness that they caused the government to be deceived by the illusion that it had to enter the economy and use its power to regulate the economy for the purpose of creating stability.

> O Elohim Peace, what beauty your name,
> consuming within us duality's shame,
> the earth is set free from burden of fear,
> accepting your peace is now manifest here.
>
> **O Elohim Peace, through your tranquility,**
> **we are free from the chaos of duality,**
> **in oneness with God a new identity,**
> **we are raising the earth into Infinity.**

7. Saint Germain, radiate into the collective consciousness the awareness that in the vision of these big financiers, this meant creating a stable situation where no smaller companies could come up and challenge the position of the big established companies.

> O Elohim Peace, with Christ at our side,
> no force of duality can evermore hide,
> It was through the vibration of your Golden Flame,
> that Christ the illusion of death overcame.
>
> **O Elohim Peace, through your tranquility,**
> **we are free from the chaos of duality,**
> **in oneness with God a new identity,**
> **we are raising the earth into Infinity.**

8. Saint Germain, radiate into the collective consciousness the awareness that over this past century, government regulations have been used to protect the big established companies from the free market, the free competition.

O Elohim Peace, you bring now to earth,
the unstoppable flame of Cosmic Rebirth,
we give up the sense that something is "mine,"
allowing your Light through our beings to shine.

**O Elohim Peace, through your tranquility,
we are free from the chaos of duality,
in oneness with God a new identity,
we are raising the earth into Infinity.**

9. Saint Germain, radiate into the collective consciousness the awareness that the "master stroke" of these financiers was the creation of the Federal Reserve System, which served not only to prevent free competition in the banking industry. It also served to prevent the big companies from reaping the consequences of their mistakes.

O Elohim Peace, as peace now we feel,
all records of war you totally heal,
the earth is now free from forces of war,
restoring her purity known from before.

**O Elohim Peace, through your tranquility,
we are free from the chaos of duality,
in oneness with God a new identity,
we are raising the earth into Infinity.**

Part 7

1. Saint Germain, radiate into the collective consciousness the awareness that in a free economy, those who make mistakes will reap the consequences and go down or be reduced in size.

> Beloved Arcturus, release now the flow,
> of Violet Flame to help all life grow,
> in ever-expanding circles of light,
> it pulses within every atom so bright.
>
> **Beloved Arcturus, your Violet Flame pure,**
> **is for every ailment the ultimate cure,**
> **against it no darkness could ever endure,**
> **earth's freedom it will forever ensure.**

2. Saint Germain, radiate into the collective consciousness the awareness that in creating the Federal Reserve as the lender of last resort, the big banks could make bad investments, and the system would protect them from going down.

> Beloved Arcturus, thou Elohim Free,
> we open our hearts to your reality,
> we have no attachments to life here on earth,
> we claim a new life in your Flame of Rebirth.
>
> **Beloved Arcturus, your Violet Flame pure,**
> **is for every ailment the ultimate cure,**
> **against it no darkness could ever endure,**
> **earth's freedom it will forever ensure.**

3. Saint Germain, radiate into the collective consciousness the awareness that independent banks are being taken over by the big banks who are a part of the Federal Reserve System and therefore are backed by the taxpayers, for the taxpayers are liable for the money that the system creates out of nothing.

> Beloved Arcturus, be with us alway,
> reborn, we are ready to face a new day,
> expanding our hearts into Infinity,
> your flame is the key to our God-victory.

> **Beloved Arcturus, your Violet Flame pure,**
> **is for every ailment the ultimate cure,**
> **against it no darkness could ever endure,**
> **earth's freedom it will forever ensure.**

4. Saint Germain, radiate into the collective consciousness the awareness that a critical mass of the people need to use their freedom to go beyond the illusions and the lies fed by the mainstream press and educate themselves about the reality of how the economy works. We must be the watchmen on the wall.

> Beloved Arcturus, your bright violet fire,
> now fills every atom, raising them higher,
> the space in each atom all filled with your light,
> as matter itself is shining so bright.

> **Beloved Arcturus, your Violet Flame pure,**
> **is for every ailment the ultimate cure,**
> **against it no darkness could ever endure,**
> **earth's freedom it will forever ensure.**

5. Saint Germain, radiate into the collective consciousness the awareness that it is a myth that a free democratic government can stay out of the economy. It is absolutely necessary that a modern government will keep a watchful eye on the economy and will regulate.

> Beloved Arcturus, your transforming Grace,
> empowers us now every challenge to face,
> with your Freedom's Song filling the ear,
> we know that to God we're ever so dear.

> **Beloved Arcturus, your Violet Flame pure,**
> **is for every ailment the ultimate cure,**
> **against it no darkness could ever endure,**
> **earth's freedom it will forever ensure.**

6. Saint Germain, radiate into the collective consciousness the awareness that regulation should not be to give an advantage to the elite, to the establishment, but to ensure free competition.

> Beloved Arcturus, we surrender all fear,
> we're feeling your Presence so tangibly near,
> as your violet light floods our inner space,
> towards the ascension we willingly race.

> **Beloved Arcturus, your Violet Flame pure,**
> **is for every ailment the ultimate cure,**
> **against it no darkness could ever endure,**
> **earth's freedom it will forever ensure.**

7. Saint Germain, radiate into the collective consciousness the awareness that the government must make sure that an elite or establishment cannot form, but that the people always have recourse to take their business elsewhere and to create smaller businesses that compete with the big ones.

> Beloved Arcturus, bring in a new age,
> help earth and humanity turn a new page,
> your transforming light gives us certainty,
> Saint Germain's Golden Age is a reality.

> **Beloved Arcturus, your Violet Flame pure,**
> **is for every ailment the ultimate cure,**
> **against it no darkness could ever endure,**
> **earth's freedom it will forever ensure.**

8. Saint Germain, radiate into the collective consciousness the awareness that a free democratic government cannot allow businesses to go beyond a certain size. It is not a free economy if businesses are allowed to become so big that they cannot only out-compete smaller businesses but that they can actually drive the market.

> Beloved Arcturus, illusions you pierce,
> no serpent can stand against angels so fierce,
> no forces of darkness can stop Violet Flame,
> all discord on earth it will instantly tame.

> **Beloved Arcturus, your Violet Flame pure,**
> **is for every ailment the ultimate cure,**
> **against it no darkness could ever endure,**
> **earth's freedom it will forever ensure.**

9. Saint Germain, radiate into the collective consciousness the awareness that when businesses become too big, they can create a situation where their financial instruments destroy the entire system.

Beloved Arcturus, we love Saint Germain,
and therefore we call forth again and again,
your Violet Flame to flood all the earth,
so Saint Germain's eyes are filling with mirth.

Beloved Arcturus, your Violet Flame pure,
is for every ailment the ultimate cure,
against it no darkness could ever endure,
earth's freedom it will forever ensure.

Part 8

1. Saint Germain, radiate into the collective consciousness the awareness that it is the duty of a government to protect its citizens against the consequences of companies becoming so big that they can dominate the marketplace and therefore hold a monopoly.

O Saint Germain, you do inspire,
my vision raised forever higher,
with you I form a figure-eight,
your Golden Age I co-create.

**O Saint Germain, what love you bring,
it truly makes all matter sing,
your violet flame does all restore,
with you we are becoming more.**

2. Saint Germain, radiate into the collective consciousness the awareness that we cannot allow monopolies that are either protected by government regulations, or protected by non-regulation so that once a company has become so big that it dominates the market, it can destroy any competition to itself.

O Saint Germain, what Freedom Flame,
released when we recite your name,
acceleration is your gift,
our planet it will surely lift.

**O Saint Germain, what love you bring,
it truly makes all matter sing,
your violet flame does all restore,
with you we are becoming more.**

3. Saint Germain, radiate into the collective consciousness the awareness that laissez faire is not an option on this planet, as long as so many people are blinded by the duality consciousness and there are fallen beings in embodiment.

O Saint Germain, in love we claim,
our right to bring your violet flame,
from you Above, to us below,
it is an all-transforming flow.

> **O Saint Germain, what love you bring,**
> **it truly makes all matter sing,**
> **your violet flame does all restore,**
> **with you we are becoming more.**

4. Saint Germain, radiate into the collective consciousness the awareness that a government cannot let the market take care of itself. The government must protect the people, not only from the elite but even from the people's own blindness when they are blinded by the duality consciousness.

> O Saint Germain, I love you so,
> my aura filled with violet glow,
> my chakras filled with violet fire,
> I am your cosmic amplifier.

> **O Saint Germain, what love you bring,**
> **it truly makes all matter sing,**
> **your violet flame does all restore,**
> **with you we are becoming more.**

5. Saint Germain, radiate into the collective consciousness the awareness that it is not enough to have a constitution based on principles, for that constitution will be undermined by people who do not see the truth behind those principles.

> O Saint Germain, I am now free,
> your violet flame is therapy,
> transform all hang-ups in my mind,
> as inner peace I surely find.

> **O Saint Germain, what love you bring,**
> **it truly makes all matter sing,**
> **your violet flame does all restore,**
> **with you we are becoming more.**

6. Saint Germain, radiate into the collective consciousness the awareness that in the Aquarian Age it is necessary to raise up people in all aspects of government, in the media, in business and in other branches of society who have the vision that beyond man-made ideas there is a greater reality.

> O Saint Germain, my body pure,
> your violet flame for all is cure,
> consume the cause of all disease,
> and therefore I am all at ease.

> **O Saint Germain, what love you bring,**
> **it truly makes all matter sing,**
> **your violet flame does all restore,**
> **with you we are becoming more.**

7. Saint Germain, radiate into the collective consciousness the awareness that it is only when we reach for that greater reality that we can create a sustainable civilization, a civilization that does not collapse through financial crisis, war or other manifestations of people's consciousness.

> O Saint Germain, I'm karma-free,
> the past no longer burdens me,
> a brand new opportunity,
> I am in Christic unity.

**O Saint Germain, what love you bring,
it truly makes all matter sing,
your violet flame does all restore,
with you we are becoming more.**

8. Saint Germain, radiate into the collective consciousness the awareness that if we allow any aspect of society to be dominated by the duality consciousness, then we will experience a crisis that will threaten the collapse of the entire society.

O Saint Germain, we are now one,
I am for you a violet sun,
as we transform this planet earth,
your Golden Age is given birth.

**O Saint Germain, what love you bring,
it truly makes all matter sing,
your violet flame does all restore,
with you we are becoming more.**

9. Saint Germain, radiate into the collective consciousness the awareness that the only way to avoid this cycle of ups and downs, the so-called business cycle, is to reach for something that is beyond the duality consciousness.

O Saint Germain, the earth is free,
from burden of duality,
in oneness we bring what is best,
your Golden Age is manifest.

> O Saint Germain, what love you bring,
> it truly makes all matter sing,
> your violet flame does all restore,
> with you we are becoming more.

Part 9

1. Saint Germain, radiate into the collective consciousness the awareness that as long as we have a business world based on the duality consciousness, we will have a business cycle of ups and downs. Sooner or later this system will collapse.

> Divine Director, I now see,
> the world is unreality,
> in my heart I now truly feel,
> the Spirit is all that is real.
>
> **Divine Director, send the light,
> from blindness clear my inner sight,
> my vision free, my vision clear,
> your guidance is forever here.**

2. Saint Germain, radiate into the collective consciousness the awareness that we need to recognize the flaws in the current system and reach for the ideas that can manifest a sustainable system that avoids these ups and downs.

> Divine Director, vision give,
> in clarity I want to live,
> I now behold my plan Divine,
> the plan that is uniquely mine.

21 | Invoking an economy for the people

**Divine Director, send the light,
from blindness clear my inner sight,
my vision free, my vision clear,
your guidance is forever here.**

3. Saint Germain, radiate into the collective consciousness the awareness that will awaken the people who have an in-depth knowledge of the economy and can receive the ideas from the ascended masters that are absolutely necessary to pull society out of the current financial crisis.

Divine Director, show in me,
the ego games, and set me free,
help me escape the ego's cage,
to help bring in the Golden Age.

**Divine Director, send the light,
from blindness clear my inner sight,
my vision free, my vision clear,
your guidance is forever here.**

4. Saint Germain, radiate into the collective consciousness the awareness that will awaken those who have the potential to be open to higher ideas and allow them to step forward and play their intended role.

Divine Director, I'm with you,
my vision one, no longer two,
as karma's veil you do disperse,
I see a whole new universe.

> **Divine Director, send the light,
> from blindness clear my inner sight,
> my vision free, my vision clear,
> your guidance is forever here.**

5. Saint Germain, radiate into the collective consciousness the awareness that will awaken the people to recognize these new ideas as the voice of reason, the voice of higher principles.

> Divine Director, I go up,
> electric light now fills my cup,
> consume in me all shadows old,
> bestow on me a vision bold.

> **Divine Director, send the light,
> from blindness clear my inner sight,
> my vision free, my vision clear,
> your guidance is forever here.**

6. Saint Germain, by the authority of the Christ within me, I hereby call forth the Light that will push society over the brink so that the right people come to the forefront and their ideas are recognized as what is necessary to take society forward.

> Divine Director, heart of gold,
> my sacred labor I unfold,
> o blessed Guru, I now see,
> where my own plan is taking me.

> **Divine Director, send the light,
> from blindness clear my inner sight,
> my vision free, my vision clear,
> your guidance is forever here.**

7. Saint Germain, by the authority of the Christ within me, I hereby call forth the Light that will judge the fallen beings who have been and are manipulating the financial system.

Divine Director, by your grace,
in grander scheme I find my place,
my individual flame I see,
uniqueness God has given me.

**Divine Director, send the light,
from blindness clear my inner sight,
my vision free, my vision clear,
your guidance is forever here.**

8. Saint Germain, by the authority of the Christ within me, I hereby call for the fallen beings in the financial system to be removed from embodiment and for the light to consume all of the matrices they have created in order to distort and obstruct the divine economy.

Divine Director, vision one,
I see that I AM God's own Sun,
with your direction so Divine,
I am now letting my light shine.

**Divine Director, send the light,
from blindness clear my inner sight,
my vision free, my vision clear,
your guidance is forever here.**

9. Saint Germain, by the authority of the Christ within me, I hereby call forth the Light that will take down the financial system of the fallen ones and bring forth the system of the ascended masters that can replace the old system and manifest a golden age economy.

> Divine Director, what a gift,
> to be a part of Spirit's lift,
> to raise mankind out of the night,
> to bask in Spirit's loving sight.
>
> **Divine Director, send the light,**
> **from blindness clear my inner sight,**
> **my vision free, my vision clear,**
> **your guidance is forever here.**

Sealing

In the name of the Divine Mother, I call to all ascended masters for the sealing of myself and all people in my circle of influence in the creative flow of the Divine Mother, the River of Life. I call for the multiplication of my calls by all ascended masters so that we form the perfect figure-eight flow of "As Above, so below." Thus, I accept that this is fully manifest, because the mouth of the Lord, the Divine Mother that I AM, has spoken it. Amen.

www.ingramcontent.com/pod-product-compliance
Lightning Source LLC
Chambersburg PA
CBHW021147230426
43667CB00006B/289